Hanukkah Lamp in form of Menorah, with four enamel medallions
representing biblical scenes, silver-gilded, German.
Museum, Jewish Theological Seminary of America.

HANUKKAH

THE FEAST OF LIGHTS

Compiled and edited by

EMILY SOLIS-COHEN Jr.

PHILADELPHIA

THE JEWISH PUBLICATION SOCIETY OF AMERICA

5716–1955

Copyright 1937 by

THE JEWISH PUBLICATION SOCIETY OF AMERICA

Sixth impression, 1955

 60

PRINTED IN
THE UNITED STATES OF AMERICA

THE EDITOR ACKNOWLEDGES HER SPECIAL INDEBTED-
NESS TO JUDAH M. ISAACS WHO FIRST SUGGESTED
THE COMPILATION OF THIS BOOK AND WAS HELPFUL
THROUGHOUT ITS PREPARATION

AND TO SOLOMON GRAYZEL FOR INVALUABLE AID AND
COUNSEL DURING THE PREPARATION OF THE BOOK AND
FOR HIS KINDNESS IN SEEING IT THROUGH THE PRESS

CONTENTS

PREFATORY

PART ONE

HANUKKAH AND ITS SIGNIFICANCE

vii

PART TWO

HANUKKAH IN LITERATURE

PROSE

PART THREE

FOR THE YOUNG

PART FOUR

COMMEMORATION OF HANUKKAH

LIST OF ILLUSTRATIONS

TO THE READER

If you have already glanced through this book beginning with the last pages—Hebrew style—you may well be wondering at the strange combinations and juxtapositions you have found. Sober history side by side with poetry; plays and riddles with synagogue music; excerpts from the Apocrypha, the Talmud, and the Prayer-Book, with stories in modern guise for young and old. Chosen from a wide field and covering a substantial portion of recorded history, these diversities have only one reason for being in the same volume. They help us to understand the festival of Hanukkah which itself dates back to an event which took place twenty-one hundred years ago.

This Feast of Lights lasts eight days and it may be expected that in that space of time you will feel responsive to many moods· We have arranged this Hanukkah book in such a way that you can turn to whatever pleases you at any moment. It may be that you prefer poetry to rabbinical discussions, or history to games, or riddles to dramas. Some of you will be adults and others will be children. Whatever your mood, your age, or your shade of thought, if you are at all interested in Hanukkah, you will find something in these pages to help you remember a glorious page in the history of an ancient people that has survived.

With Hanukkah greetings,

THE CONTRIBUTORS

FOREWORD

When the question was asked: "What is Hanukkah?" the Rabbis answered with the story of the one unpolluted cruse which contained but enough oil for one day's burning and yet, miraculously, sufficed for eight. We may know more history than those Rabbis did, but we cannot get any closer to the real miracle of Hanukkah than they, when they told this symbolic story. For, at the time when the Temple was rededicated, the future of Judaism still appeared insecure. No one could have foreseen that the faith of this little people would soon affect the religions of the pagan world, and survive for many centuries. The miracle of the oil is but another way of stressing the miracle of Judaism and its continuance.

More than twenty-one centuries have elapsed since Syro-Grecian and Hasmonean clashed in battle. It cannot be said that Jewish life has been easy since that critical moment. The attitude that demands uniformity of religion and culture as indispensable to the unity of the State, did not vanish with Antiochus. On the contrary, he has had many successors. The troubles of Judaism in our day, though apparently different, are in reality traceable to the same conception of society. Mental and spiritual uniformity is the cry of all little souls, whose aim is to remake the world in their own image. Against that point of view the Maccabees struggled, and it may legitimately be argued that their example inspired similar steadfastness in many succeeding generations, both of Jews and of non-Jews. The fight against spiritual regimentation, begun by them, has been continued by the Jewish minority wherever it has lived. That is the universal element in the Hanukkah story, and it needs emphasis today as much as at any time in the past.

But it is not only as a call to resistance that the story of Hanukkah has served as a source of inspiration to the Jewish people. The purity of the Jewish faith has always been connected with the need for sacrifice, and since the days of the Maccabees such sacrifice evokes their memory, and the memory of the men and women of their generation.

Hellenists there were among the Jews of that day. Would they have been more numerous, and would the Jews as a whole have adopted a greater measure of Greek culture had not Antiochus attempted to force it upon them? Perhaps so; especially as to philosophy and science. Judaism has not been unreceptive to noble thought, from whatever source. Greek Alexandria indicates the possibility of mutual and harmonious influence. A millenium later we behold Judaic teachers discussing Aristotle and Ptolemy with a respect equal to that accorded Rab and Samuel. But that was—a millenium later. "In the days of Mattathias . . . the Hasmonean, and his sons" Jews saw only "the wicked Kingdom of Javan arising to destroy" their cherished religion; the attempt of a tyrant to impose upon them laws, beliefs, customs and ceremonial rites inferior to their own. To conform would have been easier than to resist; but they preferred to resist, and to remain loyal to what they held to be nobler and better. So Mattathias is reported as saying:

"Though all the nations that are under the king's dominion obey him, and fall away every one from the religion of his fathers . . . we will not hearken to the king's words, to go from our religion either to the right hand or to the left."

So, also, subsequent generations found in the rites of Hanukkah a ceremonial symbolizing their own problems, and inspiring them to like loyalties. This is the real significance for history of the events of that day.

Thus it becomes clear that in Jewish life the outstanding element of Hanukkah is not the victory of arms, nor the national glory and power won by subsequent Hasmonean conquests. The meaning of the festival is spiritual, not martial. True, it emphasizes Jewish solidarity; but that is a solidarity of sacrifice and devotion. Significantly, the *Haftarah* chosen for the Sabbath of Hanukkah—a choice preserved in both the Sephardic and the Ashkenazic rituals—is not a chapter from the historical books telling of a national victory, nor one from the Prophets foretelling the ultimate triumph of Judaism, but one which speaks of the sins of the high priest, of the inadequate, if desirable, material hopes of the lay ruler, and sounds its keynote in that famous phrase of the faith by which Judaism has survived: "Not by strength and not by might, but by My Spirit, saith the Lord of Hosts" (Zech. 4.6).

For centuries, the feast of dedication has been celebrated in the Jewish home and in the Synagogue. Each generation has drawn from it renewed inspiration for meeting its own peculiar problems. If in this, our own day, there is lack of unanimity as to the message brought by the Hanukkah lights, the differences are on the surface. The fundamental message remains the same—so long as Jews are sincere and loyal, the light of Judaism will not grow dim.

THE VICTORY OF THE SPIRIT[1]

Louis D. Brandeis

Hanukkah, the Feast of the Maccabees, celebrates a victory —not a military victory only, but a victory also of the spirit over things material. Not a victory only over external enemies— the Greeks; but a victory also over more dangerous internal enemies. A victory of the many over the ease-loving, safety-playing, privileged, powerful few, who in their pliancy would have betrayed the best interests of the people, a victory of democracy over aristocracy.

As part of the eternal world-wide struggle for democracy, the struggle of the Maccabees is of eternal world-wide interest. It is a struggle of the Jews of today as well as of those of two thousand years ago. It is a struggle in which all Americans, non-Jews as well as Jews, should be vitally interested because they are vitally affected.

The Maccabees' victory proved that the Jews—then already an old people—possessed the secret of eternal youth: the ability to rejuvenate itself through courage, hope, enthusiasm, devotion and self-sacrifice of the plain people. This will bring again a Jewish Renaissance.

[1] From an address delivered in Boston, 1912.

PART I

HANUKKAH AND ITS SIGNIFICANCE

GIFTS

EMMA LAZARUS[1]

"Oh, World-God, give me Wealth!" the Egyptian cried.
    His prayer was granted. High as heaven, behold
Palace and Pyramid; the brimming tide
    Of lavish Nile washed all his land with gold.
Armies of slaves toiled ant-wise at his feet;
World-circling traffic roared through mart and street;
His priests were gods; his spice-balmed kings enshrined,
    Set death at naught in rock-ribbed charnels deep.
Seek Pharaoh's race to-day, and ye shall find
    Rust and the moth, silence and dusty sleep.

"Oh, World-God, give me Beauty!" cried the Greek.
    His prayer was granted. All the earth became
Plastic and vocal to his sense; each peak,
    Each grove, each stream, quick with Promethean flame,
Peopled the world with imaged grace and light.
The lyre was his, and his the breathing might
Of the immortal marble; his the play
    Of diamond-pointed thought and golden tongue.
Go seek the sunshine-race, ye find to-day
A broken column and a lute unstrung.

"Oh, World-God, give me Power!" the Roman cried.
    His prayer was granted. The vast world was chained
A captive to the chariot of his pride.
    The blood of myriad provinces was drained

[1] From *Poems of Emma Lazarus*, Houghton, Mifflin & Co., Boston, 1899.

3

To feed that fierce, insatiable red heart.
Invulnerably bulwarked every part
With serried legions and with close-meshed Code;
    Within, the burrowing worm had gnawed its home;
A roofless ruin stands where once abode
    Th' imperial race of everlasting Rome.

"Oh, Godhead, give me Truth!" the Hebrew cried.
    His prayer was granted. He became the slave
Of the Idea, a pilgrim far and wide,
    Cursed, hated, spurned, and scourged with none to save.
The Pharaohs knew him, and when Greece beheld,
His wisdom wore the hoary crown of Eld.
Beauty he hath forsworn, and Wealth and Power.
    Seek him to-day, and find in every land;
No fire consumes him, neither floods devour;
    Immortal through the lamp within his hand.

JUDAISM AND HELLENISM

MILTON STEINBERG

ACCORDING to a Jewish tradition which is transmitted both by Josephus and by talmudic literature, Alexander the Great, on his way to Egypt, came face to face with the High Priest of the Temple at Jerusalem. The meeting between Alexander and the priest is probably a legend with no basis in fact. And yet, like so many myths, this one, if it does not possess literal accuracy, is nevertheless spiritually true. It symbolizes one of the most dramatic confrontations in the history of humanity. For, from the moment when Alexander touched the Orient until the hour when Christianity became the state religion of the Roman Empire, the culture of the Jew and the culture of the Greek were in continuous contact with each other. In the folk-picture of the conqueror and priest facing each other there is then to be discerned a parable of the collision of two great civilizations.

For, as it happens, the two groups that wrestled with each other in Palestine in the 2nd century B.C.E. represented more than artificial and meaningless national affiliations. They were the bearers and protagonists of distinct cultures, of different systems of living, each of which possessed virtues proper to itself, but neither of which was complete without the other. Through the triumph of Jewish arms, then, there was preserved for mankind a cluster of religious and ethical values which have been a vastly beneficent influence on subsequent generations. Of the larger implications of their actions the Maccabees themselves could have been only vaguely aware. As they saw it, they were fighting for freedom, for the faith and traditions of their fathers. Unwittingly, they fought also for certain concepts indispensable to adequate human living, which in the ancient world they alone possessed and which became the common possessions of mankind at large only through their heroic efforts.

Alexander was more than a conqueror. He was, after all, a pupil of Aristotle. He felt that it was his function to civilize the lands he subdued. Into the Orient, then, he brought deliberately the whole wealth of that civilization which had grown up in Hellas. With him went the epics of Homer and Hesiod, the poetry of Alcaeus and Sappho, the drama of Aeschylus, Sophocles, Euripides and Aristophanes. The artistic standards which made the Acropolis, the philosophy of Plato and Aristotle, the deepest roots from which later sprang Stoicism, Epicureanism, Scepticism and neo-Platonism — all these were Alexander's gift to the East.

Within a short time the entire Orient was Hellenized. From India to the Hellespont, from Egypt to the Black Sea, peoples of diverse stocks learned to speak Greek, came to dress like Greeks, to worship like Greeks and to think like Greeks. The native cultures of these Oriental countries were not completely obliterated, but they were well concealed underneath a Hellenistic veneer, so that although the older Egyptian civilization still persisted and the ancient Babylonian genius still lived, both these spiritual forces expressed themselves in the language and patterns of the Greek world.

For six hundred and fifty years thereafter the whole of the civilized world remained Hellenistic. From this fusion of the Orient and the Occident, from this syncretism of Hellenism and older cultures sprang as brilliant and as graceful a civilization as man has ever known. It is now a world which is dead and half-forgotten, this ancient Greek-Oriental world. And it may be necessary to draw once more some of its lineaments that its picture may be restored.

It was, in the first place, a world which was infinitely rich in material things. At the wharves of Alexandria merchants bartered in all the products of all the lands of the world. Silks, spices and gems from the East were traded for furs and amber from the Baltic. In the banking houses of Rhodes elaborate financial enterprises were planned and launched. In Alexandria and Antioch highly organized governments ruled over vast empires.

The cultural life of the Hellenic Orient was fully as brilliant as its economic activity. There was no field of human endeavor in which this age did not excel. The same architectural genius which had created the unparalleled majesty of the Acropolis now built the Pharos of Alexandria and the Colossus of Rhodes. The tradition of Phidias and Praxiteles lived again in those sculptors who carved out the Laocoön and the Dying Gaul. In scientific research also this world distinguished itself. It produced the Euclid who systematized geometry, the Ptolemy who charted the heavens, and the Aristoxenus who wrote on harmonics. The museum of Alexandria with its zoölogical and botanical gardens was no accident. It was a logical expression of the scientific interests of a civilization that had been born when the West met the East. And the library of Alexandria with its vast collection of books — that, too, was a symbol of this Oriental-Greek world. The poetry of Apollonius of Rhodes, and of Callimachus, the Idylls of Theocritus, the satires of Lucian, the biographies of Plutarch, the essays of Theophrastus, the history of Polybius, and the geography of Strabo and Pausanias — all these were fitting successors to the literature of classic Greece. Certainly, until the dawn of the modern era no other society has created literary masterpieces in such variety and profusion.

Closely akin to this literary activity ran a great philosophical tradition. The Stoicism of Zeno and Chrysippus, Epictetus and

Marcus Aurelius, the Hedonism of Epicurus and Lucretius, the Scepticism of Carneades and Sextus Empiricus, and the neo-Platonic school which attained its climax in Plotinus — all these give vivid indication of the fact that the intellects of this age wrestled with the problem of truth, the riddle of the universe and man's place in it.

Affluent in its possession of physical things, colorful in its art, glorious in its literature, and searching in its philosophy, this was indeed a magnificent world, a world startlingly like our own.

The Jew, to be sure, could not but be affected by this dazzling culture. The upper strata of Jewish society in Palestine were Hellenized as completely as the aristocracies of other lands. In Egypt, where Jews were fully exposed to Hellenism, Greek culture profoundly permeated Hebraic life. Books like those of Philo, the Wisdom of Solomon, and Fourth Maccabees show how deeply the Jewish community of Alexandria was influenced by the dominating civilization of its day. But as a whole, Palestinian Jewry stood unyielding in the face of all the seductions of Hellenism. And when Antiochus IV attempted to force the Greek way of life upon the Hebrews the Maccabees rose in rebellion.

Considering the overflowing richness of the Hellenistic world, its elegance, and its culture, one is tempted to brand the Maccabees and their followers as blind obscurantists, as benighted half barbarians who out of pure perversity resisted the transmission to themselves of elegance, beauty and truth.

And yet, the objection of the Jew to this Greek world, to its science, its art, its philosophy, and its amenities was not the blind, unreasoning hatred of an uncultured group for intelligence. It sprang from an intuitive but none the less profound and accurate judgment on the part of the Jews concerning Hellenism. There were in Greek life certain deep and fundamental voids. certain basic lacks, which the ancient Jew perceived. And there was in

the Jewish tradition a body of religious and moral values for
which the Maccabees fought justifiably. Almost by instinct, the
Jew recognized that his culture possessed attitudes and ideals of
which the Greeks were unaware but which were eternally necessary for man's blessedness and his salvation.

In the first place, the Greek world had no living religion. The
old pagan idolatry was dead. With the passing of the Olym-
pian gods philosophers took refuge in metaphysical abstractions.
The masses, left without a satisfying faith, turned to a cynical
scepticism, shot through with the blindest superstition. Men
believed in nothing and yet exhibited astonishing credulity in
accepting any belief no matter how incredible. Organized religions have been accused of fostering superstition, and in instances,
unfortunately numerous, the charge is justified. But it is equally
true that when disciplined faiths disintegrate, men, far from
being freed from faith and superstition alike, tend to take re-
course to religious vagaries. The Hellenistic world is a classic
case in point. The pagan, as Pliny testified, worshiped blind
chance as the dominant power behind the world. But in a universe in which caprice rules, any ritual act, any charm or formula
may possibly have efficacy. Whence it came to pass that ma-
gicians, astrologers and writers of amulets grew in number as
organized religion decayed. The ancient Greek, in addition,
wanted, as men always have, some faith to give meaning to his
life. Unable to find it in his own world, he turned religious fad-
dist, moving restlessly with tides of religious fashion from one
cult to another. Now it was the Magna Mater, now it was
Mithra, now Isis, now Serapis, now some fantastic meteoric
stone worshiped as a god in some isolated Oriental hamlet. How
desperately this world needed a religion can be seen from the
eagerness with which it ultimately embraced Christianity.

The Jew considered this pagan world which had no faith and

no assurance as to the universe, which maintained a system of
state-endowed temples housing gods in whom no one really
believed, which taught religions from which all vitality had fled.
He viewed this society with its cults and fads, its blind superstitions and its religious stupidities. He concluded naturally that
he possessed one thing which the pagans did not have — a
reasonable and intelligible faith concerning the universe, a faith
which told him that the universe was not a matter of blind
chance, but the manifestation of a cosmic mind, that his life was
not a meaningless accident, but an integral and infinitely significant part of a universal drama. He rejected the Greek world
because it offered no adequate religion such as he found in his
own tradition.

Of equal weight in impelling the Jew's rejection of Hellenism
was his awareness of a profound difference in morals between
the two worlds. One of the ancient rabbis, contrasting Judaism
and Hellenism, remarked, "Three distinctive characteristics are
to be found among Jews. They are merciful, they are chaste,
and they are charitable." In this epigram are to be detected
moral distinctions between Greek and Jewish society which the
ancient Jew perceived.

The Jew almost alone in the ancient world had a sense of the
dignity of the life of every human being. His tradition taught
him that man was created through the infusion of the dust by
the spirit of God, that each human being therefore was a divinity
in miniature, and consequently of infinite moral significance.
For that reason he was taught to detest all form of human exploitation, of the violent imposition by one man of his will upon
others. In his schools of law, these ideals were given practical
application through a reluctance to inflict capital punishment,
and through the attempt to mitigate human slavery by so protecting the rights of the bondsman as to make the possession of

a slave economically unprofitable. In contrast, the Greek world was entirely without a sense of reverence for the sanctity of life. The Hellenistic social structure was built upon a brutal slavery. From Plato and Aristotle to the last days of Roman paganism, only rarely were even the best spirits among the Greeks moved to protest against this extreme exploitation of men and women. To be sure, Hellenistic literature does contain discussion on the morality of human bondage. But these discussions, while they reveal an inner moral disquietude, tend to end either with a rationalization of the *status quo* or with the advice to the slave to find his freedom in inner self-emancipation. In any event, the slave economy of the Graeco-Roman world was very little disturbed by moral protest. Observing the amphitheater where human beings were done to death for the amusement of blood-thirsty mobs, the Jew concluded, as Walter Pater did centuries later, that "what was needed was the heart that would make it impossible to witness all this; and the future would be with the forces that could beget a heart like that." He knew that the Greeks abused their slaves. He perceived that Greek society was founded upon violence, that in it the world belonged to the strong. He, who had learned to reverence man as an incarnation of God, rejected the Greek world because, in addition to having no adequate faith, it had also no respect for life, no recognition of the inviolability of the human soul.

Almost alone, too, the Jew had standards of chastity. Jewish society had developed a tradition of sexual continence that avoided sensual bestiality without being ascetic. The Greek world, on the other hand, by and large, vacillated between complete and abandoned self-indulgence and extreme, insane flight from the flesh. It exhibited, on the one side, the sensual excesses of the Gardens of Daphne, and, on the other, the rigid asceticism of the later neo-Platonists. It is significant that no Jew ever found it necessary to boast of one of his great rabbis, as Plato, in the *Symposium*, boasts of Socrates, that he was not a homosexualist. This distinction in moral standards was reflected in a difference in the tone of family life and in the position of women. The normal Jewish world reverenced the marital state, and insisted on its spiritual significance and indispensability — in marked contrast to the Hellenistic family in which the wife served to breed children and from which the cultured Greek fled to find his social outlets in the companionship of cultivated courtesans, known as *Hetaerae*. In all that brilliant world with its science and its arts, the Jew then possessed an attitude toward sexual relationships which in its wholesomeness was distinctly superior to that of the society which surrounded him.

And, last of all, the Jew was unique in his recognition of the virtue of charity. From Plato through the Stoics, there is rarely to be discerned in Greek thought any vestige of compassion for the human underdog, for those who fail in life. Plato has no scruples of kindness in consigning the masses of men to bondage in his ideal state. Aristotle insists that some human beings are naturally slaves. The Stoics generally despise the great masses of men as *typhloi* or blind fools. Only the Jew had a doctrine of charity and of sympathy for the oppressed. Only he had the feeling that man attains his truest humanity in the giving of himself to those who falter in the struggle for existence. In all the Greek world there was rarely heard a sentiment akin to that of the sages of Israel, "Seest thou a righteous man persecuting a righteous man, know thou that God is with the persecuted; a wicked man persecuting a wicked man, know thou that God is with the persecuted; a wicked man persecuting a righteous man, know thou that God is with the persecuted; and even when the righteous persecutes the wicked, by the very fact of his persecution, God is with the persecuted."

This is not to say that the Jewish world was one of pure ethical light and the Hellenistic completely a realm of shadow. Not all Jews were saints and not all teachers of Judaism expounded an undiluted and ideal saintliness. Nor was Hellenism without mitigating religious and moral virtues. Among the Stoics there is often to be found a vivid religious philosophy — a series of doctrines concerning God and the world which these Stoics maintained not for themselves alone but which they sought to communicate to the masses of men through public lectures. In the *Gorgias* of Plato, which expounds the proposition that it is preferable to suffer wrong than to inflict it, an individual Greek spirit flamed into an ethical idealism which was of a piece with much that motivated Judaism generally. On occasion among the Stoics there are heard notes of compassion for suffering humanity, of a sympathetic sensitivity to the pains of men, individual and collective. Indeed, among the Stoic legalists there appeared the axiom that all men are by nature equal — a proposition which, almost in the exact terminology in which these Stoics phrased it, appears in the American Declaration of Independence; it reflected an attitude which unfortunately was never competently applied by those who maintained it to the society of their day. There were currents of humaneness, movements of compassion, tides of a fuller religious life in the Hellenistic sea. But by and large and in essence the religious and moral distinctions which we have indicated above are unshakably valid. As a whole, each of these two traditions held virtual monopolies on attitudes and values of which the other possessed only fragmentary specimens.

It was because of this inherent difference in tone that the Jew rejected Hellenism. The Greek world had wealth, science, art, and literature. They were not enough. It had no adequate faith and it had too little heart. It was inevitable that this world would fall into decay; that it would collapse into barbarism, that it would be conquered eventually by a religion born of Judaism, which supplied a rationale that made life significant and which conveyed standards of mercy, chastity, and compassion. In the very moment of its flowering, Hellenism was doomed, because the intellect and the sense of the aesthetic are not sufficient for man. As Santayana put it,

> "Oh, world, thou choosest not the better part!
> It is not wisdom to be only wise."

The two worlds, as a matter of fact, did not exclude each other completely. On Palestinian Jewry, because of its rejection of the Greek-Oriental way, Hellenism had but little influence. On Jewry outside of Palestine, especially on that Egyptian Jewry which centered around Alexandria, the imprint of Hellenism was real and pronounced. We have already had occasion to refer to Jewish writings such as The Wisdom of Solomon, The Fourth Maccabees, and above all, those of Philo, as indications of how profoundly the Jew in the Diaspora responded to the values of the enveloping society. But the major consequence of the meeting between Judaism and Hellenism and of the interplay between them is to be found neither in Judaism nor in Hellenism but in a way of life which emerged from the two of them, in Christianity. The coöperative rôle which both societies played in preparing the way for the triumph of Christianity was very large. The Septuagint, the translation of the Bible into Greek, had beaten a path for the first Christian missionaries. The propaganda which for several centuries Judaism had maintained among the pagans, seeking to win them to the Jewish way of life, had prepared an apperceptive mass in the minds of the Greeks and the Romans, and had given them in advance of the Apostolic Church a preliminary understanding of the central positions common both to Judaism and Christianity. Indeed, the existence of pagan converts and sympathizers with Judaism in every large city throughout the Roman Empire provided a responsive audience to Paul and those who came after him. The work of men like Philo which synthesized Hellenistic philosophy with Jewish religious and moral intuitions supplied the early Christians with a systematic ideology on the basis of which, after some slight modifications, they could appeal to the Hellenistic intellectuals.

And yet, the Christian synthesis, without prejudice to those virtues which are inherent in it, was not a truly successful synthesis of Hellenism and Judaism. Jew and Christian will not agree, of course, as to whether or not it did violence to the spirit of Judaism. But that it did do violence to the spirit of Hellenism is clearly evident. For having abstracted from the Greek world the material for its dogmatics, its theology, its literary expression and some of its forms, Christianity failed to carry over into itself the aesthetic values, the intellectual freedom and the spirit of scientific research which are most truly distinctive of Hellenism. In brief, a number of essential and truly characteristic qualities were lost in the fusion.

A great opportunity presented itself to mankind when Judaism and Hellenism met — an opportunity which unfortunately was not seized in its entirety. Had these two worlds interpenetrated each other peacefully, an ideal pattern for man's living might have been created. This would have preserved the intellectual alertness and aesthetic sensitivity of Hellenism in synthesis with the Hebraic religious outlook and ethical values. Such a fusion would have abstracted the virtues of both cultures and enabled them to supplement each other. Mankind still entertains the hope that the time may yet come when Hebraic faith and ethics will be harmoniously fused with Hellenistic science, philosophy, and art, into a pattern of living richer than either alone.

But if these cultures could not at the time of the Maccabean rebellion be forced into a syncretism, it was extremely important for man's future that they be maintained independently. The values for which the Jews fought were fully as necessary for mankind as those which the Greeks sought to impose upon them. The long service which the Hebraic genius has rendered to humanity in the past, and the possibility of an ultimate synthesis in the future between the Hellenistic and Hebraic spirits are due to the courage of a band of Judaean insurrectionists who fought, not only for freedom and faith, but also for values indispensable for man's salvation.

PALESTINE

TIME OF THE MACCABEES

(acc. to I. Maccabees)

Damascus

Sidon

PHOENICIA

Tyre

LITANY

Abila
Tyriorum

PRESENT BOUNDARY

Kedesh

Hazor   MEROM

Maked !

Acco

GALILEE

Bosr

Arbela   SEA OF
KINNERETH

Karnaim

Alma

Dor

JORDAN VALLEY

Ephron

Casphon ?

Mizpah !   Raphon !

GREAT

SEA

Beth-shean

GILEAD

Bosra

SAMARIA

Samaria

Jaffa

Ramathaim

Hadid

Lod

Modin   Bethel

Ephraim   Jazer   Rabbath Ammon

Jamnia   Ekron   Beth-horon   Dock

Ashdod   Gezer   Emmaus   Mizpah   Michmash   Jericho

Kedron   JERUSALEM   JUDAEA

AMMON

Ascalon   Timnah   Adasah   Bethlehem

Madeba

Beth-zachariah   Wilderness
of Tekoa

Mareshah   Tekoa   Beth-zur   SEA
OF THE
PLAIN
OR
SALT
SEA

GAZA   Tapuah   Hebron

Adora

IDUMAEA

MOAB

NABATEANS

Akrabim

PRESENT BOUNDARY

Jerico

Mishal   Ramoth

Conquests by Judah Maccabee.

Conquests by Jonathan (3 districts)

Further conquests by Jonathan

Jewish territory at end of Macc. wars

Resettled a controlled territory by Jews

Jewish territory in time of Alexander Janai

◆   Fortified places

②   Macc. battles { 1-10 by Judah
10-14 by Jonathan
15 by Simeon

HANUKKAH AND ITS HISTORY

Solomon Grayzel

I

The First Hanukkah: 165 Before the Common Era

THE last outpost marched through the gates; the heavy wooden doors were swung shut, and the iron bolts moved into their sockets. Erect, and gloomy, the captain of the small band of Syrian soldiers stood in the narrow court awaiting the report of his returning outpost. Its corporal saluted, "Just outside the walls of the City." He went on. Without moving, the Captain again calculated the chance of holding out until the Syrian army, defeated in the field, would reorganize and come to his aid. The Acra fortress was none too strong; his trained soldiers none too many. As to these self-despising Jews, . . . his eyes wandered to where, silent, frightened, the bolder among them stood huddled in a corner. What good were they who were the cause of this trouble! Smart uniforms, smooth tongues, loud protestations of loyalty. Better in games of skill than any of his soldiers, on the field of battle, could they do a tenth as well as even those uncouth farmers who were now approaching Jerusalem? That army of farmers and their leader Judah, by what power were they able to defeat a Syrian host? . . . Their mysterious God? . . . The Captain knew a moment of fear.

Before the walls of the City, Judah the Maccabee and his army halted. The great moment had come; Jerusalem was before them. No resistance was to be expected to their entrance into the City. The Syrian garrison was small; even with the support of the somewhat larger number of Hellenist Jews, the best the invader could hope to do would be to defend the Acra, and perhaps make an occasional sortie. To the attack, therefore! His own followers knew Judah's plan: it was to take the Acra by assault, and thus cleanse the City entirely of all foreigners and apostates. The command was to move forward. With an exultant shout the Judaeans crossed the ruined wall. As it began its march through the City, the army of Judah sang.

Silent streets, deserted houses! Is this Jerusalem, the joyous, the populous city? In the poorer section, into which the army first entered, the very streets were covered with weeds. The inhabitants had been dispersed long ago by the invading Syrians. Some had remained to become martyrs. Some of the army, themselves fugitives, recalled Eleazar, the aged scribe, and Hannah and her seven sons. The singing began to die down; the army was saddened. Onward they marched, through wider streets, by handsomer houses. Here, too, a stillness as of the grave. The residents had but recently fled; this time before the conquering Jews. Here and there, in front of a home, stood a low, carved stone table. Angry mutterings now began to rise from among the army. They knew these stone tables; these were altars, altars upon which Jews had offered sacrifices to pagan gods. The marchers cursed them, and called for vengeance.

To reach the Acra it was necessary to pass close to the Temple. No word of command was spoken, yet officers and men gravitated toward the center of holiness. They came close; they stopped. They saw dilapidated walls, doors torn from their hinges and hanging awry, curtains in tatters, grass, weeds. Over all hung a deathly stillness, and in the center, above a gold altar, the statue of a god — a dead god in a dead sanctuary. There could be no further talk of an attack upon the Acra. Against his better judgment Judah yielded. He did not even argue.

The Temple became a bee-hive of activity. Fighters became builders. Feverishly they worked to repair the walls, the doors, the curtains. They gathered all the utensils and put them aside, for these had been desecrated. The idol was taken out of the Temple area, and stepped upon by thousands of feet until it was ground into a fine dust. But what to do with the altar? Upon it sacrifices had been performed by pious priests; its stones were therefore sacred even though defiled. It was taken apart, stone by stone, and put away into a corner. Pious hands built a new altar. Pious hands prepared bread for the table inside the hall. Pious hands prepared new utensils.

For weeks this activity went on. No one thought any longer of fighting against the Acra. Judah barely persuaded the men to take turns watching the fortress, lest the foe within break out and undo the work that had been done. Finally all was ready; all, that is, except the Menorah, the sacred candelabrum, to replace which no material was at hand. A celebration was in order. But for what day should it be set? A happy thought occurred to someone. The twenty-fifth of Kislev was but a few days hence, and it marked the third anniversary of the desecration of the Temple. Indeed, what could be more fitting than that the rededication should take place on that day?

The day came, and it was celebrated gloriously. Priests were found in the army, and they performed the sacrifices. As some of these soldier-priests entered the chambers they discovered some old and obviously long unused iron spikes. They attached small torches to them and made a Menorah, a rough, soldier-Menorah, but in a proper setting. Palm-branches were held by hands that had held swords. *Hallelu-Jah* was sung by throats

that had shouted a battle-cry. A new poem was recited by the
Levites:

> "I extol Thee, O Lord, for Thou hast delivered me, and
> hast not caused mine enemies to rejoice over me."

Not far off, the Syrian Captain stood on the watchtower of
the Acra, relieved and puzzled.

That was the first Hanukkah.

II

ORIGIN OF HANUKKAH

How did this event, this Hanukkah, come to be and how does
it fit into the history of the Jewish people? Who are the men
mentioned in connection with the story, and why is it so important that we still remember it after twenty centuries? This is
a much longer story. To tell it we must go back some centuries
before the event, and follow the changes among the Jewish
people in connection with the transformation of the Near East.
For the story of Hanukkah reveals why they alone, and not
one of all the petty nations who were their jealous neighbors,
none of the great empires who contended for dominion over them,
survived as a conscious and historic group.

Alexander the Great will be the focal point for the first part
of our story, since his coming to the East marks a definite era
in the history of all that part of the world. The touch of his
conquering sword awakened hither Asia. New administrative
methods, new men, new ideas replaced the lethargic system of
the unwieldy, loosely bound, though on the whole benevolent
Persian Empire. The eastern world was ready for this change,
and not even a generation of warfare which followed upon the

Conqueror's death while his generals were dividing the spoils of the conquest, did anything to hinder the spread of Greek civilization. The very soil responded to the new manner of life, and because of the modernization of the methods of agriculture, began to produce more abundantly. Commerce began to flourish because of the intimate connection between East and West. The population of the Asiatic lands bordering on the Mediterranean increased rapidly.

In the territory under Greek influence lived a little nation, small in area and in population. Before the coming of Alexander into the East the Greeks had hardly heard of this people. Even the name which the Greeks gave to its land was *Philistia*, after the Philistines who lived upon the coast. Nonetheless, vague rumors had reached the Greeks of a people dwelling inland who were devoted to agriculture and to an Invisible God of Heaven whose law of life its scribes were expounding. Travelers brought word to Greece of this "nation of philosophers who worship the sky."

Two centuries before the coming of Alexander, the Jews, this inland people, having returned from Babylonian exile, had reconstituted their nation under the milder overlordship of the Persian king. They rebuilt the temple in the City of Jerusalem, and, failing to reëstablish the Davidic Dynasty, they lived under the rule of the High Priest of the House of Aaron who combined with his religious functions autonomous secular power. Comparatively little is known about the history of the Jews during these two centuries. Their neighbors, Philistines, Ammonites, and Samaritans, had tried to hamper the establishment of the nation, but the militant tactics of Nehemiah and the spiritual activity of Ezra defeated their plots and set the small nation on the road to mental and physical independence. Though we know practically nothing of what happened after these two leaders had done their life's work, it is clear that the age which followed their activity was spiritually a highly productive one. It was then that the Torah and the prophetic books are said to have received the form in which we now have them. It was then that the small community was finally weaned away from those idolatrous practices against which the prophets had inveighed and which continued to characterize the religion of the peoples about them. Above all, it was then that the class of teachers known as Scribes, *Soferim*, was active, and so thorough was their teaching that when the avalanche of Greek civilization was sweeping everything before it, the Jewish mode of life was strong enough to offer successful resistance.

As a matter of fact, for a full century after the coming of Alexander, Judaea continued to be unaffected by Greek ways. Their neighbors had succumbed easily. The cities in the district once known as Philistia, as well as those of Ammon, Moab, and Edom, had given up the very gods in whose names they had fought the Hebrews of bible days; they had identified these gods with one or another of the gods of Olympus, adopted Greek dress and even Greek speech, and thus disappeared as entities from the pages of history. The Jews, to be sure, were also affected by the coming of the Greeks, but not at all in the same way. When the new Egyptian city of Alexandria was built, many Jews were brought there, and they soon became an important section of that city's population, and contributed greatly to its commercial development. The Syrian emperors, in their turn, brought many Jews out of Babylonia and settled them in the newly constituted cities of their empire. These Jews naturally learned Greek ways of dress and of speech and other externals of Greek civilization. In the matter of religion, however, which played a central part in the constitution of the Greek city, the Jews held aloof, though this complicated their life and led to friction with their neighbors. But in Judaea proper, small and somewhat removed from the great highways of the world, the inhabitants were not subjected to such external influences, and therefore continued in the even tenor of their ways.

But a situation soon developed which made the continuance of such isolation impossible. It has ever been the fate of Palestine to be a bone of contention between whatever power controlled Egypt and whatever power controlled Syria. Soon after the death of Alexander, Judaea fell to the lot of Egypt and the Ptolemy family which ruled over it. In the last quarter of the third century before the Common Era the rulers of Syria, descendants of Seleucus, one of Alexander's generals, began to reassert their claim to the land. They did, in fact, cast an avid eye upon Egypt altogether, and the district of Lower Syria, of which Judaea was a part, was the first step in the realization of their ambitions to be the successors of Alexander. In the year 198 before the Common Era, Judaea was finally incorporated into the Syrian state, and the Seleucid kings were faced with the problem of making that incorporation permanent.

How did the Jews themselves feel about this change in their overlord? When a nation becomes of international importance it is but natural that the preferences of its people should be divided on the basis of public and private interests. One in religion, Jews the world over felt a sympathy for each other. Those of the Diaspora, that is of the lands outside of Palestine, were accustomed to send their annual contribution for the support of the Holy Temple in Jerusalem. Small as the individual contributions were, they aggregated vast sums. On the other hand, the Jews of Judaea could not but feel flattered or outraged according to the treatment meted out to their fellow-Jews in Diaspora lands. Now the Ptolemies of Egypt started out by being favorably disposed to the Jews of Alexandria, but for reasons into which we need not go here, their policy underwent a change at the very time when the Syrian Empire sought to win Judaean sympathy to itself. What is more, the High Priest may have realized that, since the majority of the Jews of that day lived in Asia and under Syrian power, it was more to the advantage of the Temple for Jerusalem to be connected politically with this majority than with the comparatively smaller population then residing in Egypt. By and large, therefore, it would seem that the Jews of Judaea were satisfied with the change of rule. They little dreamed what troubles it would bring upon them within the short space of thirty years.

It is well to bear in mind that the Jewish victories which are celebrated on Hanukkah were not only of political and religious importance, but of social importance as well. A social transformation was taking place within Jewish life which, in a very real sense, formed the basis for the religious and political uprising of the Maccabees. The beginnings of this social change were small. While Judaea was still under Egyptian rule, a certain Jew by the name of Joseph ben Tobias, of noble ancestry and related to the High Priest, took advantage of the anti-Egyptian inclinations of the High Priest and of the Egyptian king's need of money, to have himself appointed chief tax-collector for the entire province of Syria. Supported by an Egyptian army he filled the hearts of the Jews and pagans of Palestine with fear, and his own pockets with money. In the loose administration of the time, being a tax-collector meant more than collecting taxes; it meant economic dictatorship. Joseph and his sons, generally known as the Tobiades, along with the officials he appointed, achieved two things; they made Jews disliked by the gentiles, and they established Jerusalem as a commercial center, with themselves and their henchmen as a powerful aristocracy. Thereafter Jerusalem was no longer on a by-path in the Greek world; Judaea's isolation was ended.

The Jewish theocracy was now turned into an oligarchy. The priests had until now formed the aristocratic element of the population. Their duties were in the Temple, and their income was from the Temple treasury. Organized into a *gerousia*, an advisory council to the High Priest, they were the chief authority of the autonomous state. Now, as a result of commerce, a class was added to the Judaean population whose claim to power rested on its wealth. Like the Tobiades, this wealthy class became identical or identified itself with the ruling powers.

Commerce and wealth brought these people in touch with Hellenistic attitudes and manner of life. Individual material success was the order of the day. The common people of that day, that is of the time when the Tobiades were rising to power, have left no documents from which their feelings at the changed order could be gauged. But in the wise words of Ben Sira, who wrote the book Ecclesiasticus, now a part of the collection known as the Apocrypha, some modern scholars see a reflection of the situation which then obtained. Thus in Chapter 13, vss. 18–20, Ben Sira says: "What agreement is there between the hyena and the dog? And what peace between the rich and the poor? As the wild ass is the lion's prey in the wilderness, so the rich eat up the poor. As the proud hate humility, so doth the rich abhor the poor." Again and again he returns to this subject. A class struggle was on the horizon.

For the most part, however, the Jews were a peasant people, while wealth was centered in the cities. They must have heard of the ways of the wealthy, though their actual contact with them, while painful, could not have been frequent. Something in addition to economic pressure was needed to change social cleavage into actual revolt. This something soon appeared in the nature of a hellenization of the upper stratum of Jerusalem society, so thorough as to shock the conservative and loyal population.

Their economic ambitions drove the Tobiades and their followers farther on the road to hellenization. In order to increase their commercial opportunities it seemed necessary to place Jerusalem on an equal plane with other ambitious cities. Privileges of self-government were needed, none of which could be obtained unless Jerusalem adopted a thoroughly Greek constitution. No doubt a great deal of social prestige went hand in hand with these economic advantages. But all this could be done only after the conservative element of the population had been either won over or cowed, and especially after the actual rule over the land, lodged in the High Priest, had been obtained by the elements favorable to the "reform."

Scandalized as the pious elements of the Jewish population in and out of Jerusalem were, by the gymnasia which were now built in the City, by the new manners and the new clothes of Greek style affected by the young bloods of the aristocracy, and by the neglect on the part of the young priests of their sacred duties in the Temple, they still had no power to make their objection heard.

The hellenizing Jews then proceeded with the second part of their plan, namely to capture the High Priesthood. But this was an hereditary office, and not even a priest could succeed to it unless he were in the direct line of descent. Nevertheless, they thought they could effect a change for the better by means of political maneuvering. For most of the Tobiades had made peace with the powers that were in the land, since that was to their economic advantage. Onias III, the High Priest of that day, on the other hand, was not only not in sympathy with the plans of the Tobiades, he was not even sympathetic to the rule of the Syrian power, as his forefathers had been, and would have liked to return Judaea to the rule of Egypt. He recognized the advantages of a western over an eastern alliance. To undermine the authority of the High Priest with the Syrian king the hellenizers told the king of large sums of money which were found in the Temple treasury, especially that some of this money belonged to a man who was pro-Egyptian in sympathy. At once a royal official was dispatched to Jerusalem. Legend has since embellished his visit. He is supposed to have forced entrance into the Temple, and to have been met there by a fiery horseman with two assistants, who beat him so that he had to be carried out unconscious. Legend or no legend, the fact is that Heliodorus, the official in question, left Jerusalem and the Temple treasury intact.

Thus the first attempt to dislodge Onias III failed, but the thought that the Temple in Jerusalem had money stuck in the mind of the Syrian king. Antiochus IV, surnamed Epiphanes, which means "God Manifest," was now on the throne. He was a peculiar person; so queer, in fact, that some of his subjects called him "Epimanes," i.e., "the mad one." But there was nothing at all queer about his policy; it was characteristic of the age as well as of the man. He saw a chance for the realization of the old Syrian dream to conquer Egypt. That required money, and the loyalty, at least, if not the active coöperation of the border lands. To him the hellenizers turned once more with a proposal that they would pay liberally for a change in the high priesthood—especially since the loyalty of Onias was questionable—and for a Greek constitution for Jerusalem. The suggestion was that Onias be replaced by his younger brother, who was more amenable to Tobiad aims. That was done. Jason (Joshua), brother of Onias, became the High Priest, and Jerusalem received a new name, Antiochaea, after the Syrian king, to symbolize its new standing as a thoroughly Greek city.

If the conservative elements of the population were horrified by these changes: that the high priesthood should be bought and that a pagan power should have a hand in the appointment to it; that Jerusalem should bear a Greek name, and that Temple money should be spent for the introduction of Greek customs; they were destined to be still more horrified by the next act in the drama. For about three years Jason remained High Priest, and so subservient to the hellenizing influences that they could find no fault with him. But this very subservience made them look upon him as a tool. If the high-priestly office could be bought for money, why not buy it for one of their own leaders? Menelaus was the Grecianized name of the man who had such ambitions. His Hebrew name may have been Honiah, i.e., Onias, and in all likelihood he was a priest, though even that has been doubted; he certainly was not in the traditional line of succession to the office. By promising a huge sum of money to Antiochus he received the appointment. Then began a civil war within the City of Jerusalem between the adherents of Jason, who with all his faults could at least lay claim to being of the legitimate line, and the extreme hellenizers, to whom Jewish tradition no longer possessed any sacredness at all.

Menelaus won. A reign of terror began in Jerusalem, which could be justified before the Syrian authorities only on the ground that the enemies of Menelaus were the enemies of Antiochus. Yet Antiochus' interest in Menelaus was purely financial. He was threatened with removal unless he paid what he had promised, and to do so he had his brother steal and dispose of some of the sacred vessels in the Temple. This was sacrilege, a crime which horrified even the pagans. To protest against this the ex-High Priest Onias came out of his hiding. Menelaus, however, hired an assassin to dispose of him.

Menelaus, nevertheless, could be secure only so long as Syrian arms could be called upon to uphold him. It was abundantly clear that even the population of Jerusalem, accustomed as it was to hellenizing efforts, did not consider him their representative, but that of the Syrian power and of a coterie of rich men. When a rumor spread that Antiochus had been killed on an Egyptian expedition, Jason again appeared upon the scene. Around him the populace of Jerusalem rallied, and Menelaus had to flee for his life. Unfortunately Antiochus was not dead, but only enraged that he had been cheated of the fruits of his victory over Egypt by the arrogant power of Rome. When he heard what had happened in Jerusalem, he ordered his appointee reinstated, and, in order once for all to do away with the "nonsensical" opposition of the Jewish masses, he outlawed their customs and traditions. Circumcision and adherence to the dietary laws were forbidden, and upon the altar of the Temple was placed the statue of Zeus, so that sacrifices might be brought to the god whose manifestation on earth Antiochus considered himself to be.

Surely Antiochus did not realize what he was doing. He thought that he was merely hastening a process of the results of which he had no doubt. The other peoples, neighbors of the Jews, had succumbed quickly and easily to the lure of the hellenistic life. As far as he could see the presumably "intelligent" Jew had also yielded. If the masses of this obdurate people refused to yield, he was there to force them. Moreover, Antiochus saw the High Priest as his appointed official, and could not appreciate the Jewish attitude which saw the High Priest as the Elect of God. Whether the hellenizing Jews realized the situation is a matter more open to doubt. They had not foreseen because they had not intended any such *dénouement* to their plotting ambitions. But the die was cast. Between the might of Syria and the weakness of Judaea there was no choice.

They had imbibed the spirit of Greek individualism; personal
life and success was their ideal. As far as they were concerned
the experiment of Jewish nationhood was over, and they were
willing to share the City of Jerusalem with the new pagan inhabitants whom Antiochus was going to settle there after the
Jews who had opposed him were slaughtered or dispersed. They
were willing to live under the high-priesthood of Menelaus, and
in the shadow of the Temple in which the God of Heaven was
identified with Zeus, just as hellenized Tyre identified its Melkart
with Heracles, and Askelon identified its Astarte with Aphrodite.

The last days of the Jewish people seemed to have arrived.
Groups of Syrian soldiers went from town to town and from
village to village, enforcing the new decrees. The unorganized
peasantry had no means of resistance. The best they could do
was to flee to the hills of Judaea, there to hide until the period
of wrath was over. It is about this phase that the stories of
heroism and martyrdom, such as that of Hannah and her seven
sons, and of old Eleazar, are told. In themselves these stories
are not incredible, though it was probably not Antiochus himself who figured in these incidents.

It was but natural that the bands of fugitives should begin
to think of organized opposition. It may be that even before
the final blow fell the pious opponents of hellenization came to
be known as Hasidim.[1] Against them the decree of Antiochus
was aimed, and from among them organized resistance could
be expected. Their piety was their strength; it was also their
weakness. They refused to fight on the Sabbath, even in self-
defense. The story has come down about a band of a thousand
who permitted themselves to be destroyed rather than desecrate

---

[1] They have no relation to the Hasidic movement started by R. Israel in
the 18th century.

the day of rest. Under such circumstances even organized re-sistance was useless.

One such band of fugitive Hasidim soon came to stand out above the others. It was led by a family of priests from the little town of Modin, but a short distance from Jerusalem. Whether because of an ancestor by the name of Hasmon, or for some other reason, they were known as Hasmoneans. The fact that they were priests gave them prestige; and the fact that they had lived outside of the City made them share pietist views. The old father, Mattathias, had incurred the enmity of the Syrians by refusing to participate in a heathen sacrifice, and by leading his five sons in an attack upon the Syrian troop that had come to enforce the decrees against Judaism. With the Hasidim among their townsmen they took to the hills, and then pursued the usual policy of attacking small bands of soldiers and hellenized Jews. There was one thing that distinguished them from all similar bands; they adopted the view that for purposes of self-defense fighting on the Sabbath was permissible. This, along with the unmistakable signs of military ability shown by one of the sons, Judah, very quickly attracted other Hasidim, so that at last the Jewish people had a miniature army in the field.

Judah the Maccabee stands out as among the few great military leaders whom the Jewish people produced. Since his followers are known as Maccabees, and the entire movement as the Maccabean Revolt, it might be in place to say a word about the origin of Judah's surname, *ha-Maccabee*. Unfortunately this word has not come down in Hebrew characters, as the orig-inal Hebrew sources have been lost. What is extant is the Greek *Makkabaios* transliterated back into Hebrew. The result has been a variety of guesses. The most unlikely—though most common among Jews because it is in the very spirit of the Revolt

—is that the word "Maccabee" is an acrostic derived from the initial letters of the biblical verse, *Mi Kamoka Ba-elim Ihvh*,[1] "Who is like unto Thee among the gods, O Lord." The assumption is that this sentence was inscribed upon Judah's banner. Another explanation would trace the name from the Hebrew word for hammer, *Makkeb*, thus making of him a sort of Judah Martel. Again it has been suggested that the word should be read *Mazbi*, i.e., the General. The most recent suggestion has been that the name was really *Makabiah*, meaning "Named by the Lord." Whatever it might have meant, Judah's name soon began to strike terror in the hearts of his enemies. The unexpected had happened; the Jews were in organized revolt.

The Syrian forces of the district began to bestir themselves. It is not likely that Antiochus himself, or any of his more important officials, would as yet have taken much note of this rebellion of a poorly armed, peasant population. It was obviously the task of the local authorities to put down what seemed to be a minor insurrection against royal authority. In this task, however, they found enthusiastic support among the gentile neighbors of Judaea.

In this we have a phase of the Maccabean struggle to which attention has been called but recently. Yet it is here that we have an indication that back of the religious and political causes for the Rebellion was one of wider significance, namely the movement of the Jewish population. The small territory upon which the second Jewish Commonwealth was built after the return from the Babylonian Exile was bound to become insufficient. At that very time, however, new Greek colonies and the spurt in the general population of the Syrian Empire brought

---

[1] The letters which in Hebrew stand for the name of God and are pronounced *Adonai*.

new pagan powers on every side of the small Jewish state. But the Jews could not forget that historically all that land was theirs. They did not, to be sure, lay claim to it at this time. Nevertheless, as their overflow population sought new homes in Alexandria, in Asia Minor, and in the Greek Isles, it was natural for many to settle in cities and lands nearer home; in Galilee, on the Phoenician coast, and across the Jordan. To the religious differences, and to the dislike aroused by the Tobiades, was now added economic friction with Jewish competitors. Still, as long as an autonomous Jewish state was in existence, and its leaders stood well with the Syrian court, the pagans could not give vent to their hostility. Clearly it was to their advantage to have the Jewish state destroyed or at least weakened. That is why they responded so eagerly to the call for aid on the part of the local authorities in putting down the Jewish insurrection. As usually happens, they did not wait for the Jews to be definitely defeated, but at once began to harass and attack the Jews who lived in their midst.

The first Syrian force that went to meet Judah was under the leadership of Apollonius, presumably the military governor of the district of Samaria. His force must have been small, and Judah easily overcame it. Apollonius was killed, and thereafter Judah used his captured sword in battle. Then came Seron, another official of the Palestinian district, with a larger force. Judah met him at Beth Horon, a few miles to the northwest of Jerusalem, and defeated him in a surprise attack. Only then did the Syrian authorities realize that a real effort would have to be made, and they dispatched two generals, Nicanor and Gorgias, with a large force, to overwhelm the Jewish rebels. It was in this battle that Judah showed himself to be a consummate strategist. Moreover, he knew the roads of hilly Judaea, and his smaller army was much more mobile than the large force that opposed him. Taking advantage of a temporary division of the enemy, he attacked each army in turn, and put them to flight with great slaughter. The booty provided the Jewish army with ample supplies; for the first time the soldiers under Judah could be said to be properly equipped. In all these battles auxiliary forces from among the neighboring peoples participated as soldiers or came in the capacity of merchant camp-followers ready to buy slaves from among the anticipated Jewish captives.

In spite of these three victories Judah's chances for success were still slender. So tremendous was the Syrian superiority in resources that the Jewish rebellion would have been squelched easily, had not difficulties arisen for Syria in other directions. If, therefore, we define the term miracle as an unexpected coincidence, the miracle of Hanukkah occurred at this point. Chance worked in favor of the Jews, so that at the moment when the Syrian Court should have been planning to send a large force to dispose of the rebellion in the border province near Egypt, it was compelled to go forth on an expedition in Parthia. Antiochus no doubt thought that he could afford to wait to settle the score with the Jews. For about a year there was a lull in the fighting against Judah and his army.

The Maccabean forces used the respite to advantage. The inadequate force that defended Jerusalem could not withstand the army of Hasidim. In triumph and exultation Judah led his band into the sacred City. The hellenizers scattered before him, or shut themselves up in the fortress which Antiochus had built near the Temple. The desolation which had come upon the City during the three years of civil war saddened the conquerors, and they now proceeded to remove every trace of pagan occupation. Three years after its defilement the Temple was cleansed, the statue of Zeus removed, and the altar upon which pagan sacrifices had been brought replaced by a new one. Once more the lights were kindled in the House of God, and pious priests officiated in it. For eight days the Jews celebrated the Feast of Rededication, the Feast of Hanukkah.

It is well to remember that the celebration of Hanukkah does not mark the end of the Maccabean war, but the end of religious oppression, that is the reëstablishment of Jewish worship destined not to be interrupted by the Syrians thereafter. Nevertheless, Hanukkah cannot be separated from the successful termination of the war, for, had it ended in failure, it is not unlikely that the first Hanukkah would have been also the last.

Judah continued the struggle. He further utilized his respite from Syrian attacks to wreak vengeance upon those neighboring cities whose gentile population had shown itself hostile to the Jews. Expeditions were sent to Galilee, to Transjordania, and to the cities on the coast. The first two expeditions were successful. Perhaps Judah would have liked to annex the conquered territory to Judaea, but with another invasion from Syria still threatening, he did not dare to do so. Nor would the Hasidim, who constituted his fighting force, have been willing to have their battles for their faith turned into a war of annexation. That was therefore left for the Hasmonean successors of Judah to accomplish. He contented himself with showing the pagans that the Jews were not helpless, and with transporting some of the most dangerously situated Jews back within Jewish territory.

Now the danger from the North became real. Lysias, whom Antiochus Epiphanes had left as regent of his western kingdom and the guardian of his son while he himself went off to Parthia, at length bestirred himself to settle matters in Judaea. With a large force he descended upon Jerusalem, and Judah was not equal to meeting him in battle. After a spirited fight during which one of his brothers lost his life, Judah was shut up within

Jerusalem, and his army began to suffer the hardships of a long and painful siege. Once more, however, fate intervened to the advantage of the Jewish cause. Antiochus died in the course of his Parthian campaign, and, fortunately for the Jews, he appointed, just before his death, another general as guardian of his young heir Antiochus V. Hearing of this, Lysias was anxious to leave Jerusalem and hurry north to meet his rival. When, therefore, things looked their blackest for the Jews, their enemy suggested a cessation of hostilities. The terms of peace offered the Jews gave them back their former status: freedom of faith, practice and worship, with no efforts at hellenization by force. The one right which Lysias reserved for the Syrian Crown was the right to appoint the High Priest. The new appointee was not Menelaus who was so obnoxious to the Jews, but a man by the name of Alkimus, or Eljakim, who evidently belonged to the moderate Hellenizers.

To the vast majority of the Hasidic Party these terms were highly satisfactory. They had fought the war because their religious scruples had been outraged, and now that the Syrians had promised not to interfere, they were willing to lay down the sword and return to the plow. Judah, however, saw the situation in a more realistic light. He did not trust the Syrians, and even less did he trust the hellenizing Jews from among whom the new High Priest was chosen. He aimed at nothing short of independence. As a matter of fact, Alkimus, supported by Syrian soldiers, no sooner came into power than he had some sixty of the popular party executed. There is nowhere any direct reason offered for this act. Presumably Alkimus wanted to strengthen himself with the pro-Syrian group, or he may have resented the demands of the popular party for a share in the government. The result was that Judah's forces, reduced to a small number because of the peace, and until now in hiding, once more began to grow. Alkimus began to clamor for a return of the Syrian force.

The Syrian general Nicanor appeared with a fair-sized army and a host of elephants. Judah defeated him. Nicanor was killed, and the Jews set the day down as a minor holiday—the 13th of Adar. Shortly thereafter, however, a larger force appeared, and the position of Judah was clearly hopeless. With but eight hundred followers around him, he spurned the advice to run away. He fought his last fight, and fell upon the field of battle.

The death of Judah ended the Maccabean War. A few of his followers, under the leadership of his two remaining brothers, Jonathan and Simon, escaped across the Jordan, and awaited a favorable opportunity to complete the work of Judah. The opportunity was not slow in coming, but the details are beyond the limits of this story. Religious freedom had been attained, but, whether the Jews realized it or not, that was not all they had fought for. For the time being the old group of wealthy men and priestly aristocrats was still in the saddle. They had learned to be more wary in the hellenization of the Jews, but they had not yet learned that Judaism had vitality beyond their strength to extinguish. Behind them still stood the power of Syria, ever willing to take a hand in internal Jewish affairs. Around them lived the gentiles, whose cities were like dikes trying to stem the expansion of a people who had to have more room. The aristocrats and Hellenizers did not realize that the common people had learned their own power and would not again permit others to ride roughshod over them. Before their very eyes the Syrian Empire was disintegrating. One by one its outlying provinces were falling away, while dynastic dissension weakened it from within. In the distance stood the rising power of Rome watching this process with great satisfaction. In fact, Judah the Maccabee and later on his brother, Jonathan, made alliances with Rome against the power of Syria. Above all, the common people among the Jews had gained the consciousness that their own point of view and their own civilization should and could be preserved.

Judah died in 160 before the Common Era. In 152 Jonathan, his brother, became High Priest and autonomous ruler of Judaea. In 135 Simon, the last of the brothers, was appointed hereditary ruler and High Priest by a popular assembly representative of all the people. The Hasmonean Era had begun, and the Hasmonean kings began to extend their dominion.

This religious and national victory is celebrated on Hanukkah.

III

THE HISTORY OF THE FESTIVAL

Holidays, too, may be the playthings of fate; of this Hanukkah is an example. In a very real sense, as we have seen, it contains features which make it comparable to both Passover and Purim. Like the former it marks a time when Jewish life was preserved from the danger of being absorbed by a different culture; like the latter it celebrates a deliverance from the hands of one who plotted the annihilation of the Jewish group. Yet no *seder* takes place on Hanukkah, nor is the synagogue service materially prolonged. The story of Mordecai donning sackcloth has been included in the Bible, whereas Judah's girding of the sword has not. Small candles are lit, and small gifts distributed. Work is permitted as usual, and not even a special dish, or a special kind of cake, marks the days as different from any others. Is this discrimination intentional? Has the long memory of the Jewish people failed in this solitary instance? The truth of the matter is that the history of Hanukkah as a holiday reflects the history of the Jewish group.

For the sake of completeness it must be said that there are some modern scholars who would see in Hanukkah a survival of something far older than the story of the Maccabees. They allege that in remote antiquity, before the Hebrew people broke with pagan ways, they, like so many of the others, were wont to celebrate the winter solstice. Pagan mythologies are well supplied with gods who are said to die with the approach of winter, and for whom their worshipers then proceed to look with lighted torch. The Jews, these scholars say, may have given up the belief in such a deity, but retained the custom of lighting fires at that season of the year. That may be the origin of our Hanukkah candles, just as it may be the origin of the Christmas lights.[1]

Whether or not we accept any such suggestion, it is interesting to note that even Jewish tradition connects the origin of Hanukkah with something that happened before the Maccabean dedication of the Temple. One of the main sources for our knowledge of the Maccabean age, the Second Book of Maccabees, happily preserved in the so-called Apocrypha, tells, in its first chapter, why the twenty-fifth of Kislev was chosen for the dedication. The story goes that when the exiles returned from Babylon and rebuilt the Temple, the fires on the altar were kindled in a most miraculous way, by means of a liquid fire which had been hidden away at the destruction of the first Temple. In commemoration of this miracle—so the story seems to imply, though the author of II Maccabees does not say so

[1] See the works of O. S. Rankin cited in the Bibliography.

I desire to express my thanks to Professor Julian Morgenstern for permitting me to see his as yet unpublished article on *Ancient Semitic Fire-Festivals and Fire-Ceremonies.*

specifically—fires used to be kindled by the Jews. Now, the day upon which this miracle was supposed to have taken place was the twenty-fifth of Kislev, and it was, therefore, a sort of strengthening of an ancient holiday when the Maccabees chose that same day to rededicate the Temple which they restored.

How much of this story can really be believed? The theorizers mentioned above might say that all this talk of an ancient miracle of fire, and of a celebration instituted in its honor, tends to strengthen their hypothesis. But it really is not necessary to read such meanings into the Second Book of Maccabees. The explanation is much simpler. The author of this book was trying to persuade the Jews of Egypt to observe the holiday of Hanukkah. That, as a matter of fact, is why he wrote the book. For a variety of reasons the Egyptian Jews had no interest in Hanukkah. Their ancestors had not been threatened by Antiochus. What is more, the head of Judaism in the land of Egypt was a descendant of that Onias who was High Priest when all the trouble started. Consequently, he must have regarded himself as the rightful claimant to the office in Jerusalem which the Hasmoneans occupied after the victory against the Syrians was won. It was not to be expected, therefore, that Egyptian Jews should find any interest in a holiday established by, and in memory of the Maccabeans. Naturally the author of a book which urged Hanukkah upon the Jews of Egypt was likely to look for other, non-Maccabean arguments to prove the sacredness of the day. Right close at hand he found an old tradition. Was it based on fact, or was it purely fancy? He did not know; but it was useful, and he seized upon it to drive home his point.

As a matter of fact, the same book offers another, much more plausible reason for the original celebration of those days. It calls Hanukkah a "Second Sukkot," and offers the explanation that when Judah's pious followers had finally cleansed the Temple, they bethought themselves of the fact that in the stress of the last campaign they had been prevented from observing Sukkot. This omission they then proceeded to rectify. "Therefore they bare branches and fair boughs, and palms also, and sang psalms unto Him that had given them good success in cleansing His place." Presumably they also dwelt in booths. That, too, may be why Hanukkah is celebrated eight days, for it equals the number of the days of Sukkot. As to the lights, they may have been no more than mere concomitants of the celebration. After all, it is quite a natural thing for people to kindle lights in connection with a holiday. We do so to this day.

To be sure, there is another theory. When the Syrians were masters of the City, it was common practice for them and the disloyal Jews to have small private altars right outside the home upon which a family sacrifice would be offered every so often in honor of a pagan god. The Hasidim destroyed these altars, and as a sort of counterbalance they instituted a ritual of lighting candles in honor of Israel's God. These were to be placed at the entrance to a house, where the pagan altars had stood, or at least so as to be visible from the street.

The First Book of Maccabees, as well as the Second, states that after the first Hanukkah was over the Jews of that day decided to establish the holiday as an annual event in the Jewish calendar. It has been generally assumed that the First Book of Maccabees was written some time between the years 135 and 105 before the Common Era. If that is so, we may go a step farther and assume that down to about the year 125, to speak in round numbers, the holiday was still observed. But there is strong reason to believe that it soon fell into disuse. For how else is one to explain the curious facts that in the literature of the subsequent age Hanukkah is very rarely mentioned, and that such sages as Shammai and Hillel, who lived around the year 25 before the Common Era, seem to have no tradition as to whether a Jew is supposed to start with one light and add one on each succeeding night, or with eight lights and subtract one? Had the holiday been well known among the people, so elementary a question would have been settled long before.

The conclusion seems to be inevitable that for a period of one hundred years Hanukkah was practically nonexistent. It may be that the Jews of Palestine continued to kindle a light on the twenty-fifth of Kislev. If they did so, it was because of an ancient tradition about a miracle when the Temple was rebuilt long before the Maccabees. But of the last named, their victories, their martyrs, and their holidays, the memories were vague indeed.

What might account for this oblivion of a holiday so promisingly launched? The answer generally given is based upon the political and religious differences developed among the Jews after the Judaean State had become independent. The complete autonomy for which Judah the Maccabee had fought and died, was finally achieved by his brother Jonathan. He was master of Judaea, and was freely acclaimed as High Priest by the Party of Hasidim. A few years later, Jonathan, too, lost his life in defense of his country. Thereupon a solemn convocation of the Jews met in a great Assembly, and elected Simon, the last remaining brother of Judah, hereditary ruler and High Priest. For seven years Simon ruled. The nation was loyal to him, and he was loyal to the traditions for which he had fought in former days. Simon's son was readily accepted as his successor, for the days of comradeship and glory were still fresh in the people's minds, and they loved the Hasmonean for his family as well as for himself. Each anniversary of Hanukkah must have been reunion time for the old soldiers. Proudly they recounted their experiences, and pledged renewed loyalty to the cause for which they had fought . But the generation of original Hasidim was passing away. New men and new problems brought the era of good will to an end.

If in their piety and naïveté the Hasidim had ever dreamed that with the expulsion of the Syrians and their obnoxious ways an age of peace and brotherhood would reign within Judaea, they must have become disillusioned very quickly. The progressive disintegration of the Syrian Empire was making Judaean independence ever more secure. Economic prosperity was also increasing. What is more, those ancient enemies, the hellenistic cities, rivals in culture and in trade, were now lying defenseless. They invited conquest by the ambitious Hasmonean kings. But the increase of wealth and political dominion brought back those very conditions which had been at the basis of the rebellion against the Syrians. The common people became dissatisfied again. They had no interest in wars of conquest, and they resented the un-Jewish manners of their Hasmonean king and his Court. A breach was inevitable.

It began during the reign of Simon's immediate successor, his son John Hyrcan, though it was probably not so sudden a breach as Jewish tradition would have us believe. With the parties that thus developed this discussion is not concerned. It is sufficient to note that from such a situation Hanukkah as a holiday was bound to suffer. Even under ordinary circumstances the fervor of the observance of those days would die down with the death of the original generation. Had the Hasmoneans continued to be popular, it is not unlikely that the holiday would have been encouraged among the people as a tribute to the dynasty. But quite the contrary was the case. The common people no longer saw any reason for thanking God for the Hasmonean tyrants. They certainly did not feel the need for celebrating a second Sukkot. As a result, the religious teachers of the day, bitterly opposed to the ruling house, permitted the memory of Hanukkah to dim.

The surprising thing, therefore, is not that Hanukkah was well-nigh forgotten, but that one hundred years later it was once more revived. The reason for this restoration must again be sought in the changed conditions among the Jewish people. By internal dissension and civil wars Judaea again lost its independence. This time it was the Roman Eagle, greedy for power, that sank its talons into the Jewish State and never again let go. Rome deprived Judaea of practically all it had conquered, and gave independence to the pagan cities. By the grace of Rome the weakest of the Hasmonean descendants was ruling as a sort of tribal prince. But his every movement was guarded by the family of the Idumaean convert to Judaism, Antipater, who was completely subservient to the Roman power. There were still a few Hasmoneans alive, and they tried again and again to regain their throne and the people's independence. As in the days of the Maccabees, groups of Jewish patriots began to roam the country. The Romans and their hirelings, Antipater and his sons, called them bandits. But those "bandits" were very popular with the common people who looked upon them rather as rebels against Rome. If only among the remaining Hasmoneans another Maccabee would arise to bring the great deliverance!

That was the period, it would seem, when the Second Book of Maccabees was written. The Judaeans had begun to recall the Maccabean era; it was desirable to get the Jews of the Diaspora to join in Judaean hopes for throwing off the Roman yoke. But to undertake such propaganda openly might have been dangerous. Hence the purely religious connotation of the holiday was emphasized. It was represented as the day of miracles not only during the liberation from Syria, but also when the Second Temple was rebuilt.

The movement to regain Jewish independence failed. One by one the last remnants of the Hasmonean House fell under the hand of Herod. But the hope did not die out that God would send a leader as He had sent Mattathias and his sons. Thus, cautiously, the idea of Hanukkah was revived, and soon thereafter Hillel and Shammai were compelled to take cognizance of the popular custom, and regulate it by law. Perhaps they too would have preferred to make a really important festival of it. But by that time Herod was ruling with a heavy hand, and any such revival of a holiday of independence would surely have been construed by him for what it really would have been, an expression of hope for the downfall of Rome. Nor could the teachers of the day fall back upon the excuse that Hanukkah had been ordained by God, for the Maccabean story had been written too late to be considered as among the Jewish sacred books. Therefore, while they spoke much about Purim, all that they could do with regard to Hanukkah was to validate the current custom—the kindling of the lights.

Years passed and legends began to form around the Maccabean story. Josephus, who wrote around the year 100 of the Common Era, was the last to tell the story in fair historic form. But his books were not for the Jews, nor were they long read by them. The two Books of the Maccabees, not being included in the sacred collection of Jewish literature, also dropped out of sight among the Jews. All that was left was a vague memory, and a Feast of Lights. It was a situation that called for embellishments of the story, and such soon developed. Hence the story of the miracle of the cruse of oil which should have lasted for one day, but burned for eight, and all the other legends contained in the Scroll of Antiochus, a booklet composed centuries later, but containing the accumulated legends till that time. Hence also the story, which has even crept into the prayers, that Judah's father, the aged Mattathias, had been a High Priest. In some way, moreover, Hanukkah became connected with the Jewish woman's devotion to her people. No doubt the story of Hannah contributed to this; though one need not limit one's self to this one instance. The Jews always recognized to what extent their survival has been due to the loyalty of the Jewish women.

In general, legends, too, are historical events. They are not the history of the events which they take as their basis, but they are the historical material for an understanding of the mind, the hopes, the attitude to life, of the people who create them, and of those who believe them. The more the possibility of a physical restoration receded into the background, the more the purely religious interpretation of the holiday came to the fore. It was then that the old name, Feast of Lights, was replaced by the name Hanukkah—Feast of Dedication. The former was the only name by which Josephus and his contemporary, the author of the Gospel of St. John, knew the holiday. But soon Hanukkah assumed a significance greater than the celebration of a military victory, greater even than the hope of regaining independence. The Temple, standing for religious life, the Altar, standing for self-sacrifice, the Menorah, standing for Law and study, were considered more important, and the Maccabees were remembered because they saved and rededicated these objects. Hanukkah, then, came to represent the survival of Jewish culture, and the continuance of Jewish life, a symbol of the unswerving obedience of the Jew to God and to the Torah.

As a religious holiday, Hanukkah was sometimes the cause of trouble for the Jews. In talmudic days in Babylonia, the Jews lived among a people to whom fire was sacred. There were

periods of persecution when the Jews suffered for their use of
lights to celebrate Hanukkah, and the Rabbis of the day had
to legislate exactly where the Hanukkah lights might or might
not be placed, and under what circumstances they might even
be extinguished. On the whole, however, it has been a holiday
of merriment and lightheartedness. New customs began to
develop in its celebration; songs were written in honor of the
day, and the Hanukkah Lamp gradually became a characteristic
symbol in the Jewish home. Hanukkah became a season of joy
and thanksgiving.

Again, in our own day, the meaning of Hanukkah is under-
going a change. Influences, both Jewish and environmental,
have been helping to strengthen the ceremonies connected with
it, and to make its message more eloquent. Others will discuss
those phases of the holiday. But whatever the transformations
it is still destined to undergo, Hanukkah will continue to serve,
as it has served for two thousand years, to keep alive the eternal
hope that God will not forsake His people and that over might
right must triumph.

THE MACCABEAN SPIRIT IN ZIONISM

HORTENSE LEVY AMRAM

SOME twenty-one hundred years ago, a small band of men
gathered in the defense of their altar and of the right to
worship their God in their own way. The barbarity of their
enemies forced them to the use of arms, though they were a
people of peace and few among them inclined to violence as a
weapon. But the passion of their devotion and the inspiration
of their leaders turned them temporarily from the ways of peace
to the ways of war, and they achieved their purpose. This was
the preservation of the Jewish people.

Twenty-one hundred years is a long time in the history of
men and during it these people have often been threatened
with extinction; more often the threat has been not to wipe them
out but to degrade them and to degrade their souls. Each time
some small group has stretched its hands toward unaccustomed
tools and, urged by the impulse which once turned farmers,
artisans and scholars into an army, changed themselves to meet
the threatening emergency.

One of the most insidious threats which Judaism has faced
came when during the Middle Ages the Jew was denied any contact with the land and, forced into the alleys of congested cities,
forgot the feel of a plough in his hand and the cultivated soil
under his feet. The soul of the Jew starved for these things and
in recent generations, seeking contact again with the warm earth,
he thought to find it through the avenue of *Haskalah*, the enlightenment which was brought to these ghetto dwellers from
the outside world. There were many who believed that a more

substantial type of life would come if they could absorb that
outside culture, and so books, journals and newspapers were
published for them in pure biblical Hebrew. Many a young
talmudist devoured secular learning in phrases of the ancient
language. Science and the arts thrilled young men who before
had known only the learning of Torah and Talmud. "Enlightenment" dazzled them and many became lost, estranged from
their old traditions, yet unable to absorb new ones. But others
found through *Haskalah* a new direction and these gradually
banded together to fight a different sort of battle for the preservation of Judaism. Its broad secular education prepared
them for the leader who was to come, and in due time Theodor
Herzl united these various groups into an unwarlike army that
set forth to reconquer their land by peaceful methods.

Prior to Herzl's formulation of a practical method of rehabil-
itating the Jewish people, various groups, especially in East
Europe, had looked toward colonization in Palestine as the
solution of their individual problems. Notable among these
were the *Hoveve Zion* group, those Lovers of Zion who actually
started colonies on a small scale, which, however, proved largely
unsuccessful. They had almost no resources except in ideals and
leadership, and in these they were rich, as some of the most inspired thinkers and writers of their time directed their efforts.
Few among them actually reached Palestine, fewer were able to
strike root, but the ferment of their activity spread and, joining
the general awakening of the Enlightenment, paved the way for
the larger movement.

It remained for the unspeakable insult offered to the Jew by
the Dreyfus case to turn the thoughts of Theodor Herzl, journal-
ist and litterateur, to search for some protection against another
such experience. What he learned during that famous trial seared
his spirit and inflamed him to prophetic vision. In the short

space of two months he wrote his *Jewish State*. It was the spark needed to kindle Jewish thought throughout the world; with one impulse those who read it recognized in its writer the leader they had been awaiting.

Between Herzl and Maccabeus, separated by twenty-one centuries, there are many similarities and but few differences. Outstandingly they are alike in that the one man was no more a statesman when the suffering of the Jews awakened his sympathy than the other was a soldier when called upon to lead his people in war. Of the differences between them, the most important is that they came from opposing sides, in that Maccabeus took up the struggle to save traditional Judaism while Herzl came from what today corresponds to the Hellenistic party of the earlier times. But both leaders were unprepared for their tasks and both achieved success through the force of native genius and the power of their magnetic personalities.

The dream of a return to Palestine began coloring the thoughts of Jews from the moment of their dispersion, about two hundred and forty years after the Maccabean revolt. Although it took many forms in the succeeding centuries, the dominant strain was in substance nationalistic, thus preparing the people to read Herzl's great book. He spoke in words they understood, illuminating his precise and detailed plan by inspired phrases. The modern Jew realized that he might once more be at home in his own land and a great desire was born to materialize what for ages had been but a dream.

The opportunity to put Herzl's plan into action came through two world wars: World War I brought the Balfour Declaration, and World War II resulted in the establishment of the Republic of Israel. The story of the intervening thirty years bears so many parallels to the story of the Hasmonean era that Judah the Maccabee himself could hale the modern Israeli as a fellow-fighter in a cause similar to his own. The efforts to destroy the Jews and Judaism in modern times were not confined to Palestine; if anything, they were more wide-spread, crueler and more thorough than those of Antiochus the Mad twenty-one centuries ago. Now, as then, imperialist ambitions played a part in the struggle for Palestine; in our century, as in that of the Hasmoneans, subtle as well as brutal attempts were made to destroy the influence of Judaism. Our losses, too, were heavy: six millions were martyred in Europe and many thousands gave their lives to repel the invasion of those who sought to destroy the new State. These were tragic and heroic years, both before and after May 14, 1948, when Israel declared its independence; and they proved that the Maccabean spirit lives on.

Then began the redemption of those who were in bitter straits. From the Displaced Persons' camps they came, from the stockades at Cyprus, from the ghettos in North Africa, from the stifling atmospheres in Iraq, Iran, and Yemen. All of these unfortunates were received with open arms, despite the sacrifices which their coming entailed for the Jews already in the land. For great and generous as were the contributions of the Jews in the United States and in other lands of the dispersion, they could not possibly suffice to prepare the soil or to build the factories needed to give employment to so large an influx of men and women. There had to be a fairly long period of adjustment, of self-discipline, of self-denial. This too, was met in the Maccabean spirit. A vital and promising democracy is being built in the land where the ideals of the prophets first were heard.

One of the most powerful weapons in the hands of the army of returning Jews was that of social ideals. Before the Balfour Declaration was thought of, as early as 1884, Professor Herman Schapira suggested the idea of a Land Fund to which

Jews everywhere should contribute and with which land in Palestine would be purchased. This idea evolved into the Jewish National Fund, which buys the land in the name of the Jewish people. Theoretically, there is to be enough land for all, and none shall become the property of any one man, who might leave it to his son, who in turn would augment it through purchase, marriage and the like, until in the Holy Land the old tragedy might again develop of a few powerful landowners pitted against the landless masses. To this end, the land belonging to the Jewish National Fund is leased to those who use it. In the case of individuals, their families may release it; in the case of colonies, the people may come and go, but the land remains with the colony. Its use is assured to those who improve it, in return for a small rental which covers taxes and other expenses connected with it. But it may not be sold, it may not be exploited unfairly, it may not be left idle. It must be used by Jews for Jews.

Beyond all others, however, the strongest of their weapons was the conviction that only by the work of his hands and the sweat of his brow could the Jew be saved and a true Homeland rebuilt. Dreamers turned practical, they came with songs that glorified work and a new battlecry was adopted, the cry of 'Avodah—Labor. In the days of the Maccabees, the fight was for Judaea, the hill country around Jerusalem. This one is taking place in the valleys, against the malaria mosquito, against the thistles and the nettles and the rank grass. Judah Maccabeus conquered armed battalions who held the citadel. The Haluzzim are conquering the marshes and the waste lands, turning valleys and plains once more into garden places where the vine and the fig, the grape and the orange, spread abroad into great sheets of green.

To save the land through the force of arms took the Maccabees three and a half years. To redeem the soil after centuries of neglect has already taken a generation, if one counts from the earliest settlements of the present era. But in that short span, miracles have been accomplished. The most obvious is the physical fact of marshes drained, roads built, modern cities rising on the sand, industry and agriculture taking on the aspect of modern commercial countries. At first, the changes came imperceptibly; since 1925 there has been a marked increase in the speed, so that it might be safely said that a decade ago Palestine was still a primitive country while today it has many of the adjuncts of western civilization. True to their traditions, the new settlers built schools and hospitals, laboratories and libraries, almost before they thought of factories. Like the army of the Maccabees, the new army of pioneers was composed of all types of Jews. Some left their homes for Palestine in search of security, some in search of an ideal. From the first, scholars arrived with shoemakers, and pitiful *Luftmenschen* of the Ghettos side by side with trained mechanics and engineers. This fortunate mixture tended to give the new community material for a well rounded, normal development.

But before such a picture was visualized by even the most ardent of those who dreamed of Zion rebuilt, an American woman, Henrietta Szold, saw the need for health work among the Jews then living in Palestine, and with a woman's instinct for the immediate task, she began what she thought of as a limited undertaking, but which has in time grown into the vast body known as the Hadassah Medical Organization. It started as a simple attempt to help women and children in their fundamental physical needs. It has become a health system as complete and balanced as that of any of the smaller European countries. A sudden and unforeseen increase in the rate of communal growth has resulted in this system being outstripped, not in quality or variety of service. but in quantity. There is a greater demand made upon the Hadassah hospitals and clinics than they can meet.

The same is true of the educational work. This began haphazardly. The first of these modern Maccabeans fought with the hostile forces of nature and with their suspicious and often dangerous Arab neighbors. Theirs was a difficult campaign. The first battle was against swamps and woods. Ammunition in the shape of seeds and plants, cattle and poultry, ploughs and spades, were as difficult to buy, and as expensive, as guns and high explosives. And they were more important. At first, all the efforts of the pioneers were concentrated upon clearing the land and starting their farms. Gunpowder had to figure in their campaigns, too, and the guards and night watchmen, the *Shomerim*, laid their milking pans away and took up their guns to patrol the lonely settlements likewise unprotected from marauding tribesmen. Houses were constructed hastily, often by men using tools for the first time in their lives, so that the workmanship was crude. The walls leaked air and the roofs leaked water. The beaten earth which made the floors became chilled and damp, and the dreaded enemy, malaria, entered the camps. It was no world for little children. There was place only for men and women, young and hardy, who could fight in the great battle to save the traditions of their fathers.

They fought their battles well, learning slowly to handle tools as the Maccabeans had learned to handle weapons. The day came when they could foresee victory, an ultimate victory made of many smaller ones. They foresaw the hostile swamps conquered and the hostile fields subdued, and they foresaw the life of peace rewarding their labors. It was time for a new generation, born on the land, part and parcel of the Palestinian soil. And the new generation came, growing lustily in the clean air and the glowing sun.

Each little group undertook to educate its children in its own way. When the groups became stable colonies, the schools were merely larger. There was need for a unified school system built upon modern educational methods. Slowly such a system is evolving. Each year sees greater unity, although at no time has a central system forced particular methods upon any group. Among the colonists, and among those who live in the new urban centers, there are schools for the children of the *Mizrahi*, and schools for those with the Labor point of view, as well as schools expressing moderate conservatism. There are schools which train the pupils in science and the trades. And all alike turn their eyes toward the Hebrew University which crowns Mount Scopus as a fitting pinnacle for this new Jewish educational system.

Regardless of the bias of particular groups, one great idea unifies the schools of modern Jewish Palestine as no mere pedagogical method could do. That is the fundamental Jewishness of their approach. The language of all the schools is Hebrew, and the purest and most beautiful Hebrew possible. This powerful means of unifying the Jews from all parts of the earth had been in the making through the *Haskalah* period in Eastern Europe, but in Palestine its influence was largely the result of one man's efforts. Eliezer Ben Yehudah realized that a Jewish State could be built only by a people united by a single language and what could that be but Hebrew? His love of the language was both that of the scholar and that of the artist, and he fostered its use in the face of impossible difficulties. His own home was the first where pure Hebrew was the medium of ordinary communication. Also, he edited a Hebrew weekly. And gradually others rallied to his support. Finally in one school, it became the language of instruction. But there were those who still clung to the languages of their childhood and they resented the tendency toward the renascence of what to them was a dead language. Their position was strengthened by others to whom Hebrew was a holy speech and not for common use. Gradually, however, it was adopted in all schools and children carried its use home to their elders. Inevitably it became the language of the Jews of Palestine until now it is as unquestioned as any native tongue. In it the children study the history of their people as other children in other lands study theirs in the vernacular. Moreover, Israel's children study from the greatest of all history books, the Bible. They study the Bible for Hebrew. They study the Bible as the Bible. It is the most important textbook in the schools. After a few years of this constant contact with such a book, they are curiously influenced. Something of the past, of the old dignity of expression, of the stability which comes from a sense of life's continuity, affects them and little children often express their childish thoughts in terms that savor of the Prophets. In other lands, children celebrate their national holidays and the Jewish children of those lands share in the celebrations which are also theirs, but the celebration of the festivals of their forefathers are difficult, often artificially fostered. In Israel, the Jewish child celebrates these with the unthinking devotion which children give to these joyous symbols of the past. There is no inner conflict; there can be none. They are purely and simply Jewish and Israeli, and the festivals take their places in the seasons' march as naturally as the seasons themselves come and go.

In the streeets of the Jewish city of Tel Aviv, all the children gather on the twenty-fifth day of Kislev, as their forefathers gathered twenty-one hundred years ago, to celebrate the Feast of Lights. Dressed in white, garlanded with flowers, they stream through the streets, each bearing a lighted taper, singing the songs of Hanukkah. And their elders who watch them feel their hearts well with joy and with relief, for before them they see the new consecration of the Light, the renewed assurance that once more the fighting spirit of the Maccabees has triumphed and the soul of Judaism has been preserved for the unborn generations that will follow.

HANUKKAH IN MUSIC

Abraham W. Binder

IN ancient days, as in our own, victory over the enemy was
always the signal for an outburst of poetry and song. The
musical instrument and the battle-song always played an important part in the conduct of warfare. Even during the Maccabean period, war trumpets were placed on coins as symbols
of victory.[1] When Israel crossed the Red Sea after throwing
off the yoke of Egyptian bondage, Moses and the children of
Israel burst into the immortal Song of the Sea.[2] It is said that
the prayer '*Alenu* recited at the end of every service was composed by Joshua after the victory of Jericho,[3] while the Song of
Deborah bears witness to Israel's victory over the Canaanites.[4]
David's dance before the Ark of the Covenant after he recaptured it from the Philistines was another act of thanksgiving.[5]
When Judas Maccabeus entered Jerusalem with his followers
and recaptured the Temple, it was indeed the signal for festivity
and song. This celebration was both vocal and instrumental.[6]
The singing consisted of the *Hallel* (Psalms 113 to 118), for it
was a belated observance of Sukkot, a festival always celebrated

---

[1] Sachs, *Musik des Altertums*, Breslau, p. 90.

During the summer of 1931 when I visited the excavations of Beth Tsur,
which was at one time a Maccabean encampment, Dr. Sellers showed me
some coins of this type ascribed to the Maccabean period.

[2] Ex. 15.1; 17.10.

[3] *Sefer Kol Bo*, 16.

[4] Judg. 5.

[5] II Sam. 6.14.

[6] I Macc. 4.54.

with the singing of *Hallel*.[7] Psalm 30, the Psalm of Dedication, was most likely sung at the rededication of the Temple by the Maccabeans, and thereafter was assigned especially for Hanukkah.[8] "The circumstances which had preceded the Maccabean achievements and the solemnity of Hanukkah sufficiently explain the selection of this Davidic Psalm with its tune of thankful but self-abasing joy."[9]

If there were no doubt that the name Maccabee was derived from *Mi Kamoka Ba-elim Adonai* (Who is like Thee among the mighty, O Lord?), and that this was the rallying-cry of Judah and his followers, it could also be assumed that "Who is like Thee among the mighty, O Lord?" was a battle-song as well as a song of victory.[10]

With the appearance of the legend about the cruse of oil, and the consequent injunction to kindle lights during Hanukkah week, the three benedictions were adopted for the beginning of the Hanukkah service (see p. 314). These benedictions, as well as *Ha-nerot Ha-lalu* (*Haneros Halolu*) and '*Al Ha-nissim*, were known as early as the days of the Amoraim. *Ha-nerot Ha-lalu* was originally recited after the first benediction.[11]

How these benedictions were chanted originally is unknown. The tune generally used today by Ashkenazic Jews in Western countries is as indicated on p. 68.

Then *Ha-nerot Ha-lalu* is chanted. In accordance with the Hebraic custom of including laws and philosophies with prayer, this contains injunctions to govern one's conduct during the hours the lights are burning[12] (see p. 70).

[7] II Macc. 10.6; cf. above, pp. 40–41.
[8] *Soferim* 18.2.
[9] Jennings & Lowe, *The Psalms*, Book I, pp. 117–118.
[10] Shoiss, *Das Yontef Buch*, New York, p. 259, note 1.
[11] *Soferim* 20.6.
[12] Singer, *Daily Prayer Book*, London, p. 274.

The service then continues with the Hymn of Thanksgiving.

Ma'oz Zur, Rock of My Salvation, is a late addition to the service of the Kindling of the Lights.[13] It was composed in the middle ages by one Mordecai, whose name as author appears in an acrostic, and was first sung in the home, and later was introduced into the synagogue. *Ma'oz Zur* is known to have had in 1450 a tune other than the one now popular. The present tune, obviously of German character, may be traced to two German folk tunes of the 16th century.[14] As very often happens, two strands of these tunes were joined, the last four bars attached, and hence the tune which we know now. (See pp. 316 ff.)

Besides the Hallel which is recited at the morning service on all eight days of Hanukkah, *'Al Ha-nissim*, the only special addition made to the regular liturgy, is added to the *'Amidah*. In this prayer, thanks is given to God for the miracle of deliverance through the sons of Mattathias, and the important points of the Hanukkah story are beautifully set forth, stressing the fact that idealism and heroism are not always to be found in the multitude.[15] (See p. 325.)

This being the only special prayer in the Hanukkah liturgy, it was naturally dwelt upon, and sung elaborately. It was also added three times daily during the week of Hanukkah to the grace recited after all meals. A popular Eastern European version, of which we give merely the introductory section, is the one indicated on p. 72.[16]

The Jew was never content just to sing the hymns and prayers which the liturgy prescribed for each holiday, but he also invented

[13] Ibid., pp. 274–275.
[14] Idelsohn, *Jewish Music*, p. 205.
[15] S. Singer, op. cit., London, pp. 51–52.
[16] A. W. Binder, *Chanukkah Songster*, New York, p. 20.

songs and poetry about each of his holiday celebrations, to supplement his liturgy. The earliest published collection of poems
with music, designated by the author as folk-songs, is Elchanan
Kirchan's *Simhat Ha-nefesh*, published in Fürth, in 1727.[17] This
book consists of songs and melodies (notated) for all holidays,
and such special occasions as weddings and circumcisions.

These are poems set to popular melodies of the day[18] as, for
example, the special song to be sung during the eight days of
Hanukkah. The song develops thus: (1) the time when Hanukkah
should be celebrated, (2) the way it should be celebrated,
(3) rules about kindling of the lights, (4) ritual, (5) women's
duties on Hanukkah, (6) story of the Syrian invasion, (7) miracle
of the cruse of oil, (8) story of Judah, (9) Antiochus' edicts,
(10) moralizations on ablutions for women, (11) Hannah and
her seven sons, (12) alms for the poor, (13) conditions of the
day. The last stanza gives us a clue to the conditions existing
in the community where Kirchan lived (see p. 74):

> "We are hated in the exile,
> Dear Lord, turn it away.
> Day and night, we are in turmoil,
> Send *Mashiah* in our day."

The other songs in this book, which in their day were very
popular and highly considered, are in the same style, containing
laws and customs for each holiday and always some moraliza-
tion. During the evenings of Hanukkah week, songs such as
these were heard around the table as well as puzzle-songs.[19]
Games and riddles also provided amusement.

---

[17] Republished in 1926, New York, edited by Dr. J. Shatzky.
[18] Ibid., pp. 44 and 47.
[19] *Jewish Encyclopedia*, vol. VI, s. v. Hanukkah.

The Jewish community looked forward eagerly to the celebration of Hanukkah, for it was the first relief from the bleakness of the late fall and early winter. Therefore the preparations for it were elaborate and expectations high. The children looked forward to a full or half vacation during this festival week.) If they did go to *Heder*, most of the time was spent in playing Hanukkah games.[20] Then there was the *Hanukkah gelt* which the children received from parents and relatives. Special foods were prepared during this week, varying with the locale, such as *Latkes* (potato pancakes), various cheese dishes, and roast duck. A Yiddish folk-song of the 19th century tells of these customs (see p. 76).

The lighting of the Hanukkah candles was, and is still, chiefly a home ceremony, but every morning and evening the *Shammash* or Beadle, without much ceremony, also kindled lights in the synagogue. However, this synagogue ceremony was performed once during Hanukkah week with pomp and musical ornamentation, if that city fortunately possessed a cantor and choir.

Between the 16th and 18th centuries it was the custom in certain European congregations to chant the service of welcome to the Sabbath (*Kabbalat Shabbat*) with orchestral accompaniment.[20a] The orchestra consisted of a fiddle, contrabass, clarinet, drum and perhaps a trumpet. Most likely what later in the 19th and 20th centuries became known in Europe and America as the Hanukkah concert had its origin in these customs.

The Hanukkah concert usually began with Psalm 30, the Psalm of Dedication. This was generally followed by the elaborate chanting of the benedictions for the kindling of the lights by cantor, choir and orchestra, and then by the singing of

[20] Ibid.
[20a] A. Levy, *Travels in Israel*.

Ha-nerot Ha-lalu. Very often the evening's program was rounded
out with the chanting of one of the Psalms of the Hallel, particularly the last section of Psalm 118 followed by *'Al Ha-nissim.*
This was also the occasion on which congregations had the opportunity of giving *Hanukkah gelt* to the cantor and choir.
These customs still persist in Palestine, America, and many
European countries.

In America, however, a new Hanukkah musical literature is
gradually being evolved to keep the light of Hanukkah alive.
Emma Lazarus, in *Kindle the Taper*, was one of the first in the
New World to give a poetic rendering to the Hanukkah story.
It has been set to music by Dr. Jacob Singer (see p. 78).

There have been later poets to use the theme in English verse,
notably Solomon Solis-Cohen, Philip M. Raskin and Elma
Ehrlich Levinger. They have been of untold help in interpreting
the spirit of Jewish life to our younger generation.

The story of the Maccabean victory has been the subject of
one of the greatest oratorios, *Judas Maccabeus,*[21] the work of
George Frederick Handel (1685–1759). It was composed in
thirty-two days, between July 9 and August 11, 1746, in honor
of the Duke of Cumberland upon his return from Scotland after
the victory of Culloden. The libretto, composed by the Reverend
Thomas Morell, is based on the Maccabean narrative as given
in the First Book of Maccabees and the Twelfth Book of *Antiquities of the Jews* by Josephus. After its first performance at
Covent Garden, April 1, 1747, it was repeated six times during
that year. Handel conducted it thirty-eight times, and its
success was greatly due to the support of the Anglo-Jewish community.[22] Despite the fact that it is almost two hundred years

[21] Upton, *Standard Oratorios,* Judas Maccabeus.
[22] Ibid.

old, some of the solos and choruses in this oratorio are still sung
and loved throughout the musical world, as for example, Judas'
call, "Sound and Alarm"; the famous triumphal chorus, "See
the Conquering Hero"; the duet, "O Lovely Peace," and the
final "Hallelujah."

Anton Rubinstein, likewise, utilized the Maccabean story for
his opera, *The Maccabees*.[23]

The same text as that used by Handel, but somewhat abridged
and rearranged, was utilized for an oratorio for children in 1917
by the author of this article and first performed at the New York
Y. M. H. A. in that year, under the direction of the composer.[24]

The Hanukkah melody of *Ma'oz Zur* was sufficiently interesting for Max Bruch (1838–1920) to have incorporated it into
his *Three Hebrew Melodies* for chorus and orchestra.[25]

In Palestine Hanukkah is one of the important and colorful
holidays of the year. The spirit throughout the land during
Hanukkah week is festive. Carnivals, concerts and gala performances are the order of the day. For the modern Palestinian
rebuilding the ancient homeland, the Maccabean spirit is an
every day inspiration. For it is the heroism of the Maccabeans
rather than the miracle of the oil that pervades the songs and
touches the spirit of present day celebrations. Not alone during
the festival of Hanukkah, but every day, is the example of the
Maccabees brought to the boy and girl in Palestine. And so it
has come about that a Boy Scout organization in Palestine is
known as *Maccabee*.

During its frequent parades through the city of Tel Aviv they
sing *Kadimah Maccabee* (see p. 79).

[23] Two excerpts from this opera may be found in the *Lieder-Sammelbuch*,
Yuval, Tel Aviv.
[24] A. W. Binder, *Judas Maccabeus*, Oratorio for Children, N. Y., Bloch.
[25] Max Bruch, *Hebräische Gesänge*, Breitkopf & Haertel, Leipzig.

Some new Palestinian folk-songs contain references to the spirit and days of the Maccabees (see p. 80).

And so music has through the ages voiced Israel's gratitude to the Lord for the heroic spirit of the Maccabees and for His deliverance from a blow which, if successful, would have meant annihilation. Through music Israel was, if but for a moment, able to forget the torment of the exile during the eight days of Hanukkah. Today, likewise, Israel, through song, endeavors to keep alive the spirit of the Hasmoneans.

MUSICAL SCORES

BLESSINGS OVER LIGHTS

Andante religioso (♩= 72) f

Bo - ruch a - toh a - do - noy E - lo -
Bo - ruch a - toh a - do - noy E - lo -

he - nu me - lech ho - o - lom A - sher kid - sho - nu b' - mitz - vo—
he - nu me - lech ho - o - lom She - o - so nis - sim la - avo - se -

sov v' - tsi - vo - - nu l' - had - lik ner
nu ba - yo - mim— — — ho - - hem

68

BLESSINGS OVER LIGHTS

shel Cha-nu - koh.   Bo - ruch a-toh a - do-
ba - z'-man ha - zeh.

A - men.

f firmly

noy E - lo-he-nu me-lech ho - o - lom She - he - ch'-yo-nu   v'-

ki - mo-nu, V' - hi - g'-yo - nu   la - z'-man ha - zeh.

ff A-men.

Arr. by A. W. B.

HANEROS HALOLU

Ha - ne - ros ha - lo - lu a - nach-nu mad-li - kin

al ha - ni - sim v'al hat'-shu - os v'al ha - mil - cho -

mos she-o - si - so la-a-vo-se-nu

al y' - de ko - ha - ne - cho ko - ha - ne - cho

ha — k'do — shim V'chol sh - mo — nas

HANEROS HALOLU

Tempo I

y'me cha - nu - koh   Ha - ne - ros ha - lo - lu   ko-desh hem v'en lo - nu r'shus l'hish - ta - mesh bo-hem   e - lo lir - o - som   bil - - - - - - vad

K'de l'ho - dos   l'shim - cho   al ni - se - cho

V'al y'-shu - o - se - cho   v'al nif - l'- o - se - cho.

ff *rall.* *mf*

By A. W. B.

AL HANISSIM

Traditional

Al ha - ni - sim v' - al ha - pur - kon v' - al ha - g'vu-ros v' - al ...... ha - t'shu-os v' - al ..... ha - mil - cho - mos she - o - si - so la - a'vo-se - nu ba - yo - mim ho - hem Ba - z'man ha - zeh.

Arr. by A. W. B.

72

ROCK OF AGES

Traditional

Mo - oz tsur ye - shu - o - si l'cho no - eh l'sha - be - ach
Rock of A - ges, let our song Praise Thy sav-ing pow - er;

Ti - kon bes t'fi - lo - si v'shom to - doh nza - be - ach
Thou a - midst the rag-ing foes, Wast our shelt'-ring tow - er.

L'es to - chin mat - be - ach mi - tsor ham - na - be - ach
Fu - rious they as - sailed us, But Thine arm a - vail - ed us,

Oz eg - mor bshir miz - mor cha - nu - kas ha - miz - be - ach.
And Thy word Broke their sword When our own strength failed us.

73

CHANUKKAH

Den finf un tsvan-tsig-sten tug, in nein - ten choi - desh kis-lev, a-

zoi ge-nant. Die teg fun Cha-nu-kkah sol - stu feirn, Das

Gott hot ge - hol - fen fun un - se-re feint. Den drum koif

CHANUKKAH

mit tair-en vachs eil, licht tsu bre - nen, Du in par-shoin

Die in dein hois seinen, Ven sich bei dir gleich ar - mut fin - den.

Mus - tu doch licht - un tsin-den Un Gott's vun-der tsu der-tse-len.

Arr. by A. W. B.

OY CHANUKKAH

East European
Yiddish Folk Song

1. Oy Chan-uk-kah oy Chan-uk-kah a yon-tef a shei-ner a
1. *O Chan-uk-kah O Chan-uk-kah glad feast of light In*
2. Ye-hu-dah hot far-tri-ben dem Soi-ne dem ro-tse-ach, und
2. *Jud-ah drove the tyr-ant from the sac-red port-al*

lust-i-ger a frei-li-cher nish-to noch a-zoin-er al-le nacht in
joy-ous-ness un-par-al-leled de-scends each night! Gail-y spins the
hot in beis ha-mik-dash ge-zungen lam-na-tse ach, Die shtodt Ye-ru-sho-
Chant-ing in the Temp-le hymns to the Im-mort-al Then Zi-on

dreid-lach shpiel-en mir Zi-dik heis-e lat-kes
tren-dle hap-py we play Hot tast-y good-ies we
la-yim, hot vie-der oif ge-lebt, un tsu a nai-em le-ben hot
hol-y took on brave life a-gain And for a glad re-demp-tion

OY CHANUKKAH

es   ohn a shier. Tsint kind - er   ge - shvin-der   die
eat   all   day.   Hear child - ren,   light quick - ly,   the
ye - der ge-shtrebt. Dar - i - ber   dem gi - bor   Ye-
all did hope a - gain. Sing child - ren,   dear child - ren

din - in - ke licht - e-lach ohn   Zogt "Al Ha - ni - sim" loibt
tap - ers so bright and so fair;   Bless   God for his mer-cy, ex-
hu - dah ha-mach-bi loibt hoich   Zoll ye - der ba-zund-er ba-
praise to Jud-ah Mac-ca - bee,   Join   boy and girl   in

Gott far die nis - sim und kumt gi-cher tanz-en in   kohn.
tol   his sal - va - tion, Our peo - ple's for-ev - er his   care.
zing-en dos vun - der und lieb - en dos folk zolt ihr   oich.
glad - some lays Sing   Is - rael's love e-tern-al - ly.

77   Arr. by A. W. B.

KINDLE THE TAPER

Emma Lazarus

Jacob Singer

Maestoso (♩ = 96)

1. Kin - dle the ta - per like the stead-fast star   A blaze on eve-ning's
2. Clash, Is - ra-el, the cym-bals, touch the lyre, Blow the loud trump-et
3. Still ours the dance the feast the glorious Psalm, The mys-tic lights of

fore-head o'er the earth; Send thro' the night its lus-ter till a - far, An
and   harsh-tongued horn; Chant psalms of vic-tory till the heart take fire, The
em-blem and the Word. Where is our Judah? Where our five branch'd palm?

eight - fold   splen - dor shine a - bove   thy hearth.
Mac - ca - be - an spir - it leaps   new - born.
Where are the li - on war - riors of   the Lord.

78

KADIMAH

Vigoroso (♩ = 96) *sempre marcato*

Palestinian folk song

ff Ka - di - mah   ka - di - mah   ka - di - mah Mac - ca-
Ho! For - ward Ho! On - ward   Ho! For-ward Mac - ca-

bee   Hey!   Hey!   Ka - di - mah   Mac - ca-
bee   Ho!   Ho!   Ho! For - ward   Mac - ca-

bee.   Hey!   Hey!   Ka - di - mah Mac - ca - bee.
bee!   Ho!   Ho!   Ho! On - ward Mac - ca - bee.

Arr. by A. W. B.

79

MI YEMALLEL

(Shir Chanukkah)

(Round)

Arr. by A. W. Binder

*This song may be sung as a round. The Tune at (*) may be taken up by a second voice.

MI YEMALLEL

el ha - am.
liv - er - ers a - rise.

Shema! . . . . .
Hear! . . . . . .

Piu espress.

Ba-ya-mim ha-hem baz'man ha - zeh
In those days sweet free-dom came to Ju-dah

Ma-ka-bi mo-shi-a u-fo-
Thru God's stal-wart priest
[and Mac-cab-

deh
ee

uv-ya-me-nu kol am yis-ra - el
In our trials our-selves our own re-deem - ers.

rit.

yit - a - ched ya - kum le - hi - ga - el. . . . . .
Ev' - ry Jew him - self a Mac - cab - ee. . . . . .

HANUKKAH AND THE MENORAH

Paul Romanoff

Introduction

Light—the symbol of a nation.
The Menorah—the light of a people.

IN FITTING glory the Menorah stood near the Ark with the Decalogue, in front of the curtain which hung before the Holy of Holies. Finely was the lamp wrought; pure its gold, pure its oil. Flowers and buds graced it, and seven branches glorified it. Three on each side faced the central shaft, the flame of which soared straight to heaven and the seat of glory. Adorning each branch a flower, a knob; a knob, a flower; a flower, a knob—like stars in three semi-circles around the globe.

For centuries the Menorah burned constantly.
In its light a nation walked.
By its inspiration a people lived.

The Menorah

When the Israelites left Egypt and were ready to pursue the life of an independent nation, they were confronted with the problem of creating a medium of religious expression. The Tent of Meeting, the Tabernacle, was erected as the center of worship. In its Sanctuary were placed the Ark which contained the Two Tablets, the golden incense-altar, the golden table for the show-bread, and the Menorah which is thus described in Scriptures:

"And thou shalt make a candlestick of pure gold; of beaten work shall the candlestick be made, even its base, and its shaft; its cups, its knops, and its flowers, shall be

of one piece with it. And there shall be six branches going
out of the sides thereof: three branches of the candlestick
out of the one side thereof: and three branches of the candlestick out of the other side thereof; three cups made like
almond-blossoms in one branch, a knop and a flower, and
three cups made like almond-blossoms in the other branch,
a knop and a flower; so for the six branches going out of the
candlestick. And in the candlestick four cups made like
almond-blossoms, the knops thereof, and the flowers thereof.
And a knop under two branches of one piece with it . . . for
the six branches going out of the candlestick. Their knops
and their branches shall be of one piece with it; the whole
of it one beaten work of pure gold. And thou shalt make
the lamps thereof, seven; and they shall light the lamps
thereof, to give light over against it.—And he made the
candlestick of pure gold: of beaten work made he the candlestick, even its base, and its shaft; its cups, its knops, and
its flowers, were of one piece with it. . . . Of a talent of pure
gold made he it, and all the vessels thereof." Ex. 25.31–39;
37.17–24.

Centuries later, when Solomon built the Temple in Jerusalem,
he set in the Sanctuary, with the golden altar and the golden
table, ten candlesticks which had been constructed by Hiram,
King of Tyre, five on each side (I Kings, 7.49). These Menorahs
were carried off by Nebuzaradan to Babylon (Jer. 5.19).

Tradition is silent as to the size, shape, and number of Menorahs
in the Temple rebuilt after the return from the Babylonian Exile.
In all probability the Menorahs of that period were modeled
after the Mosaic Menorahs. The thread of our information is
retrieved in the second century before our era, in the period of
the Maccabees, when the Menorah was to play a part in the

miraculous story of Hanukkah. It was then that tradition crowned this sacred vessel with a halo of heroism—the Light of God against the Might of Jupiter.

In the Herodian Temple there were Menorahs whose dimensions and design the Talmud uses to describe the Mosaic Menorah since such details of its appearance are lacking in the Bible. We know that its height was seventy-two inches; thirty-two inches from the tripod base to the section where the branches begin to shoot outward; twenty additional inches were taken up by the extension of the branches, with branches of four-inch thickness separated one from the other by four-inch intervals—a total of fifty-two inches. The remaining twenty inches were an elongation of the central shaft in an elaborate design of three cups, three knobs and three flowers.

The cups bore a marked resemblance to Alexandrian drinking vessels. The knobs represented the apples of Keraze, a town famous in the New Testament and mentioned in the Jewish literature of the same period   And the flowers were counterparts of those in Amudim, a town in Galilee, not far from Keraze, west of Capernaum and the Sea of Galilee.

The outstanding feature of the Menorah in the Herodian Temple was the *Ner ha-Ma'arabi*, or the Western Lamp. The wicks of the six other branches faced the western light. This remained aglow all day long and was refilled in the evening. It was the perpetual light—the *Ner Elohim*, the Light of the Lord, which was never allowed to be extinguished.

Tradition relates the wonders of this perpetual light. Its cup contained no more oil than did the cups of the six other branches of the Menorah, a quantity sufficient for the longest night of winter. None the less, it burned through the night and until the following evening. This miracle is supposed to have recurred until forty years before the destruction of the Temple.

The Menorah disappeared in the year 70 of the Common Era when the Romans destroyed the Temple. On the Triumphal Arch which the Emperor Titus erected in Rome to commemorate his conquest of Judaea there is, in relief, a representation of the Temple's despoilers carrying the sacred vessels away. Among them is a candelabrum—whether this is a reproduction of the Menorah or of one of the smaller candelabra which were in the Temple has not been determined. In all probability there were ten Menorahs in the Temple of Herod as there had been ten candelabra in the Temple of Solomon. This may be assumed from the design of the double Menorah found on the mosaic of the ancient synagogues, on the gilt-glass and on the character-istic objects in the catacombs, as well as from the written de-scription of Josephus. The two candelabra that flanked the Ark in these representations show two rows of candelabra in perspective.

The Menorah was used as an ornamental motif on the columns, capitals, and friezes of the synagogues of Capernaum, Keraze, Sarona and elsewhere in Galilee, and even in Greece. In the synagogue of Hammat-by-Tiberias a stone Menorah was un-earthed. On the murals of the most ancient synagogue, dated 245 C.E., excavated recently at its site in Dura-Europos in Syria, the Menorah was discovered painted above the seat of the Elder of the synagogue.

In the ancient synagogues of Palestine of the fifth and the sixth centuries (those of Naaran near Jericho, of Beth Alpha in Galilee, and Jerash in Transjordan) single and double candelabra cover the greater portions of the mosaic ornaments and panels. In another synagogue at Priene, Greece, there were several cande-labra engraved on the pillars and others in relief chiseled in stone, showing careful workmanship. As an architectural motif the Menorah has ornamented capitals, lintels, balustrades,

Fresco over seat of the Elder in Synagogue at Dura-Europos (Syria),
oldest dated synagogue, 245 C. E.
Courtesy of the Gallery of Fine Arts, Yale University.

Mosaic floor of the ancient synagogue at Jerash, Transjordania.

From E. L. Sukenik, *The Ancient Synagogue of Beth Alpha*, Jerusalem, 1932, p. 27.

screens, and other portions of religious edifices and of domestic and public buildings. In the Jewish catacombs and cemeteries at Rome and Venosa there have been examined murals on walls, vaults, gilt-glass, tombstones, sarcophagi, and rings bearing the Menorah as a symbol. This motif was cast on ancient Palestinian coins of the reign of King Antigonus, 40–37 B.C.E. The design appears also on ancient oil lamps of Palestine and the Diaspora modeled in clay.

An impressive description of Solomon's throne is found in an old Aramaic commentary to the Book of Esther, the *Targum Sheni*, and in the Midrash attributed to Abba Gorion. There are two rows of awe-inspiring lions and eagles, the trustworthy guards of the King, posted upon each step of the throne, ready to excute his every command. But closest to the King, on each side of him, stood a candelabrum. Each branch of one had carved on it one of the seven patriarchs, Adam, Noah, Shem, Abraham, Isaac, Jacob and Job. Each branch of the other bore the figure of one of the seven righteous men, Levi, Amram, Moses, Aaron, Eldad, Medad, and either Hur or the prophet Haggai. Hanging above each candelabrum was a golden cruse of pure oil to supply the lamps.

The Menorah rarely appeared alone as an ornamental motif. Whether it was employed as a synagogue mural, or as a floor mosaic, whether as a design on a sarcophagus, or on gilt-glass, a group of ceremonial objects always accompanied it. These loyal attendants were the palm-branch, citrus fruit, vial of oil, snuff dish, and Scroll. They were situated generally in the lower section of the Menorah on either side of the basic central shaft.

The Menorah in ancient Jewish art was usually depicted on both sides of the Ark which conformed to a standard shape, variations occurring mainly in the construction of its roof. Some

designs place the Ark in the center of the upper section, flanked
by lions, eagles or doves; while in the lower section are represented one or two candelabra and other ceremonial objects.

Many of the ornamental motifs employed by the Jews as
religious symbols derive from the flora and fauna of ancient
Palestine. Outstanding among the fruits of the earth are the
pomegranate, palm-branch and palm tree, citron, wheat-grains,
grapes, and intertwined branches and flowers. Among the birds
and beasts are the eagle, the gazelle, the dove, and the lion. The
ram was represented by its horn. The shaft of the Menorah
bears a resemblance to a Palestinian tree, tall and thin with
leafless branches turned upward.

The Menorah was not always of gold. After being shattered
by Antiochus Epiphanes, it was reconstructed by the Maccabees
in wood. In due time this more humble substance was replaced
by silver; finally, gold was restored.

The Menorah is rich in symbolism. For some beholders it
represented the creation of the universe in seven days, the central light being the Sabbath. The seven branches for other worshipers seemed earth's continents; to others the seven heavens.
In the works of Flavius Josephus it is recorded that the seven
branches represent the seven planets, to which the *Zohar*, the
classic book of the Cabala, adds that six of these branches receive
the light from the center as do planets from the sun.

In later Jewish synagogues the Menorah persisted as a symbol
and decorative motif. It is also to be found in manuscripts, on
ceremonial objects and on tombstones. It remained a symbol
of the nation until the late medieval period when it was sup-
planted by the ancient ornamental motif and cabalistic hexagon,
commonly believed to represent the Shield of David or the Seal
of Solomon.

THE HANUKKAH MENORAH

According to an ancient custom, it was forbidden to imitate the Menorah, the seven-branched candlestick of the Temple. However, there was no such ban on fashioning of a lamp of similar shape having a lesser or greater number of branches than the original. This permission encouraged the designers of the lamp for the Hanukkah service to utilize the Menorah motif and modify it for the peculiar needs of the eight-day festival. Instead of three semi-circles, four were fashioned—the central shaft being used for the *Shammash* (servant) by which all the wicks were kindled.

The most ancient lamp which might have been used on Hanukkah was discovered in Palestine and dates back to the first century of the Common Era. It is molded of clay and is typical of the Graeco-Roman period. It contains eight wicks and a single large opening for oil.

No example of a Hanukkah lamp of the period between the first century and the latter part of the middle ages has as yet been discovered. Those now on view in museums date from the time of the Renaissance and are in its spirit. But in the meantime a change had developed in the design of the Menorah mainly because the festival of Hanukkah had become a home and family celebration.

Nowadays in the House of Worship, which according to the Talmud is the Temple in miniature, an eight-branched candelabrum graces the southern wall; sometimes it stands in front of the Ark. Sometimes two are used, one on each side of the Ark. As it was not considered fitting to have an eight-branched Hanukkah lamp and a seven-branched Temple lamp rivaling each other in glory, the one chosen to become the Menorah of the Synagogue was that which in shape and pattern included both—the eight-branched Hanukkah Menorah.

In the synagogue the Hanukkah lamp had to maintain the erect position of the Menorah. Not so in the home. It was natural to fashion it so that it could be suspended from a wall or placed on a window-sill. The hanging lamp required a back of sufficient size to support it. This presented a surface on which to mold symbols in high-relief or in bas-relief. The palm tree, the grape clusters, represent the fruit of the sacred soil of Palestine; the Lion| of Judah, the dove and the eagle often appear next to the Crown of the Law to represent the union of law with the people. Lions hold between them a replica of the original Menorah of seven branches. On some lamps the Ark of the Covenant is embossed; on others, Moses and Aaron stand on either side of the Ark.

In the hanging lamps there are many variations in the shape of the eight containers for oil. Some are vials, others have the form of lions' heads with wicks projecting from their open mouths. Still others have assumed an oval shell-like shape. These cups are set along a rail in the front of the lamp. Sometimes each is on its own individual bracket. Beneath the eight receptacles small dishes—differing in shape in different lamps—are attached to collect the dripping oil.

The metals used in the construction of the Hanukkah lamp are pewter, brass, silver, often completely or partly gilded.

The standing lamp also underwent a change. The tripod from which the stem and the branches emanate became a round or angular foundation. Carvings, reliefs, enamels, miniatures, and anaglyptics, figures and ornaments of biblical motifs and symbols made the base interesting. Ornamental figures, embossed in relief were sometimes added to the central shaft giving additional height and striking dignity. A unique figure on some candelabra is that of the famed Judith standing triumphantly on the central shaft, clutching a dagger in one hand and in the other hand holding the head of Holofernes. For her act of bravery, tradition has graciously exalted her to the plane of the family of Maccabees.

Hanukkah lamps can be traced to the countries of their origin by certain characteristic ornamentation. The Moorish and the arabesque shapes reveal the work of northern Africa, western Asia or some islands in the Mediterranean. The Gothic imprint shows itself in a combination of various styles. Baroque and rococo appealed to the imagination of Jewish artists and silversmiths. Thus at times either in addition to or in lieu of Jewish symbols, there appear cupids, cherubs with horns of plenty, garlands, and baskets heaped with fruit. The influences of different lands and periods sometimes appear in a single lamp. The art of each country has left such definite traces on the Hanukkah lamps that determining their historical and geographical background makes an inexhaustibly fascinating study. Jewish symbols prevail. Even those lamps which have used characteristics of the countries in which Jews made and used them, subordinate the local characteristics to the Jewish characteristics and conceptions.

CONCLUSION

The Menorah, in its original design, or in modified form, has been used by Jews in every place of their settlement. In Africa —in imposing Alexandria, down the Nile at the Cataracts, in busy Carthage, and the populated coast; in Asia—in Yemen, Babylon, Persia, Palmyra, and on the border of the desert, in the Decapolis and Pentapolis, in the Greek colonies in Syria and Asia Minor; in Europe—in aristocratic Athens, in patrician

Rome, in the Islands of the Mediterranean, the Menorah became the symbol of its people. It shone in the synagogue, it glowed in the home, it guided the faithful Jew through this life and accompanied him in the hereafter, as a symbol on his tombstone.

The Menorah was regarded as the symbol of light and truth. It gleamed in the open air. It was kindled and protected in the home. Behind the walls of the ancient Ghettos tiny wicks glowed. In its reflection the adults forgot their fears and the children were told why the lights were lit, and heard the tale of the miracles and the valor of the heroes who had died for the faith of their fathers.

From generation to generation the flame of the Hanukkah lamp awakens memories of an heroic past, rekindles an ancient hope, and sustains a faith in the future, as pure as its sacred oil.

HASMONEAN COINS[1]

SOLOMON GRAYZEL

BEFORE the Persian Era precious metals were employed as a medium of exchange in the East. There were no coins, value being computed by weight. Silver predominated. The Persians introduced coins into their empire, retaining the power of coinage for the central government. By the 4th century B.C.E. the individual satrapies began to exercise the right to coin their own money. Still later, toward the end of the Persian Era, Satraps coined money in smaller denominations for use within the various provinces of which the Satrapy consisted. For the first time Palestine, a province of the Satrapy of Syria, had its own money.

With the arrival of the Greeks in Asia (ca. 330 B.C.E.) and the spread of hellenizing influences, some of the important towns received a Greek constitution and with it the privilege of minting copper coins, that of more valuable coins being reserved to the central government. As the Seleucid Empire broke up, in the second century B.C.E., the smaller states, thus freed, assumed rights of coinage.

In Judaea this right was involved in the Maccabean struggle. Neither under the domination of Egypt nor of the Seleucids had Judaea enjoyed the right of coinage, a right which would have been of value to the commercial life of Jerusalem. Hence those Jews who welcomed hellenization regarded the privilege of coinage as one of the ends to be attained by submission to Antiochus. By the irony of history it was not they but their

---

[1] This article is based on M. Narkis, *Matbe'ot Erez Yisrael*, Jerusalem, 1936.

93

opponents, the Hasmoneans who, through the Seleucid break-up, were destined to assume this function of government. For when Jerusalem was finally freed of the unwelcome Syrian soldiers stationed in the Acra, and when Simon son of Mattathias had been acclaimed by the Jews as their hereditary ruler, his government commenced to coin money, an act in which the Syrian overlord acquiesced. The earliest coins were apparently only of bronze, in denominations of one-half, one-quarter, and one-eighth of the shekel. Indeed, soon thereafter Syria withdrew this privilege, and coinage was resumed only under Simon's son, John Hyrcan.

From time to time coins of this period have been unearthed. On the obverse of Simon's half-shekel is a citron (*etrog*) between two branches of a palm-tree (*lulabim*), surrounded by the inscription *shenat arba' hazi* (fourth year, half). The whole is included in a border of dots. The reverse bears a date tree below the branches of which are two baskets filled with fruit. Around this is written *li-geulat zion* (to the redemption of Zion). This side, too, has a border of dots.

The quarter-shekel, smaller in size, differs from the half in that it has only two branches of the palm-tree, and the word *reba'* (fourth) instead of the word for half. The reverse differs only in the substitution of a single citron for the more elaborate decoration on the half-shekel.

The eighth-shekel, still smaller, bears a single palm branch between two citrons, the inscription *shenat arba'* (fourth year), and the usual circle of dots. On the reverse it bears a chalice, the words meaning "to the redemption of Zion," and the circle of dots.

The lettering on all the coins is not in the square Hebrew characters of the present day, but in the archaic characters.

MODIN

Birth Place and Burial Place of the Maccabees[1]

ZEV VILNAY

STRANGE has been the fate of the village in which the Maccabees lived and were buried. We do not know for certain what its true name was, whether Modin, Moda'im, or Modi'im, or Moda'itha; even the memory of its exact location has disappeared.

Upon a high hill to the west of Jerusalem the crusaders, in the 13th century, thought that they had found ancient Modin, and erected a church there. Christian travelers of the sixteenth century visited what they thought to have been the tombs of the Maccabees on the highway between Jaffa and Jerusalem in the vicinity of Latron. Toward the middle of the 19th century a book by a celebrated rabbi of Jerusalem speaks of Modin as having been located to the west of the ruins of Geba, on a high and lonely hill which the Arabs call Midan.

It is only within the last decades that scholars and archaeologists have identified the place where the village of the Hasmoneans actually stood. It is eastward of the city of Lydda, on the ancient road which goes to Jerusalem, in a place which the fellaheen call Midia. It may be that the Jewish scholar Esthori Parhi hinted at this village when he wrote (ca. 1322) concerning "Modi'im near Jerusalem . . . and it is called Mida'a."

Although Modin has been identified, the site of the tomb is still in doubt. In I Maccabees this tomb is described thus:

[1] Abstract of a chapter from a forthcoming work on *The Sacred Graves in Palestine.*

"And Simon sent, and took the bones of Jonathan his brother, and buried him at Modin, the city of his fathers. And all Israel made great lamentation over him, and mourned for him many days. And Simon built a monument upon the sepulchre of his father and his brethren, and raised it aloft to the sight, with polished stone behind and before. And he set up seven pyramids, one over against another, for his father, and his mother, and his four brethren. And for these he made cunning devices, setting about them great pillars, and upon the pillars he fashioned all manner of arms for a perpetual memory, and besides the arms ships carved, that they should be seen of all that sail on the sea. This is the sepulchre which he made at Modin, *and it is there* unto this day."

The monument was intact when Josephus wrote his history about the year 85, and even when Bishop Eusebius wrote his history two and a half centuries after Josephus. Even on the pictorial mosaic map of Palestine, discovered at Medeba, Transjordania, which dates from the sixth century, there is shown between Jerusalem and Lydda a house with two towers joined to it. The inscription in Greek says: "Modi'in now Moda'itha whence have arisen the Maccabees."

Two different spots in the neighborhood of the village Midia have been thought to be the burial place of Mattathias and his sons. Among the ruins scattered upon the side of the hill there is now a small building with a cupola where Sheikh Gharbawi (the Sheikh of the West) lies buried, of sacred memory to the Arabs of the district. Close to his grave the archaeologist Guerin in 1870 uncovered the foundations of a large building and the remains of stone pillars. He came to the conclusion that the human bones which he found there were those of the Hasmoneans. Some years later another Frenchman, Clermont-Ganneau, dug further in the same spot. He found vaults and crypts, also a large cross in the mosaic which formed the floor of one of the crypts.

On top of the hill, to the south of the grave of Sheikh Gharbawi, are several graves hewn into the rock. Nine stretch in one long line from west to east. They are trough-like in shape, and each is divided by means of a step into two sections. At the opening of each grave lies a huge stone that once served as a cover. Opposite this line of nine trough-like graves are four others, one of which is entirely different; it is a cave into which four narrow steps lead. On each wall is a shelf for the reception of the body. The rock which has sealed the entrance to this cave has, like so many others, been removed by vandals in search of treasure. A narrow opening has been left which permits the entrance of a man. There are in Palestine many hewn tombs similar to this, but it is just this tomb that the Arabs have chosen to dignify as *Kubur al-Yahud*, "The graves of the Jews." Perhaps there resides in this appellation a hint of the reverence that the Jews of old had for this particular spot.

Within the present generation Jews in Palestine have begun to make pilgrimages to this Kubur al-Yahud on Hanukkah, as though it were in very truth the burial place of the Maccabees.

HANUKKAH IN OLDEN TIMES[1]

ISRAEL ABRAHAMS

FEASTS in the Middle Ages wore a strong family likeness to one another. The forms of enjoyment were few, and taste was forced into a limited number of channels. But there was some differentiation. There were three elements in joy, each of which had a local habitation of its own: in the synagogue, in the public hall, and in the home. The three were always associated, but all the features were not equally pronounced. Each of the minor feasts chose one element as its characteristic. The Rejoicing of the Law was a synagogue function, Purim filled the streets and the Communal Hall, Hanukkah held the home as its peculiar scene.

Women made holiday on the Feast of Lights, some for eight days, some—who regarded a week's holiday as an unpardonable excess—only rested on the first and the last days of the feast, but all ceased their usual occupations at eventide, while the lights were burning. At an earlier period the illuminations were more public. I am not alluding merely to the illumination in synagogue, which has remained a never interrupted rite. But in the Middle Ages, when Jews lived in special quarters of the town, the lamps were often set outside the doors or at the windows. In Venice the Jews would embark on gondolas and row through their district, greeting each illuminated house with a benediction and a merry Hebrew chorus. Venice and its bridges were an eternal source both of fun and of trial. For the *Kohanim* were placed in a sorry plight when a death occurred. The bridges joined the whole Jewish quarter, and it was held by many that the presence

[1] From Israel Abrahams' *Festival Studies*, London, 1934.

of a corpse in any one house "defiled" all houses. Hence the "Priests" were forced to pass many a night in the open air, in snow or rain, spanning Venice with a dolorous "Bridge of Sighs."

But it early became the rule to reserve the Hanukkah lights for the interior of the house. We can easily see that an external lamp would invite extinction. The Gaonim already felt it necessary to permit Jews to forego the duty of "publishing the miracle" and light their rooms rather than their streets. Nay, the practice may be traced even further back, to early Roman days. It is obvious that this transference helped to make Hanukkah a domestic celebration. But it led to a further development of great interest in the history of Art. Illumination was common to many medieval ceremonies. By the beginning of the fourteenth century, Jews had acquired the habit of placing family candles in the synagogue, in memory of the dead, on the Day of Atonement. On every festival it was customary in some parts to bear a huge torch in front of the Scroll of the Law. There were, further, societies of young men who devoted themselves to illuminating the synagogue on all appropriate occasions. Or, again, in Germany, in the fourteenth century, at a *Berit Milah*, candles were always lit. Maharil tells us of a case of the initiation of twin boys in Mayence, on which occasion "they lit twenty-four small candles and two great ones," which, he adds, "were double the usual number."

Naturally the feast of Hanukkah had distinctive traits, but the prevalence of illumination at other times helped to spur on the medieval Jews to give the Hanukkah lights a special prestige. If the date given in the Strauss Catalogue be accurate, then as early as the twelfth century goldsmiths applied their nascent feeling for art to the construction of ornate Hanukkah lamps. One of that date seems to have been found at Lyons in the excavations of the old Jewish quarter. The metal used is bronze, and

the shape of the lamp is triangular, like the *fronton* of the Roman
Church. On this the lamps lie flat, but it was more usual, until
the eighteenth century, to construct the lamp with eight upright
stems or branches, with another extra stem to bear the *Shammash*
or attendant light. It may be well to remind readers of the purpose served by this extra candle or oil-flame. First, it was there
to serve as the "lighter," and thus obviate the necessity of kindling one light from another, an act forbidden by some ancient
authorities. But its chief function was to provide a light that
might be "used." If the illumination was indoors, it would
scarcely be possible that the family should refrain from seeing,
and perchance reading, by the aid of the Hanukkah lamps. Yet
this was opposed to the ritual law. Hence the *Shammash* was
placed higher than the rest of the lights, or in a conspicuous
position at the side, certainly not in the same line. This gave a
fresh opportunity to the artist. In another of the Strauss specimens, the lamp, standing on lions and bearing the figures of
heroes and many symbolical devices, is surmounted by Judas
the Maccabee; in his right hand he holds a sword, and in his
left he bears the head of the vanquished Lysias. Copper, gold,
silver, bronze, were all employed in these lamps. The Renaissance
clearly had some influence on Jewish taste. For, besides the
usual Hebraic emblems, such as the two tables of stone, cherubs,
several architectural reminiscences of the Temple, vines and
bells, flowers and pomegranates, lions and eagles, the widow's
cruse of oil, the seven-branched candelabrum, all for the most
part in relief—besides these and the favorite grotesques beloved
of Jewish art, there is an occasional specimen of an altogether
different kind. One of the Strauss lamps bears classical myth-
ological emblems, the center being adorned with a Medusa head!
Surely, the Renaissance penetrated fitfully even into the Ghettos.
Such costly works of art were not, as might be thought, the

rare property of the rich. That they were common is clear from
the very large number of extant specimens in various collec-
tions. Moreover, as the domesticity of Hanukkah grew, the
lamp became a prized ornament of many homes. An early
eighteenth-century authority, who is the spokesman of the
ordinary middle-class Jew of his day, insists that every one
should possess a silver Hanukkah lamp, or at least the "Shammash" should be of precious metal. Of course, the very poor
must have contented themselves with less expensive ware. Some,
indeed, used egg-shells, perhaps because of the mention of egg-
shells in the Mishna dealing with the Sabbath lamp, or in memory
of the eight eggs which a Rabbi flung into the air on the feast of
the "Water-drawing" at Tabernacles. Although a distinction
was drawn between the biblical and the post-biblical feasts,
still Jews transferred the customs of one class to the other. At
first, indeed, Hanukkah was observed exactly like Tabernacles.
The Second Book of the Maccabees tells us that, on Hanukkah,
booths were built and palm-branches borne, the *Hallel* was sung,
and in other respects, such as the Reading of the Law, the parallel
was, and is still, maintained. So, too, in the choice of *haftaras*
for the feast, the idea is uppermost that Hanukkah, like tabernacles, was a "Period of Joy." Some modern Jews are indignant
that in the formula for lighting the Hanukkah lamps, a phrase
is used implying that "God commanded" the illumination of
Jewish houses at the Maccabean festival. A medieval Italian
Rabbi was once asked the same question. His answer shows
that a good deal of common sense lies in the responses of Tal-
mudists. "I notice," he said, "that an order has just been issued
by *His Grace the Duke*; but the Duke did not issue it at all." It
may safely be said that those Jews who can see a divine authority
for Purim and only a human sanction for Hanukkah are suffering
from a serious attack of spiritual twist.

The social concomitants of the Feast of Lights were, like the feast itself, entirely domestic. Even the special foods show this. Cheese and milk foods predominated, for Judith, whose truculent heroism was associated with Hanukkah, had, in the Jewish version of the tale, carried cheese in her wallet when on her perilous visit to Holofernes. Other foods were garlic, and a kind of stew called in the Orient *Ssfing*, restricted to the first day. The evening meal took place while the lights brightened the home, or soon after the allotted half-hour had elapsed. Spirited hymns and table songs were specially written, among others by Ibn Ezra himself, for the occasion. The father then assembled his children and told them the story of the Maccabean struggle. Drinking was rare, but an extra glass was neither forbidden nor rejected. The hymns were most prolonged on the eighth night, for the children were encouraged to save up the unburnt remnants of oil from night to night and make a long holocaust on the final evening, while psalms and songs resounded. These songs had their special Hanukkah tunes in the eighteenth century, and no doubt the home tended greatly to foster that *Hazanut* which we wrongly identify entirely with the synagogue. Every one remembers how Bernstein, in his charming novel, *Vögele der Maggid*, represents Golde as repeating at home all the *Hazan's* trills and twirls. The home, too, replaced in a sense the synagogue on Hanukkah in another function. As I have shown elsewhere, house to house begging was discouraged by the medieval Jews. But at Hanukkah the practice was allowed, for the feast was a domestic rite in which the poor might participate by going round collecting doles from every household. Of course, Hanukkah too was the time for giving presents to teachers; it is even probable that their chief income was derived from the Hanukkah gifts. I say little here about the synagogue rites on Hanukkah, for they are the same now as in the past. But as Hanukkah was essentially a woman's feast, certain other points must be added. This was a favorite period for the exchange of gifts between the father of a betrothed maiden and the bridegroom elect. I think it may be worth while, as showing several things, among them the licence allowed to women on Hanukkah, to quote the 13th Article of the Statutes of the Jewish Congregation at Avignon. The following regulation is dated 1779:—

"Women and servants shall not carry nor accompany to the door of the men's synagogue children under the age of four years old, except at the moment of the sale of the *Mizvot*. In the latter case, the said children shall be made to quit immediately before the reading of the Pentateuch; but they may again come in to join the procession when the Scroll is taken back to the Ark. They may also come during the Blessings of the Kohanim. Should any child be brought in at any other time by women, the father of the child shall pay a fine of 20 livres. *Nevertheless, women may enter the synagogue on all the eight nights of Hanukkah.*"

The other amusements of the feast were all domestic in essence. There were no dramas for Hanukkah until very modern times, and these later Hanukkah plays do not emanate from Russia, but from Germany and, strange to tell, from America. Acting has only recently become a home pastime. With the Jew, his performances of plays were in the Communal Hall on Purim and at weddings, not in the home. Hence, I take it, the absence of dramas from the Hanukkah delights. Riddles, acrostics, arithmetical puzzles, *gematrias*, extravagant enigmas called *Ketowes*, to which the number forty-four—the total of the lights burned during the whole eight days—was the answer, these and similar mild joys reveal that the keynote of the feast was domestic calm and family quietude. In the fifteenth century, however, the game of cards invaded the home, and almost superseded all other amusements with Jews as it did with Christians. In many communal enactments forbidding the fascinating game as an ordinary thing, Hanukkah was almost invariably placed among the permitted times. A curious extension was given to this licence in the eighteenth century, for many argued that the freedom to play cards on Hanukkah endured for eight working days, and that the two Sabbaths which sometimes intervene must be deducted. The addition of two days was made every year, even when there was but a single Sabbath during the feast. Schudt tells us that the chief Hanukkah card games were *loo* and *à l'ombre*. He adds that many Christians were scandalized at this card-playing, as Hanukkah often comes near Christmas, just as Purim, the other card-playing period, coincided roughly with the Passion. In England this objection would not have been felt, for at the University of Cambridge the students in Milton's time were expressly permitted to play cards on Christmas. Jews, in point of fact, were often very deferential to Christmas. They sent presents to Christian friends on that festival, and, a generation ago, the Smyrna Jews went on Christmas day to church to escort a popular Consul. Far earlier, two centuries back, in Venice, Jews visited their Gentile friends at Christmas and sang and played with them to help them to make merry.

Though cards tended to monopolize the fair field of recreation, two other games have held their own on Hanukkah. With one, the arithmetical riddles, or *Ketowes*, I have already dealt. The other was the *Teetotum*, or *Trendel*, as it is called abroad. With what delight did Dukes (then in London) write to Leopold Löw at Szegedin, under the date September, 1864: "I have seen a toy in London called a *Teetotum*. It is exactly like a Hanukkah *Trendel*, with English letters instead of Hebrew on it. But why it is called by its peculiar name no one can tell me." Of course the name comes from the letter T, which is inscribed on one of the four sides of the toy: thus "T *Totum*" or *T takes all*. This reminds me of the noted Latin epigram, addressed by the boy to the twirling *Teetotum*: *"Te totum amo, amo te, Teetotum."*

It is a very ancient game, known to the Greeks and Romans. But why was it specially favored on Hanukkah? No answer has ever been given to this natural question. It may be that the *Teetotum* was regarded as a very innocent form of gambling, if that be not altogether too harsh a word to use. Many pious people never played cards or any other game of chance, but they have felt that so simple a game as this was lawful enough. But I can now supplement this with a new suggestion. The *Teetotum* is still in parts of Ireland the chief indoor recreation of the peasantry at Christmastide. Now it is well known that such games seldom change their seasons. I should not wonder if the *Teetotum* was a favorite toy elsewhere at Christmas. If so, the Jews may have transferred it to Hanukkah. For they never invented their own games, except those of the intellectual species, such as Hanukkah *Ketowes*. The *Ketowes* even gave rise to a folk proverb: *"Zechus Owes, Kein Ketowes,"* i. e., I suppose, the merit of the fathers is not the solution of life's riddle.[1] Indeed, the moral of Hanukkah is, after all, that Judaism must rely oh present effort by the children as well as on the past merits of their sires, if it is to remain in any true sense a "Feast of Light."

---

[1] (*Ketowes* also means a jest, and the saying might rather be rendered: *Zechus Owes* is nothing to make light of. *Ed.*)

QUIPS AND QUIRKS FOR HANUKKAH

Sidney B. Hoenig

Introduction

Jews have always had a gift for escaping the mental torture of persecution through imaginative and speculative sorties into the lore and history of the past, seeking even in Holy Writ for hidden symbols. If Israel was the chosen of nations, possessed of a divine mandate, then somehow the shadow of coming events must be lurking in every page, nay in every letter, of sacred writing.

Thus the medieval Jews amused themselves with anagram and word play and mystical interpretation of numbers and of letters; and with riddles and conundrums—all with that pinch of levity that made them true for the moment, but yet, as is any old man's tale, never to be accepted as "really true."

A Riddle with a Fourfold Answer

The Man-of-Old asked the Child-of-Today:

"Why did the first Hanukkah fall on the twenty-fifth day of the month Kislev?"

The Child-of-Today made reply:

"Because Judah the Maccabee drove Antiochus from Jerusalem and rededicated the Temple, and the oil intended for one day burned for eight."

The Man-of-Old smiled and said:

"But why did all this happen on that particular day? You know, history has a way of repeating itself. Perhaps the victory

107

and the dedication fell on the anniversary of a past event. Let us see."

Whereupon man and child traveled back until they found themselves at the beginning of time in the Garden of Eden. And lo and behold, they came upon an answer to part of the riddle! And the man set it down to be told again and again on Hanukkah to the little ones of Israel as *The Legend of the Winter Solstice*:

I

The Garden of Eden was flooded with sunshine. The trees grew and flourished. The birds sang. The flowers budded and bloomed, and the heart of Man was glad. At length there came a day when Adam paid heed to the whispers of Eve. He ate of the forbidden fruit. And Man and Woman were driven from the Garden to eat bread in the sweat of their brow.

During the day the sun warmed the earth. When the coolness of evening came and the day's task was ended, Adam and Eve sat quietly in the shade to eat of the bread of their toil.

Suddenly Adam noticed that the sun set earlier. Darkness followed quickly. Nights became longer, days shorter.

Was this some new punishment? Alarmed, the Man and Woman fasted and prayed. A week passed—the sun withdrew yet earlier. Adam and Eve became terrified. Was darkness to creep farther and farther upon earth and devour all living?

Lo, a miracle! On the morrow the sun tarried longer, and on the morrow, and on the morrow after. Days grew steadily longer, nights shorter.

Then Adam laughed aloud at his fears. And he and Eve feasted and made merry. They kindled fires of thanksgiving. For they knew that all was as it had been, and would ever by —that the lights in the heaven were fixed in their courses for

signs, and for seasons, for days and for years, and that while
the earth remained, seed time and harvest, cold and heat, summer and winter, and day and night would not cease.

Now the day that Adam celebrated by kindling fires of thanksgiving fell in mid-winter when the sun, they tell us, reaches a
point farthest from the middle of the earth and appears to pause
and then returns on its course.

And this day is the twenty-fifth of the month Kislev. It is
the Winter Solstice.

II

"This is only the first portion of our answer," said the Man-
of-Old. "Let us move forward through the years." So they
fared forth and joined their people in the wilderness on the trek
from Egyptian darkness into the light of freedom.

And they beheld the children of Israel assembled, awed and
expectant. For all the work of the tabernacle was finished. And
Bezalel and the wise-hearted men who had wrought with him
brought the tabernacle unto Moses, and all its furniture; the
ark of the testimony, and the ark cover; the table, all the vessels
thereof, and the showbread; the pure candlestick, the lamps
thereof, even the lamps to be set in order, and all the vessels
thereof, and the oil for the light—

And it was the twenty-fifth day of the month Kislev.

III

So, with two portions of the answer to their riddle, the questing
pair traveled farther, forward through the years to a second
redemption, the deliverance from the night of exile in Babylon.
And the people were gathered before Nehemiah and the priests.
Upon the restored altar they put the slime that had remained

in the pit. In it, seventy years before, the priests had hidden the sacred oil from the invader, and the earth of the pit had preserved this oil against what time the altar would be restored.

Suddenly the sun, which was hidden behind the clouds, burst forth in all its majesty. Its rays beat down upon the altar and lo, the residue of the oil burst into flame. Priests and people marveled at this wondrous sight, and Nehemiah decreed that henceforth a period of prayer and feasting and rejoicing should be held throughout all the generations of Israel on the anniversary of the day on which the altar and the rebuilt temple had been dedicated.

And this day was the twenty-fifth day of Kislev.

IV

"Now," said the Man-of-Old, "let us seek in the time of the Maccabees for the final portion of our answer. Is it not possible that there was some event on the twenty-fifth day of Kislev from which Judah and his soldiers drew the renewed courage that brought the small band to victory, and the Temple to its former state?"

And so they took up their quest, and found the people of Judaea in great distress. For the Syrian tyrant had declared a special feast, and had commanded that all the inhabitants of the land worship on the altars which he had set up in the holy places. The faithful among the Jews were tortured because they would not forsake the faith of their fathers.

And the king commanded that this day be called the Feast of Antiochus.

And it was the twenty-fifth day of the month Kislev.

And so it was that when the Child-of-Today had the four portions of the answer to his question, he found that the enigma was solved.

"You see," said the Man-of-Old, "History does not explain everything. The day when the sun gave promise of renewed life to the sleeping earth, the Tabernacle was dedicated by Moses; and that also was a Hanukkah—a day of dedication. Centuries later, on that day, a redeemed people returned from Babylonia, beheld a miracle of sacred oil upon the restored altar. That likewise was a Hanukkah—a day of dedication.

"It was that day which the Maccabeans chose to rededicate the defiled altar, and so to turn the mourning of the Feast of Antiochus into the gladness of the Feast of Lights."

————

The Child-of-Today asks, "Is there any new portion for our own time? Has the twenty-fifth day of Kislev ever given occasion for a new dedication?"

The Man-of-Old said, "History does not explain everything. It was on the twenty-fifth day of the month Kislev in our time—we call it the tenth of December of the year 1918— that a British general, by the name of Allenby, led the victorious forces of the Allied armies into the city of Jerusalem and delivered it."

Mystic Letters

The Man-of-Old asked the Child-of-Today:

"Why was Judah called Maccabee?"

"Because," said the Child-of-Today, "Judah used as his battle cry:

M i   מ   מי Who is
K amoka   כ   כמוכה Like Thee
B aelim   ב   באלים Among their gods
I hvh (Adonai) י   יי O Lord!

The first letters of the Hebrew words spell *mkbi* or Maccabee."

———

"I know another answer," said the Man-Of-Old. "Let us take the final consonants of the words—

Abraha *M*   אברהם
Isaa   *K*   יצחק
Jaco   *B*   יעקב

Thus the names of the three patriarchs yield the main consonants of the Hebrew word *Makkeb* meaning Hammer, as some say Judah was called.

———

The Child-of-Today countered with a question to the Man-Of-Old:

"Can you make an anagram from the name of Judah's family the Hasmoneans?"

"I think I can," said the Man-Of-Old.

חודש   *H*   *Hodesh*—the New Moon, to signify the Jewish Calendar.

שבת   *S*   *Sabbath*—the day of hallowed rest.

מועדים *M*   *Mo'adim*—Festivals.

נבואה   *N*   *Nebuah*—Prophecy.

אבות   *A*   *Abot*—The Tradition of the Patriarchs.

יחוד השם *Y*   *Yihud*—Monotheism.

These are the principles for which the Maccabees fought."

———

"Have you any way of playing with the word חֲנוּכָּה, Hanukkah?" asked the Man-of-Old. "Do you think you could make

two Hebrew words out of it?" The Child-of-Today was
sorely puzzled. At last he said, "I can think of one word—

Hanu חָנוּ "They rested."

The Man-of-Old exclaimed, "Good! I can think of the next—

Kah כָּה = twenty-five."[1]

The child was gleeful—"They rested from battle on the
twenty-fifth (of Kislev)."

MYSTIC NUMBERS

"Let us see," said the Man-of-Old, "whether we can find any
forecast of Hanukkah in the early stories through the numerical
value of the Hebrew letters."

The Child-of-Today replied in glee, "Let us go back again to
the beginning of time. Is there any reference to Hanukkah in
the story of creation?"

The Man-of-Old smiled and said:

"In the account of creation are the words *Yehi Or*, 'Let there
be light.'

י Y	(*Yod*)	equals	10
ה H	(*He*)	equals	5
י Y	(*Yod*)	equals	10

יהי YHY (yehi) equals 25

**The sum of the Hebrew letters in *Yehi*, 'Let there be,' is 25.
Thus the sentence *Yehi Or* means '25 light.' This we can inter-
pret to mean on the 25th day of the month there is to be light."**

---

[1] In Hebrew every letter has a numerical value, כ equaling 20, and ה equaling 5.

"When you are older," said the Man-of-Old, "and read the Gemara, a part of the Talmud, you will discover that the thirty-six candles used during the whole eight days of Hanukkah equal the number of treatises in the Gemara.

"And so we have the lights of Hanukkah foreshadowed in the Bible and hinted at by the Talmud."

THE SHAMMASH-CANDLE

"Is there any hidden sign about the *Shammash*-Candle, the one that lights the others?" asked the Child-of-Today.

"I think I can find you one," said the Man-of-Old, "take a pencil and figure it out. When Jacob met Esau, the Bible tells us 'The sun shone for him' (ויזרח לו השמש), *Va-yizrah lo ha-shemesh* (Gen. 32.32). The Hebrew word *Lo* (for him) consists of the letters

Lamed ל　equals 30

Vav ו　equals　6

The sum of these is thirty-six. Now, if instead of *ha-shemesh*, the sun, we put *ha-shammash*,[1] the *shammash*, we can read it, 'The *shammash* shone for thirty-six comrades.' "

———

"I prefer the explanation," said the Child, "which tells us that since we are forbidden to use any of the candles for any other purpose than to have them shed light for our feast, we must take an extra one to kindle them and to protect them."

---

[1] *Shemesh* and *Shammash* look alike in the consonantal Hebrew text.

Hanukkah Games

Games have been a characteristic feature of Hanukkah. Even games of chance, usually frowned upon, were permitted, provided, of course, that they did not degenerate into gambling. Chess, dominoes and riddles (*ketowes*) which depended upon numerical values of words were encouraged.

The most popular children's game, however, was with the Top (*Drehdel—Trendle, Galgelon.*) A square top is used. On each side is inscribed one of the four Hebrew letters, נ *Nun*, ג *Gimmel*, ה *He*, ש *Shin*. These are regarded as the initial letters of the sentence *Nes Gadol Hayah Sham* (נס גדול היה שם), "A great miracle happened there." During the entire month of Kislev children are busy carving tops from wood or casting them from lead.

The game is a sort of "put and take," each of the four letters signifying a gain or a loss or an even break. The top is spun, and anxious little heads turn to watch its course, anxious eyes are strained to see what letter looks up at them as the top comes to rest on its side. *Nun* means "nothing," *Nichts*, take nothing and give nothing. Then it is the next child's turn to spin the top. If luck is good, *Gimmel* is on top, which means "everything," *Ganz*, take everything. The next spin may be somewhat less fortunate and bring the *He*, which means *halb*, "half," take half. But the next turn may bring the greatest misfortune, since by showing the *Shin* the top will be saying *Shtell*—put in more.

Hanukkah Customs

On the eighth day of the feast children have a special holiday, called *Zot Hanukkah*, "This is Hanukkah."

What remains of the oil used in the Hanukkah lamps is given to the children to make a special illumination for their games.

This also is the time of gift giving. Children and their elders exchange presents.

Hanukkah shares with Purim in being a time in which gifts of money are distributed among those in need.

Hanukkah is often marked by the announcement of a betrothal, for it has been customary to make it the season of the interchange of gifts between men and women.

Among all peoples there are dishes that are prepared at special seasons and have a flavor peculiar to the holiday. The Jews have developed such delicacies. Often they are the ordinary food of the country of their birth; and are adapted to some special holiday.

Hanukkah Lamp, Salomon Collection, *Hebraica*, plate XV.

Hanukkah Lamp. Salomon Collection, *Hebraica*, plate XVIII.

PART II

HANUKKAH IN LITERATURE

ANCIENT WRITINGS

THE MACCABEAN REVOLT

INTRODUCTION

THE primary source for the history of the Maccabean Period is the apocryphal Books of Maccabees (see p. 41). Even Josephus, the Jewish historian, who died around the year 100 of the Common Era, drew his material from these two books. A word about the manner in which I and II Maccabees have been preserved is, therefore, in place.

The Jews produced a large number of books which were not of as high literary and religious merit as were those included in the Bible. Therefore they were not considered sacred. In other words, these books may have been widely read but their reading was not encouraged by the religious teachers as was that of Holy Scripture. This attitude was emphasized when some unorthodox sects began to make extensive use of the latter-day writings. Books of this sort, the active circulation of which was discouraged, came to be known as "hidden away" or apocryphal. The early Christians, however, made no such distinction. Holding themselves to be the heirs of the Hebrew spirit, the Christians adopted as their own the entire religious literature which that spirit had produced. Hence the Bible of the early Church, the Catholic, included the apocryphal writings, which were placed between the Hebrew scriptures and the Gospels. The later Protestant Bible excluded them. "The Apocrypha" is the general name by which the writings admitted by the Catholic Church are known. They include The Maccabees.

Thus a strange situation developed. The Jews forgot this part of their literature. The Hebrew originals were lost. Only the Church of Rome treasured the books in their Greek translation. Judah the Maccabee became a worthy in the Catholic Church, just as were Abraham, Moses, and the Prophets.

Historically I Maccabees is the more reliable of the two books.

Later other books came into being, bearing the name of *Maccabees*. One, *The Scroll of Antiochus*, has an interesting history of its own. It probably originated in Babylonia in the 7th or 8th century, and for a long time was used in the Synagogue on Hanukkah as the Scroll of Esther is used on Purim. But it has neither literary nor religious merit, and by this time is practically forgotten. A critical English translation of it by the Haham Moses Gaster is to be found in the *Transactions of the International Congress of Orientalists*, 9th Congress, 1892 (London, 1893), vol. 2, pp. 3–32.

THE TYRANNY OF ANTIOCHUS[1]

And it happened, after that Alexander, son of Philip, the Macedonian, who came out of the land of Chettiim, had smitten Darius, king of the Persians and Medes, that he reigned in his stead, the first over Greece, and made many wars, and won many strongholds, and slew the kings of the earth, and took spoils of many nations, insomuch that the earth was quiet before him; whereupon he was exalted, and his heart was lifted up. And he gathered a mighty strong host and ruled over countries and nations, and kings, who became tributaries unto him.

And after these things he fell sick, and perceived that he should die. Wherefore he called his servants, such as were honourable, and had been brought up with him from his youth, and parted his kingdom among them, while he was yet alive.

[1] Substantially according to the Authorized Version of the Apocrypha; I Maccabees 1.

So Alexander reigned twelve years, and then died. And his servants bare rule every one in his place. And after his death they all put crowns upon themselves; so did their sons after them many years: and evils were multiplied in the earth. And there came out of them a wicked root, Antiochus surnamed Epiphanes, son of Antiochus the king, who had been an hostage at Rome, and he reigned in the hundred and thirty and seventh year of the kingdom of the Greeks.[2]

In those days went there out of Israel wicked men who persuaded many, saying: "Let us go and make a covenant with the heathen that are round about us, for since we departed from them we have had much sorrow." So this device pleased them well. Then certain of the people were so forward herein, that they went to the king, who gave them license to do after the ordinances of the heathen. Whereupon they built a place of exercise at Jerusalem according to the customs of the heathen; and made themselves uncircumcised, and forsook the holy covenant, and joined themselves to the heathen, and sold themselves to do mischief.

Now when the kingdom was established before Antiochus, he thought to reign over Egypt, that he might have the dominion of two realms. Wherefore he entered into Egypt with a great multitude, with chariots and elephants, and horsemen, and a great navy, and made war against Ptolemy, king of Egypt; but Ptolemy was afraid of him, and fled; and many were wounded to death. Thus they got the strong cities in the land of Egypt, and he took the spoils thereof.

And after that Antiochus had smitten Egypt, he returned again in the hundred forty and third year, and went up against Israel and Jerusalem with a great multitude, and entered proudly

[2] In the year 175 before the Common Era.

into the sanctuary, and took away the golden altar and the candlestick of light, and all the vessels thereof, and the table of the showbread, and the pouring vessels, and the vials, and the censers of gold, and the veil, and the crowns, and the golden ornaments that were before the temple, all which he pulled off. He took also . . . the hidden treasures which he found. And when he had taken all away he went into his own land, having made a great massacre, and spoken very proudly. Therefore there was great mourning in Israel, in every place where they were; so that the princes and elders mourned, the virgins and young men were made feeble, and the beauty of women was changed. Every bridegroom took up lamentation, and she that sat in the marriage chamber was in heaviness. The land also was moved for the inhabitants thereof, and all the house of Jacob was covered with confusion.

And after two full years the king sent his chief collector of tribute unto the cities of Judah, who came unto Jerusalem with a great multitude, and spake peaceable words unto them, but all was deceit: for when they had given him credence, he fell suddenly upon the city, and smote it very sore, and destroyed much people of Israel. And when he had taken the spoils of the city, he set it on fire, and pulled down the houses and walls thereof on every side. But the women and children took they captive, and possessed the cattle.

Then builded they the city of David with a great and strong wall, and with mighty towers, and made it a stronghold for them. And they put therein a sinful nation, wicked men, and fortified themselves therein. They stored it also with armour and victuals, and when they had gathered together the spoils of Jerusalem, they laid them up there, and so they became a sore snare: For it was a place to lie in wait in against the sanctuary, and an evil adversary to Israel. Thus they shed innocent blood on every side of the sanctuary, and defiled it; insomuch that the inhabitants of Jerusalem fled because of them. Whereupon the city was made an habitation of strangers, and became strange to those that were born in her, and her own children left her. Her sanctuary was laid waste like a wilderness, her feasts were turned into mourning, her sabbaths into reproach, her honour into contempt. As had been her glory, so was her dishonour increased, and her high estate was turned into mourning.

Moreover king Antiochus wrote to his whole kingdom that all should be one people, and every one should leave his laws; so all the heathen agreed according to the commandment of the king. Yea, many also of the Israelites consented to his religion, and sacrificed unto idols, and profaned the sabbath. For the king had sent letters by messengers unto Jerusalem and the cities of Judah, that they should follow the strange laws of the land, and forbid burnt offerings, and sacrifice, and drink offerings, in the temple; and that they should profane the sabbaths and festival days, and pollute the sanctuary and them that were holy, and set up altars, and groves and chapels of idols, and sacrifice swine's flesh, and unclean beasts, and that they should also leave their children uncircumcised, and make their souls abominable with all manner of uncleanness and profanation, to the end that they might forget the law and change all the ordinances. And whosoever would not do according to the commandment of the king, he said, he should die. In the selfsame manner wrote he to his whole kingdom, and appointed overseers over all the people, commanding the cities of Judah to sacrifice, city by city. Then many of the people were gathered unto them, to wit, every one that forsook the law; and so they committed evils in the land; and drove the Israelites into secret places, even wheresoever they could flee for succour.

Now the fifteenth day of the month Kislev, in the hundred

forty and fifth year, they set up the abomination of desolation upon the altar, and builded idol altars throughout the cities of Judah on every side; and burnt incense at the doors of their houses, and in the streets. And when they had rent in pieces the books of the law which they found, they burnt them with fire. And wheresoever was found with any the book of the covenant, or if any consented to the law, the king's commandment was that they should put him to death. Thus did they by their authority unto the Israelites every month, to as many as were found in the cities.

Now the five and twentieth day of the month they did sacrifice upon the idol altar, which was upon the altar of God. At which time according to the commandment they put to death certain women, that had caused their children to be circumcised. And they hanged the infants about their necks, and rifled their houses, and slew them that had circumcised them. Howbeit many in Israel were fully resolved and confirmed in themselves not to eat any unclean thing. Wherefore they chose rather to die, that they might not be defiled with meats, and that they might not profane the holy covenant; so then they died. And there was very great wrath upon Israel.

The Heroism of Mattathias [1]

In those days arose Mattathias, the son of John, the son of Simeon, a priest of the sons of Joarib, from Jerusalem, and dwelt in Modin. And he had five sons, John, who was surnamed Gaddis; Simon called Thassi; Judas, who was called Maccabeus; Eleazar, called Avaran; and Jonathan, whose surname was Apphus. And when he saw the blasphemies that were committed in Judah and Jerusalem, he said: "Woe is me! Wherefore

[1] I Maccabees, 2.

was I born to see this misery of my people, and of the holy city, and to dwell there, when it was delivered into the hand of the enemy, and the sanctuary into the hand of strangers? Her temple is become as a man without glory. Her glorious vessels are carried away into captivity, her infants are slain in the streets, her young men with the sword of the enemy. What nation hath not had a part in her kingdom, and gotten of her spoils? All her ornaments are taken away; of a free woman she is become a bondslave. And, behold, our sanctuary, even our beauty and our glory, is laid waste, and the Gentiles have profaned it. To what end therefore shall we live any longer?" Then Mattathias and his sons rent their clothes, and put on sackcloth, and mourned very sore.

In the meanwhile the king's officers, such as compelled the people to revolt, came into the city Modin to make them sacrifice. And when many of Israel came unto them, Mattathias also and his sons came together. Then answered the king's officers, and said to Mattathias on this wise: "Thou art a ruler and an honourable and great man in this city, and strengthened with sons and brethren. Now therefore come thou first, and fulfil the king's commandment, like as all the heathen have done, yea, and the men of Judah also, and such as remain at Jerusalem, so shalt thou and thy house be in the number of the king's friends, and thou and thy children shall be honoured with silver and gold, and many rewards." Then Mattathias answered and spake with a loud voice: "Though all the nations that are under the king's dominion obey him and fall away every one from the religion of their fathers, and give consent to his commandments, yet will I and my sons and my brethren walk in the covenant of our fathers. God forbid that we should forsake the law and the ordinances. We will not hearken to the king's words to go from our religion, either on the right hand or the left."

Now when he had left speaking these words there came one
of the Jews in the sight of all to sacrifice on the altar which
was at Modin, according to the king's commandment. Which
thing when Mattathias saw, he was inflamed with zeal, and his
reins trembled, neither could he forbear to show his anger according to judgment; wherefore he ran, and slew him upon the
altar. Also the king's commissioner, who compelled men to
sacrifice, he killed at that time, and the altar he pulled down.
Thus dealt he zealously for the law of God, like as Phinehas did
unto Zimri the son of Salu. And Mattathias cried throughout
the city with a loud voice, saying: "Whosoever is zealous of the
law and maintaineth the covenant, let him follow me." So he
and his sons fled into the mountains, and left all that ever they
had in the city.

And then came unto him a company of Hassidaeans, who
were mighty men of Israel, even all such as offered themselves
willingly for the law. Also all they that fled for persecution
joined themselves unto them, and were a stay unto them. So
they joined their forces and smote sinful men in their anger,
and wicked men in their wrath; but the rest fled to the heathen
for succour.

Then Mattathias and his friends went round about, and
pulled down the altars; and what children soever they found
within the coast of Israel uncircumcised, those they circumcised
by force. They pursued also after the proud men, and the work
prospered in their hand. So they recovered the law out of the
hand of the Gentiles, and out of the hand of kings, neither suffered they the sinner to triumph.

Now when the time drew near that Mattathias should die, he
said unto his sons: "Now hath pride and rebuke gotten strength,
and the time of destruction, and the wrath of indignation. Now

therefore, my sons, be ye zealous for the law, and give your
lives for the covenant of your fathers . . . Be valiant, and show
yourselves men in the behalf of the law; for by it shall ye obtain
glory. And, behold, I know that your brother, Simon, is a man
of counsel, give ear unto him alway; he shall be a father unto
you. As for Judas Maccabeus, he hath been mighty and strong,
even from his youth up; let him be your captain, and fight the
battle of the people. Take also unto you all those that observe
the law, and avenge ye the wrong of your people. Recompense
fully the heathen, and take heed to the commandments of the
law.''

So he blessed them, and was gathered to his fathers. And
he died in the hundred forty and sixth year,[1] and his sons buried
him in the sepulchres of his fathers at Modin, and all Israel
made great lamentation for him.

THE MACCABEE[2]

Then his son Judah, called Maccabeus, rose up in his stead.
And all his brethren helped him, and so did all they that held
with his father, and they fought with cheerfulness the battle
of Israel. So he got his people great honour, and put on a breastplate as a giant, and girt his warlike harness about him, and
he made battles, protecting the host with his sword. In his
acts he was like a lion, and like a lion's whelp roaring for his
prey. For he pursued the wicked, and sought them out, and
burnt up those that vexed his people. Wherefore the wicked
shrunk for fear of him, and all the workers of iniquity were
troubled, because salvation prospered in his hand. He grieved
also many kings, and made Jacob glad with his acts, and his

[1] In the year 167 or 166 B.C.E.
[2] I Maccabees, 3.1–9; 4.28–59.

memorial is blessed forever. Moreover he went through the cities of Judah, destroying the ungodly out of them, and turning away wrath from Israel; so that he was renowned unto the utmost part of the earth, and he received unto him such as were ready to perish . . .

In the next year Lysias gathered together threescore thousand choice men of foot, and five thousand horsemen, that he might subdue them. So they came into Idumaea, and pitched their tents at Bethsura, and Judah met them with ten thousand men.

And when he saw that mighty army, he prayed and said: "Blessed art Thou, O Saviour of Israel, who didst quell the violence of the mighty man by the hand of Thy servant David, and gavest the host of strangers into the hands of Jonathan the son of Saul, and his armourbearer; shut up this army in the hand of Thy people Israel, and let them be confounded in their power and horsemen. Make them to be of no courage, and cause the boldness of their strength to fall away, and let them quake at their destruction. Cast them down with the sword of them that love Thee, and let all those that know Thy name praise Thee with thanksgiving."

So they joined battle; and there were slain of the host of Lysias about five thousand men, even before them were they slain.

Now when Lysias saw his army put to flight, and the manliness of Judah's soldiers, and how they were ready either to live or die valiantly, he went into Antiochia and gathered together hired soldiers, and having made his army greater than it was, he purposed to come again into Judea.

Then said Judah and his brethren: "Behold, our enemies are discomfited; let us go up to cleanse and dedicate the sanctuary." Upon this all the host assembled themselves together, and went up into Mount Zion. And when they saw the sanctuary desolate, and the altar profaned, and the gates burned up, and shrubs growing in the courts as in a forest, or in one of the mountains, yea, and the priests' chambers pulled down; they rent their clothes, and made great lamentation, and cast ashes upon their heads, and fell down flat to the ground upon their faces, and blew an alarm with trumpets, and cried toward heaven.

Then Judah appointed certain men to fight against those that were in the fortress, until he had cleansed the sanctuary. So he chose priests of blameless conversation, such as had pleasure in the law, who cleansed the sanctuary and bare out the defiled stones into an unclean place. And when as they consulted what to do with the altar of burnt offerings, which was profaned, they thought it best to pull it down, lest it should be a reproach to them, because the heathen had defiled it; wherefore they pulled it down, and laid up the stones in the mountain of the temple in a convenient place, until there should come a prophet to show what should be done with them. And they took whole stones according to the law, and built a new altar according to the former; and made up the sanctuary, and the things that were within the temple, and hallowed the courts. They made also new holy vessels, and into the temple they brought the candlestick, and the altar of burnt offerings, and of incense, and the table. And upon the altar they burned incense, and the lamps that were upon the candlestick they lighted that they might give light in the temple. Furthermore they set the loaves upon the table, and spread out the veils, and finished all the works which they had begun to make.

Now on the five and twentieth day of the ninth month, which is called the month of Kislev, in the hundred forty and eighth year, they rose up betimes in the morning, and offered sacrifice according to the law upon the new altar of burnt offerings, which they had made. Look, at what time and what day the heathen had profaned it, even in that was it dedicated with songs, and cetherns, and harps, and cymbals. Then all the people fell upon their faces, worshipping and praising the God of heaven, who had given them good success. And so they kept the dedication of the altar eight days, and offered burnt offerings with gladness, and sacrificed the sacrifice of deliverance and praise. They decked also the forefront of the temple with crowns of gold, and with shields; and the gates and the chambers they renewed, and hanged doors upon them.

Thus was there very great gladness among the people, for that the reproach of the heathen was put away. Moreover Judah and his brethren with the whole congregation of Israel ordained that the days of the dedication of the altar should be kept in their season from year to year by the space of eight days, from the five and twentieth day of the month Kislev, with mirth and gladness. . . .

The Valor of Eleazar[1]

Not long after this the king sent an old man of Athens to compel the Jews to depart from the laws of their fathers, and not to live after the laws of God; and also to pollute the temple in Jerusalem, and to call it the temple of Jupiter Olympius; and that in Gerizim by the name of Jupiter the Defender of strangers, as they did desire that dwelt in the place.

The coming in of this mischief was sore and grievous to the people; for the temple was filled with rioting and revelling by the heathen. . . . The altar also was filled with profane things, which the law forbiddeth. Neither was it lawful for a man to keep sabbath days or ancient feasts, or to profess himself at all

[1] II Maccabees, 6.

to be a Jew. And in the day of the king's birth every month they were brought by bitter constraint to eat of the sacrifices; and when the feast of Bacchus was kept, the Jews were compelled to go in procession to Bacchus, carrying ivy.

Moreover there went out a decree to the neighbour cities of the heathen, by the suggestion of Ptolemy, against the Jews, that they should observe the same fashions, and be partakers of their sacrifices: And whoso would not conform themselves to the manners of the Gentiles should be put to death. Then might a man have seen the present misery. For two women were brought for having circumcised their children; these, when they had openly led them round about the city, the babes hanging at their breasts, they cast down headlong from the wall. And others, that had run together into caves near by, to keep the sabbath day secretly, being discovered to Philip, were all burnt together, because they made a conscience to help themselves for the honour of the most sacred day.

Now I beseech those that read this book, that they be not discouraged for these calamities, but that they judge those punishments not to be for destruction, but for a chastening of our nation . . . But let this that we have spoken be for a warning unto us. And now will we come to the declaring of the matter in few words.

Eleazar, one of the principal scribes, an aged man, and of a well favoured countenance, was constrained to open his mouth, and to eat swine's flesh. But he, choosing rather to die gloriously, than to live stained with such an abomination, spit it forth, and came of his own accord to the torment, as it behoved them to come, that are resolute to stand out against such things, as are not lawful for love of life to be tasted.

But they that had the charge of that wicked feast, for the old acquaintance they had with the man, taking him aside, besought him to bring flesh of his own provision, such as was lawful for him to use, and make as if he did eat of the flesh taken from the sacrifice commanded by the king; that in so doing he might be delivered from death, and for the old friendship with them find favour.

But he began to consider discreetly, and as became his age, and the excellency of his ancient years, and the honour of his grey head, whereunto he was come, and his most honest education from a child, or rather the holy law made and given by God: therefore he answered accordingly, and willed them straightways to send him to the grave. "For it becometh not our age," said he, "in any wise to dissemble, whereby many young persons might think that Eleazar, being fourscore years old and ten, were now gone to a strange religion; and so they through mine hypocrisy, and desire to live a little time and a moment longer, should be deceived by me, and I get a stain to mine old age, and make it abominable. For though for the present time I should be delivered from the punishment of men: yet should I not escape the hand of the Almighty, neither alive, nor dead. Wherefore now, manfully changing this life, I will show myself such an one as mine age requireth, and leave a notable example to such as be young to die willingly and courageously for the honourable and holy laws."

And when he had said these words, immediately he went to the torment: They that led him changing the good will they bare him a little before into hatred, because the foresaid speeches proceeded, as they thought, from a desperate mind.

But when he was ready to die with stripes, he groaned, and said, "It is manifest unto the Lord, that hath the holy knowledge, that whereas I might have been delivered from death, I now endure sore pains in body by being beaten: but in soul am well content to suffer these things, because I fear Him."

And thus this man died, leaving his death for an example of a noble courage, and a memorial of virtue, not only unto young men, but unto all his nation.

Hannah and Her Seven Sons[1]

And it came to pass that seven brethren also with their mother were at the king's command taken and shamefully handled with scourges and cords, to compel them to taste of the abominable swine's flesh. But one of them made himself the spokesman and said, "What wouldest thou ask and learn of us? for we are ready to die rather than transgress the laws of our fathers." And the king fell into a rage, and commanded to heat pans and caldrons: and when these forthwith were heated, he commanded to cut out the tongue of him that had been their spokesman, and to scalp him and to cut off his extremities, the rest of his brethren and his mother looking on. And when he was utterly maimed, the king commanded to bring him to the fire, being yet alive, and to fry him in the pan. And as the vapour of the pan spread far, they and their mother also exhorted one another to die nobly, saying thus: "The Lord God beholdeth, and in truth is intreated for us, as Moses declared in his song, which witnesseth against the people to their faces, saying, 'And he shall be intreated for His servants.'"

And when the first had died after this manner, they brought the second to the mocking; and they pulled off the skin of his head with the hair and asked him, "Wilt thou eat, before thy body be punished in every limb?" But he answered in the language of his fathers and said to them, "No." Wherefore he also underwent the next torture in succession, as the first had done.

[1] II Maccabees, 7.

And when he was at the last gasp, he said, "Thou, miscreant, dost release us out of this present life, but the King of the world shall raise up us, who have died for His laws, unto an eternal renewal of life."

And after him was the third made a mocking-stock. And when he was required, he quickly put out his tongue and stretched forth his hands courageously, and nobly said, "From heaven I possess these; and for His laws' sake I contemn these; and from Him I hope to receive these back again:" insomuch that the king himself and they that were with him were astonished at the young man's soul, for that he nothing regarded the pains.

And when he too was dead, they shamefully handled and tortured the fourth in like manner. And being come near unto death he said thus: "It is good to die at the hands of men and look for the hopes which are given by God, that we shall be raised up again by Him; for as for thee, thou shalt have no resurrection unto life."

And next after him they brought the fifth, and shamefully handled him. But he looked toward the king and said, "Because thou hast authority among men, though thou art thyself corruptible, thou doest what thou wilt; yet think not that our race hath been forsaken of God; but hold thou on thy way, and behold His sovereign majesty, how it will torture thee and thy seed."

And after him they brought the sixth. And when he was at the point to die he said, "Be not vainly deceived, for we suffer these things for our own doings, as sinning against our own God: marvellous things are come to pass; but think not thou that thou shalt be unpunished, having assayed to fight against God."

But above all was the mother marvellous and worthy of

honourable memory; for when she looked on seven sons perishing within the space of one day, she bare the sight with a good courage for the hopes that she had set on the Lord. And she exhorted each one of them in the language of their fathers, filled with a noble temper and stirring up her womanish thought with manly passion, saying unto them, "I know not how ye came into my womb, neither was it I that bestowed on you your spirit and your life, and it was not I that brought into order the first elements of each one of you. Therefore the Creator of the world, who fashioned the generation of man and devised the generation of all things, in mercy giveth back to you again both your spirit and your life, as ye now contemn your own selves for His laws' sake." But Antiochus, thinking himself to be despised, and suspecting the reproachful voice, whilst the youngest was yet alive did not only make his appeal to him by words, but also at the same time promised with oaths that he would enrich him and raise him to high estate, if he would turn from the customs of his fathers, and that he would take him for his friend and intrust him with affairs. But when the young man would in no wise give heed, the king called unto him his mother and exhorted her that she would counsel the lad to save himself. And when he had exhorted her with many words, she undertook to persuade her son. But bending toward him, laughing the cruel tyrant to scorn, she spake thus in the language of her fathers: "My son, have pity upon me that carried thee nine months in my womb, and gave thee suck three years, and nourished and brought thee up unto this age, and sustained thee. I beseech thee, my child, to lift thine eyes unto the heaven and the earth, and to see all things that are therein, and thus to recognise that God made them not of things that were, and that the race of men in this wise cometh into being. Fear not this butcher, but, proving thyself worthy of thy brethren, accept thy death, that in the mercy of God I may receive thee again with thy brethren."

Before she had yet ended speaking, the young man said, "Whom wait ye for? I obey not the commandment of the king, but I hearken to the commandment of the law that was given to our fathers through Moses. But thou, that hast devised all manner of evil against the Hebrews shalt in no wise escape the hands of God. For we are suffering because of our own sins; and if for rebuke and chastening our living Lord hath been angered a little while, yet shall He again be reconciled with His own servants. But thou, O unholy man and of all most vile, be not vainly lifted up in thy wild pride with uncertain hopes, raising thy hand against the heavenly children; for not yet hast thou escaped the judgment of the Almighty God that seeth all things. For these our brethren, having endured a short pain that bringeth everlasting life, have now died under God's covenant; but thou, through the judgment of God, shalt receive in just measure the penalties of thine arrogancy. But I, as my brethren, give up both body and soul for the laws of our fathers, calling upon God that He may speedily become gracious to the nation; and that thou amidst trials and plagues mayest confess that He alone is God; and that in me and my brethren thou mayest stay the wrath of the Almighty, which hath been justly brought upon our whole race." But the king, falling into a rage, handled him worse than all the rest, being exasperated at his mocking. So he also died pure from polluting, putting his whole trust in the Lord.

And last of all after her sons the mother died.

Let it then suffice to have said thus much concerning the enforcement of sacrificial feasts and the king's exceeding barbarities.

Dedication of the Temple[1]

And Maccabaeus and they that were with him, the Lord leading them on, recovered the temple and the city; and they pulled down the altars that had been built in the market place by the aliens and also the walls of sacred inclosures. And having cleansed the sanctuary they made another altar of sacrifice; and striking stones and taking fire out of them, they offered sacrifices after they had ceased for two years, and burned incense, and lighted lamps, and set forth the showbread. And when they had done these things they fell prostrate and besought the Lord that they might fall no more into such evils; but that, if ever they should sin, they might be chastened by Him with forbearance and not delivered unto blaspheming and barbarous heathen. Now on the same day that the sanctuary was profaned by aliens, upon that very day did it come to pass that the cleansing of the sanctuary was made, even on the five and twentieth day of the same month, which is Kislev. And they kept eight days with gladness, in the manner of the feast of the tabernacles, remembering how that not long afore, during the feast of tabernacles, they were wandering in the mountains and in the caves after the manner of wild beasts. Wherefore bearing wands wreathed with leaves, and fair boughs, and palms also, they offered up hymns of thanksgiving to Him that had prosperously brought to pass the cleansing of His own place. They ordained also with a common statute and decree, for all the nation of the Jews, that they should keep these days every year.

[1] II Maccabees, 10.1–8.

THE MIRACLE OF OIL

THE Talmud is a compilation of the law and folklore discussed in the rabbinical academies of the East. The Babylonian Talmud was brought to completion, more or less in the state in which we possess it, in the Babylonian academies about the year 500 C. E. It is divided into treatises, each dealing in the main with a separate subject. The treatise from which the following is taken deals with the laws of the Sabbath. It is characteristic of the Talmud to interrupt the subject under discussion by the inclusion of other matters suggested by the subject. And so our sages asked: *What is Hanukkah?*

Commencing with the twenty-fifth day of the month Kislev there are eight days upon which there shall be neither mourning nor fasting. For albeit the Greeks entered the temple and defiled the oil, it was when the might of the Hasmonean overcame and vanquished them that, upon search, a single cruse of undefiled oil sealed by the High Priest was found. In it was oil enough for the needs of a solitary day.

Then it was that a miracle was wrought.

The oil in the cruse burned eight days.[1]

[1] Babylonian Talmud, Shabbat 23 b.

THE OBSERVANCE OF HANUKKAH

FOR centuries the *Shulhan 'Aruk* has been the code of rabbinical Judaism for all ritual and legal questions that arose after the destruction of the Temple. Its author, Joseph ben Ephraim Caro, is the last of the great codifiers. The *Shulhan 'Aruk* was written in Caro's latter years, although its authority was not firmly established until the middle of the seventeenth century.

From this book have been taken the following injunctions for the observance of Hanukkah:

Do not fast during Hanukkah, nor on the day preceding the feast, nor on the day following.

Eat and be merry. Linger over your viands and punctuate your meals with jest and song, and relate miracles.

Buy yourself a lamp of silver to reflect the beauty of the flickering lights. Fill it with sufficient oil to burn at least half an hour. Set it in public view.

Place the eight tapers in a straight row, since no day of Hanukkah is superior to another. Only the kindler and guardian of the lights, the ninth taper, shall stand above them all.

Kindle the lights before any member of the household, child or adult, seeks sleep.

Light the *Shammash*. With it kindle first the taper on the left. Move toward the right.

Men, women and children may kindle the lamp of dedication. It is well for each member of your household to have a lamp to kindle.

Augment your contribution to the community fund so that all your brethren may celebrate Hanukkah.

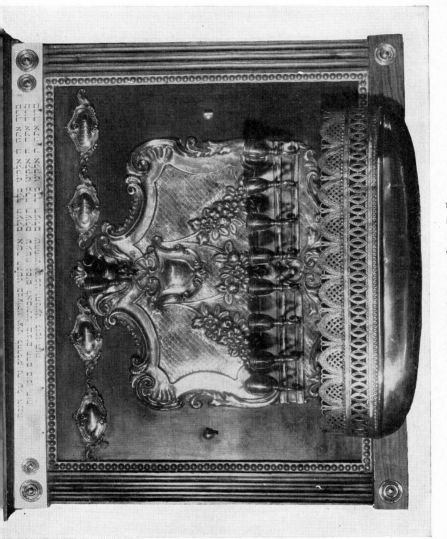

Hanukkah Lamp, silver, Italian.

Museum, Jewish Theological Seminary of America.

MATTATHIAS CHARGES HIS SONS BEFORE HIS DEATH, AND APPOINTS JUDAH WHO IS CALLED MACCABAEUS AS LEADER IN HIS STEAD

Based in large measure upon Josephus, but with many omissions of historical events and additions of the miraculous and imaginative, the *Josippon*, from which the following passages are taken, was ascribed to Joseph ben Gurion. It may have been written as early as the 6th century, though portions of it date from the 9th century. It used to be very popular among the Jews.

Now[1] the days of Mattathias drew nigh that he should die; and he called unto his five sons, and he encouraged them, and he strengthened them with his words. And he said unto them: "My sons, I know that now many wars will be waged among you, because we arose and bestirred ourselves to fight for our people and for our remnant that escaped, and for the cities of our God. And now, my sons, be jealous for the sake of your God and for the sake of His sanctuary; and fear not death, for if ye die in the battle of the Lord, ye will receive your reward, and ye will be in the land of the living with our fathers. Moreover, ye will also inherit a portion and an inheritance in the lot of their inheritance; for all our fathers were jealous for the Lord, and our God gave them grace and honor. Know ye not that Phinehas our father, because he was jealous for the God of Israel, received a covenant of salt for ever? And his priesthood was unto him, and unto his seed after him, an everlasting covenant; because he was jealous for his God, and made atonement

[1] Taken from B. Halper, *Post-Biblical Hebrew Literature*, An Anthology, The Jewish Publication Society, Philadelphia, 1921, vol. II, pp. 55–58.

for the children of Israel. And the Lord our God therefore raised him above all the sons of Aaron, our first father, and He gave him His covenant of peace. Also unto all our fathers who were jealous for our God did our God give their reward; and they found favor in the sight of God. Now, my sons, be strong and of good courage, fear not, and be not dismayed on account of these unclean nations; for they trust in their strength that perisheth and in their might that cometh to an end, but ye trust in the strength of the Lord our God which perisheth not and in the power of His might which cometh not to an end. For they trust in the multitude of their troops and in their army, but ye trust in the Lord with whom are strength and power to save by many or by few. And the power of the horse is a vain thing for deliverance, for deliverance is the Lord's. Assemble yourselves, my sons, and be like one man and of one heart; and be jealous for the God of Israel, as your pious fathers were; and the Lord, the God of your strength, will put the dread of you and the fear of you upon your enemies."

And he called unto Simon his eldest son, and charged him, and said unto him: "My son, I know that the Lord has put wisdom and understanding in thy heart. And now give, in perfect good will, thy counsel unto thyself and unto the holy people, and withhold not, I pray thee, thyself nor thy counsel from this people. And thou shalt be a father to thy brethren, and they will hearken unto thee in every matter; for the Lord our God has put in thee counsel, and wisdom and strength."

And Mattathias said again "Call to me Judah my son." And he was called unto him; and he stood before him. And he said unto him: "My son Judah, whose name is called Maccabee because of thy strength, hearken to my counsel, so that whithersoever thou turnest, thou mayest have good success, and mayest be prosperous. I know that thou art a man of war, and that

God has put in thee power and strength, so that thy heart is as the heart of a lion, which melteth not and feareth not. And now honor the Lord with thy strength which He has given thee, for everything is from Him; and go, and fight His battles without slothfulness and be not slothful to go to every side, and to every corner, in the east, and in the west, and in the north, and in the south, in the holy land, to take vengeance from the nations who defile it. And be thou unto the holy people captain of the host and war Messiah."[1]

And Judah answered his father, and said: "Behold, my Lord, my father, I will do according to all which thou hast commanded me."

And he commanded, and they brought unto him the vial of oil; and he poured it upon his head, and he anointed him leader and war Messiah. And all the people shouted with a great shout, and blew the trumpet, and they said: "Long live the leader," and: "Long live the anointed."

And it came to pass when Mattathias the priest finished charging his sons, that he expired and died, and was gathered unto his people. And Judah his son, who was called Maccabee because of his strength, arose in his stead from among his sons, to be leader and anointed. And his brethren and all his father's house and all the congregation of the pious helped him. . . .

And the wicked were discomfited through their dread of him, and the wrong-doers were dismayed through their fear of him. And it was that, when he shouted, his voice was as the voice of the roaring of a lion on the day he roars to tear the prey. And all Israel rejoiced in his deeds, and exulted in his work. And all the world was terrified because of his fame. Then were kings,

---

[1] In Yoma 72b and Horayot 12a this term refers to the priest who is anointed to encourage the army. Comp. Deut. 20.2–4.

greater and mightier than he, dismayed; and trembling seized
hold upon the chiefs of the earth and the kings thereof. And
his name went forth among the nations to the end of all the
earth; and the tales of the wonders of his mighty deeds reached
to the end of the earth. And when he was gathered unto his
people, all the seed of Israel praised him, and honored him.
And they spoke, saying: "May the spirit of the Lord cause him
to rest, and may he dwell in the secret place of the Most High,
and abide under the shadow of the Almighty, under the tree
of life."

HANUKKAH IN LITERATURE

MODERN WRITINGS

DRAMA

THE DUNGEON IN THE CITADEL

THE DUNGEON IN THE CITADEL[1]

Henry Wadsworth Longfellow

CHARACTERS IN THE ORDER OF
THEIR APPEARANCE

THE MOTHER OF SEVEN SONS
VOICES, *her six sons*
ANTIOCHUS EPIPHANES, *a tyrant*
SIRION, *Hannah's youngest son*

SCENES

SCENE   I   The ante-room of the torture-chamber
SCENE II   The ante-room of the torture-chamber

---

[1] Act II of *Judas Maccabeus.*

SCENE I

The MOTHER *is alone in the ante-room of the torture-chamber. She is listening.*

THE MOTHER

Be strong, my heart!
Break not till they are dead,
All, all my Seven Sons; then burst asunder,
And let this tortured and tormented soul
Leap and rush out like water through the shards
Of earthen vessels broken at a well.
O my dear children, mine in life and death,
I know not how ye came into my womb;
I neither gave you breath, nor gave you life,
And neither was it I that formed the members
Of every one of you. But the Creator,
Who made the world, and made the heavens above us,
Who formed the generation of mankind,
And found out the beginning of all things,
He gave you breath and life, and will again
Of His own mercy, as ye now regard
Not your own selves, but His eternal law.
I do not murmur, nay, I thank Thee, God,
That I and mine have not been deemed unworthy
To suffer for Thy sake and for Thy law,
And for the many sins of Israel.
Hark! I can hear within the sound of scourges!
I feel them more than ye do, O my sons!
But cannot come to you. I, who was wont
To wake at night at the least cry ye made,
To whom ye ran at every slightest hurt,—

I cannot take you now into my lap
And soothe your pain, but God will take **you all**
Into His pitying arms, and comfort you,
And give you rest.

A VOICE (*within*)

What wouldst thou ask of us?
Ready are we to die, but we will never
Transgress the law and customs of our fathers.

THE MOTHER

It is the voice of my first-born! O brave
And noble boy! Thou hast the privilege
Of dying first, as thou wast born the first.

THE SAME VOICE (*within*)

God looketh on us, and hath comfort in **us**;
As Moses in his song of old declared,
He in His servants shall be comforted.

THE MOTHER

I knew thou wouldst not fail! He speaks no more,
He is beyond all pain!

ANTIOCHUS (*within*)

If thou eat not,
Thou shalt be tortured throughout all the members
Of thy whole body. Wilt thou eat then?

SECOND VOICE (*within*)

No.

THE MOTHER

It is Adaiah's voice.
I tremble for him.
I know his nature, devious as the wind.
And swift to change, gentle and yielding always.
Be steadfast, O my son!

THE SAME VOICE (*within*)

Thou, like a fury,
Takest us from this present life, but God,
Who rules the world, shall raise us up again
Into life everlasting.

THE MOTHER

God, I thank Thee
That thou hast breathed into that timid heart
Courage to die for Thee. O my Adaiah,
Witness of God! If thou for whom I feared
Canst thus encounter death, I need not fear;
The others will not shrink.

THIRD VOICE (*within*)

Behold these hands
Held out to thee, O King Antiochus,
Not to implore thy mercy, but to show
That I despise them. He who gave them to me
Will give them back again.

THE MOTHER

O Avilan,
It is thy voice. For the last time I hear it;
For the last time on earth, but not the last.

To death it bids defiance and to torture.
It sounds to me as from another world,
And makes the petty miseries of this
Seem unto me as naught, and less than naught.
Farewell, my Avilan; nay, I should say
Welcome, my Avilan: for I am dead
Before thee. I am waiting for the others.
Why do they linger?

FOURTH VOICE (*within*)

It is good, O King,
Being put to death by men, to look for hope
From God, to be raised up again by Him.
But thou—no resurrection shalt thou have
To life hereafter.

THE MOTHER

Four! already four!
Three are still living; nay, they all are living,
Half here, half there. Make haste, Antiochus,
To reunite us; for the sword that cleaves
These miserable bodies makes a door
Through which our souls, impatient of release,
Rush to each other's arms.

THE FIFTH VOICE (*within*)

Thou hast the power;
Thou doest what thou wilt. Abide awhile,
And thou shalt see the power of God, and how
He will torment thee and thy seed.

THE MOTHER

O hasten;
Why dost thou pause? Thou who hast slain already
So many Hebrew women, and hast hung
Their murdered infants round their necks, slay me,
For I too am a woman, and these boys
Are mine. Make haste to slay us all,
And hang my lifeless babes about my neck.

SIXTH VOICE (*within*)

Think not, Antiochus, that takest in hand
To strive against the God of Israel,
Thou shalt escape unpunished, for His wrath
Shall overtake thee and thy bloody house.

THE MOTHER

One more, my Sirion, and then all is ended.
Having put all to bed, then in my turn
I will lie down and sleep as sound as they.
My Sirion, my youngest, best beloved!
And those bright golden locks, that I so oft
Have curled about these fingers, even now
Are foul with blood and dust, like a lamb's fleece,
Slain in the shambles.—Not a sound I hear.
This silence is more terrible to me
Than any sound, than any cry of pain
That might escape the lips of one who dies.
Doth his heart fail him? Doth he fall away
In the last hour from God? O Sirion, Sirion,
Art thou afraid? I do not hear thy voice.
Die as thy brothers died. Thou must not live!

CURTAIN

SCENE II

As the curtain rises the MOTHER *is standing before*
ANTIOCHUS

THE MOTHER

Are they all dead?

ANTIOCHUS

One only lives. (*Draws her to the curtain to look behind it*)
Behold them where they lie;
How dost thou like this picture?

THE MOTHER

God in heaven!
Can a man do such deeds, and yet not die
By the recoil of his own wickedness?
Ye murdered, bleeding, mutilated bodies
That were my children once, and still are mine,
I cannot watch o'er you as Rispah watched
In sackcloth o'er the seven sons of Saul,
Till water drop upon you out of heaven
And wash this blood away! I cannot mourn
As she, the daughter of Aiah, mourned the dead,
From the beginning of the barley harvest
Until the autumn rains, and suffered not
The birds of air to rest on them by day,
Nor the wild beasts by night. For ye have died
A better death, a death so full of life
That I ought rather to rejoice than mourn—

SIRION, *the youngest son, enters from the torture-chamber*

Wherefore art thou not dead, O Sirion?
Wherefore art thou the only living thing
Among thy brothers dead? Art thou afraid?

ANTIOCHUS

O woman, I have spared him for thy sake,
For he is fair to look upon, and comely;
And I have sworn to him by all the gods
That I would crown his life with joy and honor,
Heap treasures on him, luxuries, delights,
Make him my friend and keeper of my secrets,
If he would turn from your Mosaic Law
And be as we are; but he will not listen.

THE MOTHER

My noble Sirion!

ANTIOCHUS

Therefore I beseech thee
Who art his mother, thou wouldst speak with him,
And wouldst persuade him. I am sick of blood.

THE MOTHER

Yea, I will speak with him and will persuade him.
O Sirion, my son! Have pity on me,
On me that bare thee, and that gave thee suck,
And fed and nourished thee, and brought thee up
With the dear trouble of a mother's care
Unto this age. Look on the heavens above thee,
And on the earth and all that is therein;
Consider that God made them out of things
That were not; and that likewise in this manner
Mankind was made. Then fear not this tormentor;
But, being worthy of thy brethren, take
Thy death as they did, that I may receive thee
Again in mercy with them.

ANTIOCHUS

I am mocked,
Yes, I am laughed to scorn.

SIRION

Whom wait ye for?
Never will I obey the King's commandment,
But the commandment of the ancient Law,
That was by Moses given unto our fathers.
And thou, O godless man, that of all others
Art the most wicked, be not lifted up,
Nor puffed up with uncertain hopes, uplifting
Thy hand against the servants of the Lord,
For thou hast not escaped the righteous judgment
Of the Almighty God, who seeth all things!

ANTIOCHUS

He is no god of mine; I fear him not.

SIRION

My brothers, who have suffered a brief pain,
Are dead; but thou, Antiochus, shalt suffer
The punishment of pride. I offer up
My body and my life, beseeching God
That He would speedily be merciful
Unto our nation, and that thou by plagues
Mysterious and by torments mayest confess
That He alone is God.

ANTIOCHUS

Ye both shall perish
By torments worse than any that your God,
Here or hereafter, hath in store for me.

THE MOTHER

My Sirion, I am proud of thee!

ANTIOCHUS

Be silent!
Go to thy bed of torture in yon chamber,
Where lie so many sleepers, heartless mother!
Thy footsteps will not wake them, nor thy voice.
Nor wilt thou hear, amid thy troubled dreams,
Thy children crying for thee in the night.

THE MOTHER

O Death, that stretchest thy white hands to me,
I fear them not, but press them to my lips,
That are as white as thine; for I am Death,
Nay, am the Mother of Death, seeing these sons
All lying lifeless.—Kiss me, Sirion.

THE MAGIC TOP

A play for the puppet theater

THE MAGIC TOP[1]

EMILY SOLIS-COHEN, JR. and MARY GERSON

PRODUCTION NOTES WHEN PERFORMED IN A PUPPET THEATER

This play can be produced simply, with simple construction of puppets, properties and scenes. The materials used are inexpensive and easily obtainable: balsa or plain pine wood, cardboard, denim, cloth, velvet, and other common dress stuffs. The furniture can probably be bought in a toy shop.

Directions for construction are given in these notes. It is advisable to consult the bibliography and libraries for titles of books on how to make puppets, for complete directions.

PUPPETS

A FRIENDLY TREE. Make a large trunk, paint it brown, and construct a few branches to extend across the stage. Paint these green. A pleasant face should be near the top of the Tree, with a cloth flap for a mouth. Attach a string to this flap, so that mouth can be animated when the Tree speaks.

This Tree, being friendly, should appear alive and fresh, and give decoration to the stage. It should be braced in back, to keep it standing and mobile.

---

[1] Adapted from a story of the same name in *The Breakfast of the Birds and Other Stories*, from the Hebrew of Judah Steinberg, translated by Emily Solis-Cohen, Jr. The Jewish Publication Society of America, 1917, reprinted 1936.

It is suggested that cardboard (cut out) should be used to construct the Tree.

GALGELON, THE TOP. Make a Hanukkah top of puppet size. On its sides paint the Hebrew letters ש ,ה ,ג ,נ. The head must be hinged to the body so that it can move about while Galgelon sings and talks. The legs are short springs; the feet, attached to the springs, are to be made of balsa, or plain pine wood.

This construction is simple and effective, giving Galgelon easy action for movement, as the Top should be animated, have a lively and festive air, and dance about.

AMAZIAH. This naughty boy is about seven years of age. Make a child in the usual manner. Let him wear a tan shirt and denim trousers that reach to the ankles, and give the effect of overalls.

NADAB. This good child is aged about nine, and is dressed similarly to his brother, except that his shirt is blue.

DINAH. The mother of these boys may be dressed in a blue denim or brown chambray, wearing a full apron, tied in back. Sew a pocket in the apron to hold the coin for which she reaches.

The clothing of mother and sons should appear worn, but neat. Their surroundings should give the feeling of being spick and span. The entire coloring should be subdued.

Dinah's important movements are her entrances from out-of-doors into the kitchen. When she is near the table, talking to her sons, the movements are small. She also has simple business near the kitchen cupboard.

THE WIZARD TREE. Use heavy cardboard to make a huge tree-trunk, from which two bare branches, shaped like human arms, extend. At top of the trunk, cut holes for eyes, place electric bulbs behind them, which are to be lit whenever the Tree speaks.

Since the Tree is a wizard, and a mysterious feeling is to be engendered, it is well to paint it black or a very deep green.

INHABITANTS OF THE MAGIC FOREST

A DEER. Although the Deer is young, it is horned to make it apparent to the audience. The Deer should be painted a light gray. Its legs are to be hinged to the body, to give it supple movement.

The Deer leaps in from the wings of the stage, leaps about, and leaves in a similar fashion.

A BUNNY. Make the Bunny of a solid piece, painted tan or white. The Bunny's movements are large leaps.

A DOVE. Make of balsa wood, painted white, with hinged wings to which springs are attached, as also to the tail and head, so that the bird can fly and hover.

JUDAH THE MACCABEE. Make Judah a very simply constructed puppet. To one of the hands attach a small loaf of bread, so that when Judah extends his hand toward Nadab, the loaf will be visible.

Although it is possible to dress Judah in the Palestinian garb of his day, it might be better to have him in a short jacket of red velvet velour, with the legs painted gold, to give a regal and awesome effect.

PROPERTIES

SCENE I. Dinah's kitchen should contain a wall-cupboard, a small picture; in front stage, two chairs and a table. The chairs may be bought or constructed, and should be placed so that one boy faces the audience and the other sits at right angles to him. Have a book on the table for reading.

The table should be hinged. On its under side should be attached goodies for the feast. In the final scene the table top is flipped, so that the laden side is brought up top. Before this happens there is a black-out.

SCENE II. The Magic Forest should be indicated by framing the stage opening (side and top) in cardboard cut-outs, to give the appearance of leaves and branches, moss—in short, a forest.

The background should be blue, to indicate dusk.

LOG. Use a small, real log, painted black. Place it on the ground at side (right or left stage). On this log the boys sit.

SCENE III. The Cave should give a different feeling than the Magic Forest. Have for the cut-outs in the stage opening (top and sides) cardboard painted black, to look like cave over-hangings, stalactites and the like.

The scene opens with the stage lighted where Nadab is standing. On the opposite side of the stage, not visible to the audience, will be a platform on which a throne is set. There should be sufficient space in front of the throne for the occupant to rise and stand. When this occurs, the light should rise, so that the throne is suddenly visible, and give the effect of surprise.

The throne should be a straight-backed chair, with broad arms, painted gold. The platform should be of wood.

LIGHTING

Throughout the play, use white, gray, or light-blue background. For warm lights, use amber.

CHARACTERS IN THE ORDER OF
THEIR APPEARANCE

A FRIENDLY TREE
ITS TALKING ROOTS, *invisible*
GALGELON, *the top*
AMAZIAH, *a naughty boy*
NADAB, *his brother*
DINAH, *their mother*
THE WIZARD TREE

INHABITANTS OF THE MAGIC FOREST: $\begin{cases} a\ deer \\ a\ bunny \\ a\ dove \end{cases}$

JUDAH THE MACCABEE

SCENES

PROLOGUE	Before Dinah's house
SCENE I	Dinah's kitchen
SCENE II	The Magic Forest
SCENE III	A Cave
SCENE IV	Dinah's kitchen

PROLOGUE

The Curtain is down.   A VOICE *speaks from back-stage*

VOICE

Little children out there, have you ever played with a galgelon,
a Hanukkah Top? Of course you have. Every Hanukkah. So
you know how to spin it, and how, when it falls, a Hebrew letter,
Nun, *Gimel*, *He* or *Shin*, is on top, and you have often looked
quickly to see if the letter is the one you picked, for if it is you
will get a prize.

When the curtain goes up, watch carefully and you will see two
little boys, Nadab and Amaziah, one is good and one is
naughty, and you will see their Top, and how it led them on a
great adventure. But I won't tell you any more, for you must
meet the children, and listen to the Top, whose Hebrew name is
Galgelon.

Be sure now. Watch Galgelon carefully.

Curtain Rises

The FRIENDLY TREE *is in the center of the stage.* GALGELON,
the MAGIC TOP, *comes tripping out* (*right stage*), *spins past the*
FRIENDLY TREE *and whirls off* (*left stage*)

ROOTS OF TREE

Apparently the voices rise from beneath the ground

We, your roots beneath the ground,
Tremble at that strange new sound.
Open wide your eyes and see
What that Creature is, O Tree.

TREE

In deep tones

Neither beast nor bird I hear,
Bee, nor wasp, nor cricket clear,
Child, nor man, that Creature queer;
I must guard my nestlings dear,
And the children living near.

After a pause

Now I'll take him by surprise;
Feigning sleep I'll close my eyes.

The eyes of the TREE *close while* GALGELON *comes tripping
out again; dances by the* TREE, *whirls and spins, and finally sits
down near* TREE, *who continues*

Be you friend or be you foe,
Weaving wicked spells below?
Hold; I will not let you go
'Til you tell me whence you come,
Why you whirl and dance and hum.

TOP

Rising to his feet, sings in high pitch

I bring to little girls and boys
Jolly toys and many joys.
My name is GALGELON. Come and play,
Dance and whirl with me today.
Prizes win as I spin,
Out and in, out and in.
Watch each side,
As I glide.

Dances forward and back, turning to show each letter as named.
and finally stands with back toward audience

> *Nun* for thee
> *Gimel* for me
> *He* and *Shin* for thee—and thee.

> *After a pause faces audience*

Look now while I slow and stop,
Backward lean, a tired TOP.

> *Leans against* TREE

Whose the letter that is seen?
Nun or *Gimel, He* or *Shin?*

> *Appears to await answer, then continues*

All around the world I roam,
Where'er Israel builds a home,
Joining in the jubilation
Of the Feast of Dedication
Nes Gadol,
Wonder great—
One day's oil
Burned for eight,
Midst a people's jubilation
At their shrine's rededication.

TREE

That miracle I know full well.
Year on year within my dell
Children hymn the Maccabees,
Tell their glorious victories;
How brave Judah led the fray,

Drove invading hordes away;
How the tyrant was defied
By a woman sanctified.

TOP

Hayah Sham,
What was then will be again.
What was there is everywhere.
Wonders of that day and clime
Live again through endless time.

TREE

But you have not told to me
Why you prance and dance so free,
Why you hum and whirr and drum,
Wondrous, ageless, *Galgelon.*

TOP
Gaily dancing

I prance and dance and whirr and drone
And spin around the world alone,
Till playing children follow me,
And with their eyes a vision see;
Within their hearts . . . the Maccabee.

Turns, facing TREE, *and starts talking in a more serious tone*
Only last year two little boys, Nadab and Amaziah are their
names, thought they would not have me to play with, because
times were hard, and their mother had only a few pennies for
bread. And Amaziah, I am afraid, was naughty and he whined
and cried . . .

CURTAIN

SCENE I

Curtain rises on the kitchen of DINAH. *A table is in center of room; a cupboard is against the wall in back, facing audience.* NADAB *is sitting by the table, reading a book;* AMAZIAH *is sitting on the opposite chair, whining:*

AMAZIAH

I want a top. I want a Hanukkah top . . .

NADAB

Softly

I wish Mother would come. She can read better than I can . . .

AMAZIAH

Still petulant

Who wants to hear that story again? A top! That's the best part of Hanukkah. I want a new top, like all the other boys. (*He sobs, rubbing his eyes.*)

NADAB

Trying to pacify him

Things will be better soon, Amaziah, and then we can have a top. Maybe a real flier with wings. Maybe by next year . . .

AMAZIAH

Becoming annoyed, raising voice

I want my top now! I want it now!

NADAB

Mother said that she had only enough pennies for a loaf of bread. Like three days ago. But she said things would be better soon.

AMAZIAH

Storming

When is soon? Bread! Who wants bread? A top! A Hanukkah top. I want to spin my top.

NADAB

Shame on you, Amaziah! Stop whining and listen to this about the Maccabees. It makes you forget you don't have a top. (*Looks at book—sighs.*) I wish I had lived then . . . to fight with Judah and all . . . (*Starts reading, slowly, almost spelling words.*) "But Judah and they that were with him made their way secretly to the villages and called their kinsfolk, and they hid in caves in the mountains. And when Judah had trained his men, the enemy found them ir . . . irre . . . irresist . . .

AMAZIAH

Impatiently

I don't care what they were! I want a top! Last year no presents; this year none. One top. What's that? Joshua's mother's poor too, but she bought him a top to spin, and his letter won twice. And now he has nice toys to play with. I hate black bread! Who wants it anyhow? (*Shrieks*) Black bread—black—bread!

NADAB

Looking up

Mother wants it, Amaziah. You know that very well. She makes us eat first. She just takes a crumb and sometimes none, never a whole slice. I won't take any tonight. Not unless she does.

AMAZIAH

Starts crying again

I don't care! I want a top! that spins and whirls!

DINAH

Enters the room. She looks about, sees what is happening and whispers to herself
My poor little boys. Yes, they shall have a top. (*She walks out before the boys notice her*)

NADAB

Looking at Amaziah

Cry-baby . . . Cry-baby . . .

AMAZIAH

Still sobbing

I don't care. I want a . . . a . . . a . . .

NADAB

Impatiently

All right. Gee Whiz!

DINAH

Enters room again, holding the TOP. *Speaks cheerfully*

Look boys! I've brought you a top . . . a beautiful shiny top!

AMAZIAH

Jumping up and down gleefully

A Hanukkah Top! Mother! Nadab! See it spin. How fast! Look at the colors! How it whirls. Watch, Nadab. See how it jumps about. Look at it whirl.

NADAB

Looking at DINAH. *Shakes his head*

Poor Mother. I guess there won't be any bread.

AMAZIAH

TOP *starts spinning toward door*

Look, Nadab! Look how it capers. Look! Look! (*Becoming hysterical*) It's going out the door! (*Rushing out after* TOP) Oh, oh, my top!

NADAB

Runs after him

DINAH

Stands quietly looking after the boys

CURTAIN

SCENE II

Set—The blue sky of a late afternoon. A small log. On the opposite side of the stage there is a TREE-WITH-THE-FACE-OF-AN-OLD-MAN. *Two limbs are stretched out like the bent, gnarled arms of a man. The Forest is in total darkness. The curtain rises and lights come up. The two boys are on stage.* AMAZIAH *is seated on the log.* NADAB *is standing by the* TREE

VOICE OF A READER

Off stage

"And the Top danced up hill and down dale, and the boys ran after it. They ran for hours and hours, and finally came to the edge of a wood."

AMAZIAH

Weeping

I want my top. Where is my top? I am so tired and hungry. We've been running and running.

NADAB

Sobbing

Our poor hungry Mother, and the pennies she saved for a loaf of black bread.
The boys continue sobbing. A BUNNY *appears from behind the* TREE. *He jumps out, cocks his head, and looks at the boys.* NADAB *looks up, sees the* BUNNY. *He stops crying and says to his brother*

NADAB

Oh, oh—look Amaziah, a Bunny.

AMAZIAH

Lifts his head

Oh, Bunny, Bunny, tell to me
Where my straying top can be?
Did you meet it on your way?
Do you know where it did stay?
In the woods? on mountain side?
In the fields does it abide?

BUNNY

Pricks his pointed ears, shakes his little tail. Speaks in a quavery little voice

Mine eyes have seen no *Galgelon*,
Mine ears heard not its whirring drone.
But I met a loaf of black, black bread
Soaked in tears a mother shed,
Black, rolling bread . . .
Tears a mother shed—

AMAZIAH

Impatiently

Bunny, stop saying black bread. Where is my top? That's what
I want to know.

BUNNY

The bread I saw was really . . . (*Looks at the scowling face of*
AMAZIAH, *becomes frightened, and scuttles off with his sentence
uncompleted*)

NADAB

Turning to AMAZIAH, woefully

The loaf of bread which the Bunny saw, it was our Mother's, the very bread she meant for supper, and now today, she's hungry again. (*He sobs*)

AMAZIAH

Wails

I want my top! I want my top!

NADAB

Strains as if he hears something

There's the top now . . . No, it isn't . . .

AMAZIAH

Returns to the log and is crying. A DEER runs into the light, stops and looks at the boys

NADAB

Look, Amaziah, it's a Deer. (*Turns to DEER and in an imploring voice asks*)

> O pretty Deer,
> Sweet, pretty Deer,
> Do you know
> Where our top did go?

DEER

Looks toward boys, then speaks in deep, slow tone

Yes, kind, good boy,
I have seen your toy—
Can you guess where?

BOYS

Shake their heads

We know not where.

DEER

Then truly swear
To give a full share
Of your breakfast to me,—
For the next days, three.

NADAB

Whatever I have, be it honey cake or sour bread, you shall have it, little Deer.

AMAZIAH

Jumps up and cries angrily

But you won't have mine, not a single mouthful, not till you tell us where our top is. Where did you hide it? Deer—tell me that. (*He sobs*) I am so cold and hungry.

DEER

Looks at boys, rushes off

NADAB

Weeping

Poor Mother. It is not enough that she is hungry, but she will be so worried, because we're not at home. It's dark, and we've never been out after sundown. Dear Dove. You can see over the trees. Please fly ahead of us and lead us home.

AMAZIAH

Home? First find out if she has seen my top. Have you Dove?

DOVE

I do pity your forlorn mother, children. I am a deserted mother also. My children left our nest, and never flew back. But I am certain that you are not more than a few yards away from your village. As for your top, it is close by . . . Near you in this wood is a cave. Near this cave a wizard stands and waits for you. If you utter a word or even wink your eye, you will be caught in his snare. Remember! Do not utter a single word, nor wink your eye.

BOYS

Oh, oh, there's the wizard . . .

WIZARD

Suddenly the TREE *lights up—a weird voice cries*

Ohhhhhhhhh. What do these little boys want? What are you looking for? Come, wink at me. (*Wizard winks at them and chants*)

> Wink, Wink;
> Blink, Blink;
> Sink, Sink;
> Wink, Wink.

Nice little boys, good little boys. Can it be a top you are looking for? There was a top, a pretty top. What colors it had! It was lost, it said. Too bad, too bad! How about a little wink?

> Wink, Wink;
> Blink, Blink;
> Sink, Sink;
> Wink, Wink.

AMAZIAH

Forgetting the DOVE'S *warning*

I want my top. I . . .

NADAB

Claps his hand over AMAZIAH'S *mouth*

Sh-sh-sh. Don't say anything, Amaziah. Don't you know what the Dove said?

WIZARD

Well, since you little boys won't talk to me, I'll tell you the secret. Count the threads on your prayer-fringes. If you find eight threads in the right-hand corner, do not fear, but enter the cave. If you do not find eight threads, beware—beware.

Lights dim down on WIZARD

AMAZIAH

Looking at Arba' Kanfot he is wearing around his neck

I'm going to count my threads right now. (*He starts counting*) One, two, three, four, five, six—six . . . seven . . . the seventh one is torn. (*Weeps*) Oh, gee! I only have six.

NADAB

I'll count mine now, and see if I have eight. (*Starts counting, slowly at first, then increases tempo*) One, two, three, four, five, six, seven, eight. Mine is perfect! I'm not afraid, I'm going right into that cave and find our top.

He turns toward back-stage, as curtain falls

CURTAIN

SCENE III

Set—Cave of JUDAH. *Off to one side is a throne;* JUDAH *is seated on it.* NADAB *is standing facing him.*
The curtain rises on dark stage.
*Characters—*JUDAH MACCABEUS, *holding a small loaf of bread in hand.* NADAB.
Curtain rises in dim light, revealing NADAB. *He starts crying softly*

NADAB

How dark it is, and oh, how cold. I'm afraid I'm lost. Oh, my poor mother. My poor hungry mother. (*He starts as if he has heard a sound*) Can the top be here? No, I don't see anything. It's only my wish that makes it seem so. (*Slowly a brilliant light comes up. It appears over* JUDAH *seated on the throne. Fanfare of music*) Where am I? What a strange place this is!

JUDAH

He speaks very gently

Come here, my good little man. Do not be afraid. You have known me for a long, long time. Do you not recognize me?

NADAB

Comes a little closer, hesitatingly

No—no, and yet I'm sure I've seen you. Your face looks something like—something like . . .

JUDAH

Your own, when you look in the mirror and you pretend that you are . . .

NADAB

Breathlessly

Judah Maccabeus.

JUDAH

Shaking his head

You are right. But tell me, what brought you here now? Have you been thinking about me?

NADAB

It was a top. A *galgelon* with wings. You see, my brother Amaziah is younger than I, and sometimes he acts like a baby. He wouldn't stop crying until Mother bought us a new top. She really oughtn't to have done it, because she only had pennies enough for a loaf of bread. Many days she went hungry so we would have enough to eat, but on Hanukkah she ought to have had supper with us. Don't you think so?

JUDAH

That's the way of Mothers. But come to me. I have something for you.

NADAB

Is it our top? It did caper so prettily. My brother and I watched it and followed it out of the door, far away, until it disappeared.

JUDAH

Yes, Nadab, it is your top. Here it is. (*He extends his hand with the loaf of bread in it*) From a loaf of bread it came, and into a loaf of bread it has turned forever. Take this to your mother; tell her no matter how much she eats, there will always be more. And tell her also that whatever you want to taste will be in the loaf whenever you eat it.

NADAB

How can I thank you, Judah Maccabeus?

JUDAH

By never forgetting me, and always carrying my image in your heart, and reliving my deeds.

NADAB

Cheerfully

I know them all. How you were captain of the Maccabees, and how with but a few men you drove the tyrant from the land, and cleansed the Temple, and lit the lamp, and how you said to your men: (*Slowly and with much dignity*) "Fear not! The foe trust in the right arm of dust, in shields that may shiver, in swords that may rust. We trust in the arm of the Lord. His law is our shield and His wrath is our sword. The captain that leads you is priest of His shrine. And His glorious Name is our banner divine."

JUDAH

As I thought. You too are a Maccabee. You have it in your heart. Now turn around and close your eyes . . . (*Light fades as* NADAB *turns*) Close your eyes and take a wish . . .

NADAB

I wish . . . I wish . . .

CURTAIN

SCENE IV

Set—Kitchen of home of DINAH.

*Characters—*NADAB, AMAZIAH, DINAH.

Properties—Table, two chairs, cupboard, table cloth.

Curtain rises on dark stage . . . AMAZIAH *and* NADAB *are standing near table;* DINAH *is off to one side*

VOICE

Off stage

Open your eyes!

Lights come up full

NADAB

I wish, I wish, I wish I were home. O-h-oh . . . I am home, and there is the golden loaf of bread!

DINAH

Rushing over to the boys

My children, my poor children! I thought you were lost to me. Thank God I have found you! You have been gone so long. We have no pennies to buy bread, and now we shall all go hungry. Woe is me—woe is me. (*She sobs quietly*)

NADAB

Joyously

Look, Mother! See what I have brought you! This loaf of bread. Wish, and whatever you fancy for supper, you shall have.

DINAH

Pshaw, Nadab, you jest. Surely you would not worry Mother. It's not like you. Where did you get the bread? Not from any doorstep, I hope.

NADAB

Anxiously

Mother! But you'll never guess who did give it to me. Judah Maccabeus!

DINAH

Amazed

Judah Maccabeus! Are you ill? What's the matter with you? You are teasing.

NADAB

Indeed I'm not, Mother. It's true. Take a wish! Take a wish!

DINAH

Bends her head

I wish we could have a supper fitting the festival, wine and cakes, roast duck and white bread, and sweets for the children, and goodies heaped high. I wish, I wish, I wish . . .
Lights fade, table top is reversed, lights go on again revealing banquet

NADAB

It's true! It's true! See, Mother, all the things you've wished for. (*They laugh merrily.* AMAZIAH *has been sitting with his head in his hands, weeping.* NADAB *crosses over to him and puts a hand on his shoulder*). Don't cry, Amaziah—you can have all the things to eat you want.

AMAZIAH

I'll never be a bad boy again.

NADAB

Isn't it wonderful? If only we had a top. If only we had our top. But look, Mother— (TOP *enters room, prances around*) The Top, a gold one, too! Look, look—goody, goody, goody! (*They are very joyous. The* BOYS *jump up and down, and the curtain falls*)

CURTAIN

EPILOGUE FROM BEHIND THE CURTAIN

READER

And so they had a happy festival, and Amaziah forgot how to whine, and *Galgelon* went on spinning and spinning round the world, and maybe—who knows—the Magic Top may come to your house some day this year.

CURTAIN

THE VALIANT MACCABEES

THE VALIANT MACCABEES

EMILY SOLIS-COHEN, JR. and REMO BUFFANO

PRODUCTION NOTES

This script may be produced by human actors or by puppets or by marionettes.

The scenery should be simple and suggestive. A light blue duvetyn backdrop may be used as a permanent setting. In the first act there should be, right stage, the outline of a door and some steps leading into a house; left stage, there should be a simple tree-trunk and a low wall running across the back stage. It is from the other side of this wall that the unseen refugees talk.

For the remaining acts use the same backdrop with profile pieces set in front. Particularly in puppet or marionette production it is well to remember that the characters must have plenty of room for moving around, and the stage must not be cluttered with properties that are overlarge.

In costuming either actors or dolls, it will be most effective to use the garb of the period. This can be easily determined by consulting histories or books on the costumes of ancient Israel and of the Greek-Syrian era. It is important to make a definite color scheme for the entire play and follow it consistently. It is always well to be suggestive rather than realistic.

CHARACTERS IN THE ORDER OF THEIR APPEARANCE

ELEAZAR, *a venerable scribe*

MATTATHIAS, *a priest*

JUDAH, *his son*

REFUGEES

HANNAH, *a martyr*

DAVID, *her youngest son*

THE OFFICER OF THE KING, *a Greek*

FIRST SOLDIER, *a Greek*

JOSHUA, *a renegade*

THE BULL

SECOND SOLDIER, *a Greek*

THE ELEPHANT

A CAPTAIN, *a Hebrew*

SCENES

PROLOGUE   Before the curtain

SCENE   I   The garden of Mattathias at Modin

SCENE   II   The market place at Modin

SCENE   III   The Syrian camp at Emmaus

EPILOGUE   Before the Temple

PROLOGUE

ELEAZAR

Appears before the curtain

These are woeful times and the fate of Israel is covered in darkness. Who knows what even the next few days may bring? The tyrant, Antiochus, is not content to conquer our land—he is determined to destroy the Jews from the face of the earth. He wants no trace of them to be left; neither the laws nor those who believe in the laws. The Torah he will burn and the people he will massacre. Only those who consent to sacrifice to his gods will he permit to live. O Lord, we are in Thy hands! In Thy hands, O Lord! The tyrant has profaned our scrolls, but he will not be able to blot them all out. I am Eleazar, the scribe! Here are the fruits of my labor. (*He draws scrolls from under his cloak. Holds them up*) These scrolls I have written and brought with me, safe to Modin. Now I must take them to Mattathias, the priest, and to his son Judah, to whom Israel looks for deliverance. I must not delay longer with my precious burden. (ELEAZAR *makes his exit back of the curtain*)

SCENE I

The garden of MATTATHIAS *in Modin. In the middle background is a wall, so placed that the actors can look over the wall on people passing in the street below, to whom they speak. Only by shadows, visible to the audience, are the people behind the walls seen. They are distinguished by their voices, being those of* CHILDREN, MEN, WOMEN, *all are refugees.*

JUDAH *and* MATTATHIAS *are standing at one side of the stage, talking. Laughter floats over the wall into the garden.* MATTATHIAS *stops talking to listen*

VOICES OF CHILDREN

This is a great game. Let's play it again.
All right.
Let's begin:

A song floats over the wall. Its tune is light and jesting

> This, O Greek, is the Jew's reply,
> For the Law of God he will surely die;
> Give your gods of stone on our flesh to dine,
> Washed down with our blood,
>   'Tis a royal wine!

MATTATHIAS

What? Merriment at this unhappy hour?

JUDAH

It is a new game the boys play in Jerusalem. They call it The Gods' Feast! The refugees are teaching it to our children of Modin. "The Gods' Feast," listen, father.

Shadows of people passing on the street below the wall are seen against the background.

JUDAH

Look, father, here more refugees come. I hope they bring strong tidings.

VOICE

From other side of the wall

Ho, Sir! Can you direct me to the smithy?

JUDAH

There are several hereabouts. What tools do you seek?

VOICE

Hammers, Sir!

JUDAH

Hammers, did you say?

VOICE

Hammers. The sons of Hannah told us we would find the best hammers in Modin.

JUDAH

There are hammers and hammers. They have a price. What do you bring?

VOICE

Ten javelins from the sons of Hannah.

JUDAH

Good. (*To the second*) And you?

VOICE

Two score spearheads.

JUDAH

Good faithful ones. Enter in there in the name of the Lord.

VOICES

In the name of the Lord.
We hear them enter into the house. JUDAH *again turns to his*
FATHER *and sees him rending his garments*

MATTATHIAS

Woe is me. Wherefore was I born, to have seen the end of the
Holy City and to have dwelled there when it was seized by the
enemy and the sanctuary fell to strangers.

JUDAH

Cease mourning, father, and let us throw off this vile yoke.
Only by striking, and striking without delay, can we do that.
The sons of Hannah are gathering men. They send us arms to
store—but when will they send word to strike?

MATTATHIAS

In the Lord's good time, my son. Antiochus is not the first
tyrant who thought to destroy Israel.

JUDAH

Had I my way, he would pay for the first, and be the last.

VOICE

On the other side of the wall

Sir, Ho sir! Where is the house of the Hammer Maker?

JUDAH

Hammer Maker? How heard you of him?

VOICE

The sons of Hannah told us he lived on this street.

JUDAH

Enter in there in the name of the Lord. That is the house you seek.

VOICE OF WOMAN

It is he . . . it is he . . . I am blind, but my ears know the voice of the deliverer of Israel. Though I cannot see, I know it is he.

JUDAH

Is she blind?

WOMAN'S VOICE

Yea. The heathen took away my eyes, my husband and all my sons, but this little one.

JUDAH

But she has no little one.

HER FRIEND'S VOICE

She is stark mad, good sir. Her grief has made her mad.

WOMAN'S VOICE

He is dead, they tell me. But Elisha shall breathe on him and
he will live. Though it is neither new moon nor Sabbath, I will
seek the Prophet.

JUDAH

Go in. My brothers will take care of you. (*Calls*) Jonathan, I
send you two mothers to guard. (*After* REFUGEES *have entered
house*, JUDAH *turns to* MATTATHIAS) Each arrival makes
me more impatient to strike.

MATTATHIAS

In His own good time the Lord will avenge the pollution of
His House.

JUDAH

The silversmith Joshua has changed his name to Jason. Heard
you that? And he is urging his companions to forsake the
synagogue for the field of Greek sports. Traitors! They will
need all their training when I run them from the land.

ELEAZAR

From the other side of the wall

Peace be with you.

MATTATHIAS

The voice of Eleazar, the scribe. Welcome, my friend. You,
too, have fled to us? I have been alarmed for you, Eleazar.
(ELEAZAR *comes on the scene*)

ELEAZAR

I come not in flight, but to bring a precious word.

JUDAH

Then you must bring word from Hannah's Reuben to strike.

ELEAZAR

No, Judah, even more precious than that. Here! The sacred scroll intact. High Priests of the Lord, guard them with your lives. (*Gives the scroll to* MATTATHIAS)

JUDAH

Father, open the Torah. Read us once more the song of Moses: The enemy said I will pursue, I will overtake; my sword shall be satisfied with them.

MATTATHIAS

The scrolls! (*He fondles them*) Blessed be the Lord! (*Takes up the recitation*)

> Thou didst blow with Thy wind.
> The sea covered them.
> They sank as lead in the mighty waters.

JUDAH

Who like Thee is among their Gods, O Lord?

ELEAZAR

A valiant battle cry, Judah.

JUDAH

Yea, Eleazar, and it shall be mine.

ELEAZAR

And mine! Who like Thee is among their gods, O Lord? Mi kamoka ba-elim adonai!

MATTATHIAS

Your courage is like the young warriors', Eleazar. You have not been the best scribe in Judaea for naught.

ELEAZAR

My eyes are dim with age, but my hands are true. They remembered. They remembered. All are there—the Law, the Prophets and the Writings. What matter our slain if Eleazar can save the Law. Now I can return.

MATTATHIAS

Return? Nay, Eleazar, you must abide here safe with us.

ELEAZAR

I am safe. Though my house be watched, I shall return to it. There will I abide. It shall not be said that Eleazar grew old enough to be afraid.

MATTATHIAS

Oh, great Eleazar, the Lord be with you. (ELEAZAR *leaves*) I will go and hide these precious scrolls. (*Sounds as though of more* REFUGEES.) What, more who flee to us? (MATTATHIAS *exits into the house*)

JUDAH

I hope it is the Greeks in search of Eleazar. (*Looks over the wall*)
What! You, Hannah, and who is that with you?

VOICE OF HANNAH

Young David has come with me. (HANNAH *and* DAVID *enter*)

HANNAH

In the name of the Lord!

JUDAH

Embracing DAVID

At last you bring me word from your brother Reuben to strike.
Do you not?

HANNAH

We are ready, Judah, but not as you think.

MATTATHIAS

Enters

Hannah, welcome in the name of the Lord. I rejoice that your
son brought you to our safekeeping.

HANNAH

It is not to stay, but to say farewell we are come. We crave your
blessing before we die.

JUDAH

Then Reuben is ready for battle, and death if needs be?

HANNAH

Yes! Ready for death. It is time for battle, Judah, but my
seven sons must perish first.

JUDAH

Perish! Perish! Your sons?

HANNAH

Above all others does the tyrant fear my sons and your sons,
Mattathias. This is his plot. The Greeks will take my seven
sons in Jerusalem and the king himself will offer them riches to
forsake our law. Here in Modin they will offer you riches to
join their worship in the market place. Thus with one blow
Antiochus thinks to conquer our nation.

JUDAH

A good plot, Hannah. How did you find it out?

HANNAH

From a Greek soldier who once lay sick at our house, and who
is now close to the king. He came to us by stealth with this news.

JUDAH

So you have come to join us here, and Reuben will follow with
his army. I understand. We will wait for the enemy in Modin
and throw back their honors in their teeth.

HANNAH

That was Reuben's first plan, but I counseled my sons to remain
at home and submit.

MATTATHIAS

Submit? My ears deceive me, Hannah.

JUDAH

I do not understand.

HANNAH

Nor did Reuben, at first. Pay heed to me, Judah, as though you and your brothers were my sons too. You I bid live and fight as I have bidden my seven others perish. Can't you understand now? If my boys go to battle and are slain, they will but die. If they perish by torture—seven in one day—refusing honor and riches from the king himself—they will live and their spirit shall fight on forever. Our nation will avenge their death.

DAVID

This then is our message from Reuben. When a messenger whom ye shall choose shall bring to you word that we are dead, you will know the first blow has been struck. In every village there are such as know our password: "The Sons of Hannah." These faithful will gather to you and set the Holy City free.

MATTATHIAS

O woman of valor, you have exceeded us all!

JUDAH

We, your sons in Modin, shall do your bidding to our last hour. Stay with us and be our counselor.

HANNAH

Nay, my son. I am informed the worst tortures are ready for my own sons if they refuse to obey the tyrant. If their flesh grows weak, my presence will steel their hearts.

MATTATHIAS

David is so young and comely.

DAVID

So said our Greek friend. He begged mother to hide me—he said I was too young to die.

HANNAH

How little they know a son of Israel.

JUDAH

So you go to your death.

DAVID

Kneels before HANNAH

Bless me, mother.

HANNAH

May the spirit of my deed strengthen you and your brothers.

JUDAH

Sevenfold shall be our strength. (MATTATHIAS *leads* HANNAH *and* DAVID *off and then returns immediately*)

MATTATHIAS

The message from the tyrant has come. Read it, my son. The messenger awaits an answer.

JUDAH

Reading

Mattathias, an honorable and great man in Modin. From Apollonius, servant of Antiochus, the Illustrious, Greetings: Three days shall pass and then when the sun is at its height in the heavens we will offer a sacrifice to Zeus, who dwells on snow-clad Olympus. We bid you and your sons to join us therein in the market-place. Riches and honor shall be yours, and you shall be among the friends of the king.

MATTATHIAS

This request deserves as answer the head of its bearer.

JUDAH

Let me send a better answer that will cost them more heads. (*To soldier*) Return our greetings to your master. Say unto him, Mattathias, the Priest, and his five sons, John, Simon, Judah, Eleazar and Jonathan will witness your sacrifice. When you proclaim the day and hour to the people of Modin, tell them that Mattathias and his sons will be there. They will come. (*Soldier withdraws*)

MATTATHIAS

Yea, sevenfold shall be your strength and like a hammer shall you strike them down.

JUDAH

Raises his arm

Who like Thee is among their gods, O Lord?

CURTAIN

SCENE II

The market place in Modin. There is an altar prepared for the sacrifice. Next it is an idol, two basins, one for lustral water and the other for barley seeds. Also myrtle boughs. As the curtain rises the noise of a seething crowd is heard. (With human actors, the crowd finally comes on the stage. With puppets it can be backstage.) A GREEK SOLDIER *and an* OFFICER OF THE KING *are talking. The* SOLDIER *is sweeping the ground before the mound with myrtle boughs*

KING'S OFFICER

Well, my sons, this looks like a great day for us, after all. Antiochus will reward us well. Mattathias and his sons are coming to join our worship.

SOLDIER

Eleazar, that old man, preferred the torture.

KING'S OFFICER

Strange people, these Jews. (*Sound of surging mob*) What is that?

SOLDIER

The Jew who changed his name to Jason is coming.

KING'S OFFICER

His people are not exactly cheering him. (*Cries from the crowd*) Listen!

VOICES

What flesh he eats turns to gold. He must have chosen the name
Jason for luck. He wears the golden fleece instead of the thread
of blue.

JASON

Appears and goes directly to the SOLDIER; *he is in Greek costume*
Listen, friend soldier, tell me how one proceeds about this sacrifice of yours.

SOLDIER

Why, sir, you hold a pig by the tail in one hand and roast him
and you hold out your other hand for the god to drop gold in.

KING'S OFFICER

We Greeks pay well. Tell you that to Mattathias.

JASON

Why shouldn't you pay me? What if my own people turn on
me? Your gold is not pay enough. I'll need a bodyguard.

SOLDIER

> Antiochus is a bad man.
> To turn a Jew into a bad man
> By showing him the golden fleece
> That is the glory of his Greece.

OFFICER

We'll fix the altar for you, friend Jason. All you need do is to take a long, sharp, gleaming, glittering knife and plunge it under the horns of the beautiful bull. There is the right moment, though. If you miss the right moment, the bull will make you the sacrifice with his horn.

People pass in and out in horror. During this scene the crowd gathers. Horror is shown at the idol with noises and gestures

SOLDIER

If you wait there, friend, the sacrifice will be ready for you shortly. (JASON *leaves—or stands to one side*) Here comes the old lion and all his cubs. (*The* SOLDIER *continues sweeping.* MATTATHIAS *and* JUDAH *now enter*)

MATTATHIAS

If there is no crowd on the stage

Are we the first to arrive in this sinful place? I cannot abide to look upon that idol that is like a tombstone over Israel. Let me go home, Judah.

JUDAH

Have strength, father. Today we strike. Look into the lifeless idol's eyes and see nothing. You are my father and in my arm and heart there is great strength that did spring from you. (*Noise of crowd, welcoming* JUDAH *with enthusiasm*)

JUDAH

Father, I failed to tell you, but our message has come from the martyred sons of Hannah. I must tell our people who obeyed me and forgathered here. (*Addresses people*) Listen to me, be *y*e Greeks or be ye Jews. Eleazar the scribe is dead. Had he even pretended to disobey the Law he would be living, but he walked to his death saying, "I will be worthy of my old age." (*A sob from the crowd*)

OFFICER

I wish the priest would come. I do not like the sound of this mob. (*Bull is heard bellowing off stage*)

VOICES

Let the Jew have a ride on him first. Hang Jason to his tail. (*The* SOLDIER *enters with the bull, or if played by persons a procession of priests comes in with a white bull garlanded. Flutes are playing. Basins, one of water and one empty, are carried.*) (JASON *enters*. MATTATHIAS *starts*)

MATTATHIAS

In Greek garb! You!

JUDAH

Addressing JASON

I suppose you know, Joshua, of the doom of Eleazar?

JASON

At ninety years he had nothing to make him live.

JUDAH

While Joshua is not yet old enough to die.

MATTATHIAS

Joshua, give ear and repent.

JUDAH

Addressing the people

Give ear to the news! Hannah and her seven sons have been slaughtered. One by one they were offered riches and one by one they refused honor and went to the torture saying: "The Lord God of Hosts knows that we die for His Laws." Yea, even her youngest son did Hannah send to the torturer. After him she died.

OFFICER

Is the priest coming? I dare wait no longer. This mob is like an angry jungle. You, venerable sir (*to* MATTATHIAS) be the first to come and do the worthy thing. Sacrifice; and you and your sons shall have silver and gold and be the friends of the king.

MATTATHIAS

If all nations that your king has subdued should depart from the worship of their fathers, yet will I and my sons and my people not forsake the Law. We will not go aside from our worship, to the right hand or the left.

SOLDIER

Oh, that's very nice oratory, old father, but not very practical. Antiochus is not to be dallied with. On this altar you either eat or are eaten. Perhaps some one else will start the ceremony. Who among you is the king's friend?

JASON

I will be the first to do you homage and obey the king. (*He goes to the altar, dipping his hand in the lustral water. He bends his head to receive a garland from the hand of the priest. He takes barley grains and scatters them on the mound. He prays*) O Zeus, thou aegis-bearer that dwells on snow-clad Olympus, hear us this day. (JASON *takes the knife and raises it to strike the bull.*) (MATTATHIAS *rushes forward, seizes the knife from the hand of* JASON *and plunges it into the apostate's breast*)

MATTATHIAS

Your false god must first drink your blood. (JASON *dies*) Thus die all Thine enemies, O Lord.

JUDAH

Swinging right and left, and casting off his cloak revealing himself armed
You, traitor, are only the first to die. (*To the* SOLDIER) Soldier of Antiochus, defend your king; he like your god needs your protection.
The crowd closes in on the Greeks. The bull rushes off, noises of the crowd from backstage grow louder and louder and then slowly diminish

JUDAH

Jumps on the mound, shouting
Who like Thee is among their gods, O Lord! (*He smashes the idol*)

CROWD

The Hammer of the Lord of Hosts has dealt a mighty blow.

JUDAH

Whosoever is zealous for the Law and would fight to free Israel
let him follow us. There are other heathen altars to shatter.
(JUDAH *stands triumphantly as the curtain comes down. The
crowd chants from backstage*)

CROWD

To battle! To battle! Though small be our band
While the hosts of the tyrant are countless as sand,
    Fear not! For they trust
    In the right arm of dust.
In swords that may shiver, in shields that may rust;
    But our arm of defense
    Is the arm of the Lord.
Our shield is His Law, and His Wrath is our sword;
The heroes who lead us are priests of His shrine,
And His glorious Name is our standard divine.

CURTAIN

SCENE III

The scene is laid on a plain near the Greek camp. TWO GREEK
SOLDIERS *and an elephant are on the stage. The elephant is
trumpeting. If the play is done with actors a costume can be easily
contrived to be worn by two boys who will play the part of the elephant*

FIRST SOLDIER
(*To elephant*)

There, there, old lady, step prettily.

SECOND SOLDIER

Oh, is it you? I thought it was one of those Syrian slave traders
who have come to buy our Hebrew captives.

FIRST SOLDIER

Captives? We have to catch them first. (*Singing*)
      Six thousand strong we marched away,
      The sleeping Judah to seize and slay,
      His men to sell for a full year's pay.
      For a year's, a year's, a year's full pay.

SECOND SOLDIER

This war is a serious business, men. Stop your nonsense.

FIRST SOLDIER

Perhaps you like this better. It's truer:
      Though our general is tall and brave,
      He'll step into a green, green grave.
      For Judah's lion is very strong
      And can prolong his magic song.

(*To elephant which he starts to lead across the stage*) Here, here, old girl, don't get headstrong. Come along. Come along. We mustn't delay. They will soon be back. The general will want to ride you in the triumphal procession.

The noise of a raging battle gets louder and louder. Lights on stage grow dim

SECOND SOLDIER

What's that din? Look! It must be our men moving. Our victorious Gorgias must have bagged the whole Hebrew camp while they lay asleep.

FIRST SOLDIER

Are you sure it is our men? The banners look strange.

SECOND SOLDIER

They must be the captured Hebrew standards.

FIRST SOLDIER

What? Captured banners waving in front of our hosts?

Trumpets are heard and shouts of "Charge the Greeks," "The Sons of Hannah," grow louder and louder. Lights on back drop or off to the side in the direction of the battle gradually change from blue to red

SECOND SOLDIER

It's that demon Judah.

FIRST SOLDIER

Zeus protect us. Judah got into our camp before our men got into his.

Cries and trumpets continue

SECOND SOLDIER

Let us give the alarm.

FIRST SOLDIER

Don't be silly. Let somebody else die. Look! Look! By that red and flaming glow I should say that our camp was burning. You may rush in if you like. I must hurry. Gorgias will undoubtedly need the elephant for a long retreat.

Din of battle continues and both SOLDIERS *go off with the elephant in the direction away from the raging battle. There is an empty stage for a moment and then* JUDAH *and the* CAPTAIN *of his army enter*

JUDAH

And with their own sword shall they be slain. (*To his army which is presumably off stage in the direction in which the battle was raging*) Soldiers of Israel, fear ye not their multitude, neither be ye afraid of their assault. There is one who delivereth and saveth Israel. Be not greedy of the spoils, inasmuch as there is another battle before us. Gorgias and his hosts will soon be weary of looking for us in the mountains and will be on our heels.

CAPTAIN

See, the heathen are afraid. They flee.

JUDAH

Israel this day shall see a great deliverance.

Enter the TWO SOLDIERS

FIRST SOLDIER

To SECOND, *not seeing* JUDAH *and the* CAPTAIN
This way, friend, we can make our exit this way.

start les

CAPTAIN

Even this way is closed to you. Where would you go?

SECOND SOLDIER

To join our families, sir.

CAPTAIN

Greeks are safer with their ancestors.
Combat between CAPTAIN *and* TWO SOLDIERS *and* JUDAH.
JUDAH *kills one of the* SOLDIERS. *The* CAPTAIN *pursues
the other off stage. The* CAPTAIN *returns almost immediately
leading the elephant*

CAPTAIN

The heathen horde is scattered. Their camp is in complete ruins.
There is gold in abundance and silver and blue silk and purple
of sea and other great riches. The men are praising JUDAH
who wields the mighty hammer. Gorgias is fled. With their
own sword you slew them. Their steed is now yours, Judah.

JUDAH

Blessed art Thou, O Lord God of Israel, who didst quell the
violence of the tyrant by the hand of Thy servants.

CAPTAIN

A rededicated and holy temple shall bless the children of Israel.

JUDAH

But, Captain, we must not think our task is done. They will raise new armies.

CAPTAIN

Yea, and you will defeat them all. What matter if it be a year or two years before we enter Jerusalem. Judah, lead on!

JUDAH

As the will of God is in heaven, so let Him do.

Off stage the soldiers shout "Judah the Maccabee." There is the sound of marching men and the curtain comes down as they chant:

> No safety remaineth for Javan but flight,
> No help from blind metal, no help from deaf stone,
> The Lord, God of Hosts reigns eternal, alone.

CURTAIN

EPILOGUE

The scene depicts the entrance to the temple. JUDAH *stands before the gates. Chanting is heard from off stage*

JUDAH

The Lord hath been mindful of us. He will bless the House of Israel. He will bless the House of Aaron. He will bless all, both the small and the great.

CHANTING

Let us go into the House of the Lord. Our feet are standing within thy gates, O Jerusalem.

JUDAH

Lift up your hands to the sanctuary and bless the Lord.

CHANTING

Lift up your heads, O ye gates, and be lifted up, ye everlasting doors, that the King of Glory may come in.

JUDAH

Who is the King of Glory?

CHANTING

The Lord of Hosts, the Lord Mighty in battle, He is the King of Glory.

CURTAIN

AT THIS SEASON

By

SAMUEL PITLIK

Translated from the Hebrew

By

EMILY SOLIS-COHEN, JR.

PROPERTIES AND COSTUMING

PROLOGUE

An old man's cloak.

His beard.

His staff and knapsack.

A tree stump so designed that it holds eight containers for tapers or candles or electric bulbs.

SCENES I AND II

Palestinian costumes of the time of the Maccabees.

A short sword (Scene II).

SCENE III

Talit and headgear.

Tables and chairs or benches; a lectern.

A Hanukkah Lamp.

SCENE IV

An Ark for the Law.

A Hanukkah Lamp.

Spanish costumes.

SCENE V

Modern costume.

Couch, a table and table-cover, photographs of Theodor Herzl and Moses Mendelssohn, chairs.

A Hanukkah Lamp.

SCENE VI

A huge Hanukkah Lamp to be carried in a procession.
Banners.

MUSIC

PROLOGUE

Prelude—*Eli Eli*

SCENE I

Psalm 79, vss. 1–5, to be chanted (see score)

With God's Help to Aid Us (see score)

SCENE II

Ma'oz Zur—Rock of My Salvation

(Goldfarb, Samuel E. and Israel, *The Jewish Songster*,
Brooklyn, 1929, pt., I, p. 12); see above page 73

Psalm 24, vvs. 7–10

Idelsohn, A. H., *Sefer Ha-shirim*, Berlin, 1912, pt. II, p. 85)

Halleluhu (Dance) Psalm 150, vss. 5–6

(Altman, Shalom, *The Judaean Songster*, N. Y., 1934, p. 70)

SCENE III

Tanhum

(S. Golub, Metro Music Co., N. Y.)

SCENE IV

Adonai Melek—The Lord Reigneth (from Sephardic ritual)

SCENE V

Eli Eli

SCENE VI

Tob lihyot—Good To Live
(Goldfarb, ibid., pf. II, p. 24)

Anashim 'Alizim—A Folk Song (see score)

EPILOGUE

'Am Yisrael Hai—The People Lives Eternal
(Goldfarb, ibid., pt. II, p. 9)

בָּאוּ גוֹיִים בְּנַחֲלָתֶךָ

ש – ך – ש – קד היכל את או – טמ ך – ת – בנחל יים –גו או – ב
ba - u go-yim benahala-te-ha tim - u et hekal kod-she - ka sa

– מ ך – די – עב נבלת את נו – נת יָם – לעי לים – ש – ירו את מו
mu et yeru-sha-layim le-i-yim nat - nu et niblat aba-de - ka ma-

ער – י תו – לחי ך – די – חסי בשר ים – מ – הש עוף – ל אכל
akal le - of ha-sha-ma-yim besar haside-ka le-hay-to ya - ar

בְּעֶזְרַת אֱלֹהֵינוּ

Allegretto

נו - ל - צִי - יְ הוּ - יְ - תַת - מְ נוּ - הִי - אֶל רַת - עֶז - בְּ
be - ez - rat elo - he - nu Ma - tit - ya - hu ya - zi - le - nu

נוּ - ל - אֵ - יִן נוּ - הִי - אֶל דַה - יְהוּ רַת - עֶז - בְּ
be - ez - rat elo - he - nu yehu - dah yig - a - le - nu

ל-ל-ל ל - ל ל-ל-ל-טר ל-ל-ל ל ל - טר ל-ל-ל-טר ל-טר
tra - la tra - la - la - la la tra - la - la la - la la - la la - la

ל ל-ל ל-ל ל - טר ל - ל-ל-טר ל - טר
tra - la tra - la - la - la la tra - la - la la - la la

221A

אֲנָשִׁים עֲלִיזִים

Allegro con spirito

א - נ - שִׁים   עֲ - לִי - זִים בְּמַע - גַל מִס - תוֹב - בִּים
a - na - shim   a - li - zim bema-gal mis-to be-bim

ו - חוֹשְׁ - בִים כַּ - מָה יָ - פֶה אֶת א - הו - בָ - תִי אַר - אֶה וּמִי שֶׁ - רוּ-
ve-hosh-bim ka-mah ya-feh et a-hu-ba-ti er-eh umi she-ro-

דִי - נֶג - דִי יָ - פֶה יָ - מַד - יָ פֶה - י דִי - נֶג - דִי תִי - קַד - לֵ - רַ - צָה
zeh   lire - kod i-ti   ya-mod ya-feh neg di neg-di

221B

CHARACTERS IN THE ORDER OF
THEIR APPEARANCE

ANCIENT ISRAEL

YOUNG HASIDIM

OLD HASIDIM

FIRST MESSENGER

SECOND MESSENGER

THIRD MESSENGER

FOURTH MESSENGER

JUDAH THE MACCABEE

CELEBRANTS, MEN AND WOMEN

THE PUPILS OF RAB

RAB, ABBA ARIKA

A FATHER

A MOTHER

A CHILD

INQUISITORS

A SON

A MOTHER

A DAUGHTER

HER HUSBAND

THEIR FATHER

SCHOOL CHILDREN OF PALESTINE

HALUZIM

HALUZOT

SCENES

PROLOGUE

ON THE ROAD

As the curtain rises the score of Eli Eli *is heard. The stage is vacant. There is a large rock in forefront; near it is a stump of a tree. This stump contains eight holders for candles or lights which are not visible to the audience*

ANCIENT ISRAEL

Enters, rests on the rock, lays staff on ground. From his knapsack takes eight tapers and places them in the stump. He then rises and kindles them, reciting in Hebrew and then in English

Baruk ata adonai elohenu melek ha-'olam asher kiddeshanu bemiz-votav vezivanu lehadlik ner shel Hanukkah

Blessed art thou, O Lord our God, King of the Universe, who hast sanctified us by Thy commandments and commanded us to kindle the lights of Hanukkah.

Remains silent for a few moments contemplating the burning tapers. Then in a low voice murmurs

Miracles . . . He who performed miracles . . . Where are those days? . . . Why are they so far off? They still glow in my memory, those days . . . Miracles . . . He who performed miracles . . . In those days . . . And now, a wanderer's life, wandering . . . wandering . . . How long? Whither?

CURTAIN

SCENE I

IN JUDAEA
IN THE TIME OF ANTIOCHUS

As the curtain rises the score of Ma'oz Zur *is heard. A cave is disclosed in which* HASIDIM *are hiding from the tyrant*

VOICES OF HASIDIM
Chanting

O God, the heathen are come into Thine inheritance;
They have defiled Thy holy temple;
They have made Jerusalem into heaps.
They have given the dead bodies of Thy servants to be food
    unto the fowls of the heaven,
The flesh of Thy saints unto the beasts of the earth.
They have shed their blood like water
Round about Jerusalem, with none to bury them.
We are become a taunt to our neighbors,
A scorn and derision to them that are round about us.
How long, O Lord, wilt Thou be angry for ever?

JUDAH THE MACCABEE *enters hurriedly while the chant continues*
Wherefore should the nations say: "Where is their God?"
We that are Thy people and the flock of Thy pasture
Will give Thee thanks forever,
We will tell of Thy praise to all generations.

JUDAH
Echoes last line

We will tell of Thy praise to all generations.

HASIDIM

They rise excitedly

Judah? What has happened? What comfort have you?

JUDAH

He destroyed the idol. He slew the traitor. He summoned us
to him. (*Raises his arm and exclaims*)
Mi L'Adonai Elai! Who is for the Lord, come to me!

HASIDIM

One voice follows another rapidly

Who?
Who destroyed the idol?
What traitor?
Who was slain?
Tell us!
Tell us!

JUDAH

My father, Mattathias. He smashed the idol. He slew the
traitor. He called us to him; saying: "Who is for God, come
to me!"

HASIDIM

You talk in riddles. Tell us plainly what happened.

JUDAH

I'll tell you just as it happened. A heathen captain came to
Modin, where we live—

HASIDIM

Yes, Yes – –

JUDAH

He set up an altar and an idol and said to my father: "Thou art a ruler and an honorable and great man in this city, and strengthened with sons and brethren. Now therefore come thou first and fulfill the king's commandment, as all the heathen have done."

HASIDIM

And he threw their words in their teeth!

JUDAH

My father answered in a loud voice: "Though all the nations that are under the king's dominion obey him, and fall away every one from the religion of their fathers, and give consent to his commandments, yet will I and my sons and my brethren walk in the covenant of our fathers. God forbid that we should forsake the law and the ordinances. We will not hearken to the king's words, to go from our religion, either to the right hand or the left."

HASIDIM

What happened then?

JUDAH

When my father finished speaking, there came one of the Jews in the sight of all to sacrifice on the altar which was at Modin, according to the king's commandment. Wherefore my father ran and slew him upon the altar. Also the king's commissioner, who compelled men to sacrifice, he killed, and the altar he pulled down.

YOUNG HASIDIM

Sing

With God's help to aid us,
Mattathias will save us.
With God's help to aid us,
Judah, redeemer, be!
[*Repeat*]

OLD HASIDIM

What is all this joy about?

YOUNG HASIDIM

Strength resides not in tears; nor victory in weeping. With joy
we will prevail; and with shouting bring down the foe.

FIRST MESSENGER

Enters hurriedly

Eleazar the scribe they killed. With tortures. He would not
eat the flesh of swine. Nor even pretend to.

ALL

They chant

Woe! Woe! Woe!
How long, O Lord,
Wilt Thou be angry forever?

SECOND MESSENGER

Enters hurriedly

Hannah and her seven sons are dead.

ALL

Woe! Woe! Woe!
They have shed their blood like water
Round about Jerusalem,
With none to bury them.

THIRD MESSENGER

Enters hurriedly

I alone am left of the thousand slain on the Sabbath. We would
not desecrate the day of rest by bloodshed.

ALL

Woe! Woe! Woe!
They have given the dead bodies of Thy servants to be food
    unto the fowls of the heaven,
The flesh of Thy saints unto the beasts of the earth.

FOURTH MESSENGER

Enters hurriedly

Thus saith Mattathias the priest: "If the foe attack you on
the Sabbath, defend your lives. Life is more precious even than
the Sabbath to God, Most High."

JUDAH

Let us leave our caves. How long shall we flee to the hills?
How long shall we be afraid before the rustling of a leaf? Let
us drive forth the foe from our land. (*He raises his right arm*)
Mi L'Adonai Elai—Who is for God, come to me—

ALL

The HASIDIM *and* MESSENGERS *surround* JUDAH *and dance*

With God's help to aid us
Mattathias will save us.
With God's help to aid us,
Judah, redeemer, be!

[*Repeat*]

CURTAIN

SCENE II

DEDICATION OF THE TEMPLE

Vacant stage. Ma'oz Zur *heard off stage, left. The curtain rises on a Temple court*

PROCESSION

Procession begins from right, men first, women follow. After men have gone off stage, left—women remain on stage; all join the chant of:

> Lift up your heads, O ye gates,
> And be ye lifted up, ye everlasting doors;
> That the King of glory may come in.
> Who is the King of glory?
> The Lord strong and mighty,
> The Lord mighty in battle.
> Lift up your heads, O ye gates,
> Yea, lift them up, ye everlasting doors;
> That the King of glory may come in.
> Who is the King of glory?
> The Lord of hosts;
> He is the King of glory.   Selah.

The Procession enters the Temple, left. The women remain in the court and dance The Victory Dance[1] to the chanting of Halleluhu *by a quartet backstage.*

QUARTET

Chants from backstage

Hallelujah.
Praise God in His sanctuary;
Praise Him in the firmament of His power.

[1] For description of Dance, see p. 232.

Praise Him for His mighty acts;
Praise Him according to His abundant greatness.
Praise Him with the blast of the horn;
Praise Him with the psaltery and harp.
Praise Him with the timbrel and dance;
Praise Him with stringed instruments and the pipe.
Praise Him with the loud-sounding cymbals;
Praise Him with the clanging cymbals.
Let every thing that hath breath praise the Lord.
Hallelujah.

THE VICTORY DANCE

Four couples stand in a circle, the first opposite the third, the second facing the fourth.

Step One

Couples 1 and 3 raise arms shoulder high, elbows bent. They advance to the center with short running steps; at the center Couple 1 crosses to the opposite side beneath the arms of Couple 3.

Step Two

Couples 2 and 4 do likewise.

Step Three

Reverse *Step One;* Couple 3 crossing to own place.

Step Four

Couples 2 and 4 reverse similarly.

Step Five

Walking rhythmically to the music all dancers change hands, first left, then right, circling twice until they return to position and partners. They clasp hands and face the center.

Step Six

Couples 1 and 3 circle in their own position with short graceful steps; then they dance to the center, greet the opposite couple, bow, and dance back to position.

Step Seven

Couples 2 and 4 do likewise.

Step Eight

The four couples repeat *Step Six* simultaneously. All meet in the center, bow, and dance back to position.

CURTAIN

SCENE III

SURA ACADEMY IN BABYLONIA

The curtain is down. From behind it the music of Tanhum *is heard. The curtain rises on the Lecture Hall of the Sura Academy in Babylonia.* STUDENTS *are seated, deeply occupied in study of the scrolls. Hanukkah lights are burning. A discussion is carried on in whispers*

FIRST STUDENT

In excited tones

When I was in Palestine I heard Rabbi Johanan say that whenever Rab was discussing Torah with his teacher, Judah ha-Nasi, an onlooker would notice sparks of fire leaping from mouth to mouth.

SECOND STUDENT

Do you remember what our great teacher Rab said to his son? "Better to eke a small living from the land with hard toil than earn much from commerce and trade."

THIRD STUDENT

And I heard that when the holy book of Daniel says, "They that turn the many to righteousness shall shine as the brightness of the firmament," it meant those who teach little children.

FIFTH STUDENT

Enters and announces

Our teacher is coming. Give honor to the Prince of the Torah. *All the students rise and gaze reverently at* RAB, *who enters slowly and passes in front of them, until he reaches the high reading desk*

RAB

Peace to you, beloved pupils;
Peace to you.

STUDENTS

In unison

Peace to our Master this holy night.

RAB

Gazes at Hanukkah light

Tonight I shall repeat the laws of Hanukkah. The sages teach that every home must have its light. It is the custom among the pious to have a lamp for every member of the family. The School of Shammai says: "On the first night, kindle eight lights, and on each night thereafter, diminish their number." The School of Hillel says: "On the first night kindle one light, and on each night thereafter, increase by one."

A STUDENT

Tell us, our Master, where must we place our lights when we return home?

RAB

At the door. If you live in an upper story, you must place the light at the window overlooking the street . . . (*Musingly*) In time of danger, however, we must be content with placing the lamp upon a table within the room. (*He fingers the lamp before him*)

A STUDENT

Rushes in, breathless

The Magi are coming. Extinguish the lights.
A STUDENT *rises and extinguishes lights. Through the darkness, the voice of* RAB *is heard, speaking gently*

RAB

For Israel there is but one light, the Torah. Our foes can extinguish tapers, but they can never extinguish the light of the Torah. You, my pupils, must go forth and, in the face of the enemy, kindle the flame which neither the Magi nor any oppressor after them can quench. The sparks from the light of the Torah will illumine our exile until the day come when God shall have mercy on Zion and restore her captivity.

CURTAIN

SCENE IV

IN SPAIN

Done through Pantomime

The curtain is down. From behind it comes the hum of Adonai Melek. *The curtain rises, disclosing a cellar. Against the farthest wall is an ark for the Scrolls of the Law. A table is in the center of the room—on it is a Hanukkah Lamp*

Father and son are praying. As they finish, the mother enters. The father then moves to the Hanukkah Lamp and lights it, lips moving in blessing.

A loud knocking is heard

The boy is bidden to hide. He runs behind a tapestry. The father extinguishes the candles. The room is in darkness.

The knocking becomes louder

Finally the door is broken open. Officers of the Inquisition rush in.

The stage is lit up

The father puts his arm across his wife's shoulder.
An Inquisitor takes up the Lamp and holds it accusingly before the man and woman.
The two remain proudly silent.
Finally, the Inquisitor throws down the Lamp.
The father and mother are dragged off.
Suddenly the child emerges, snatches the Lamp from the floor and kindles it.

CURTAIN

SCENE V

IN NAZI-LAND

The curtain is down. From behind it comes the music of Eli, Eli. *The curtain rises on a large living-room on whose walls hang portraits of Moses Mendelssohn and Theodor Herzl. On a table in the center of the room stands a Hanukkah Lamp. Beside it are seated a* MOTHER, *her* SON *and* DAUGHTER, *and her daughter's* HUSBAND

SON (*about 20 years*)

I'll run away. I'll go to Palestine, away from these filthy Nazis.

MOTHER

Why Palestine? What can you do there?

DAUGHTER

Nothing, mother, for you never taught us Hebrew. In Palestine, we would be as strangers.

SON

Strangers in Palestine? Never. I can learn Hebrew quickly, and so can you. We can learn also to till the soil.

SON-IN-LAW

But I cannot leave so quickly. A doctor cannot run away. There are the sick I must tend.

Cries heard at the door

Jew! Jew!

The sound of blows is heard, and a voice calling

VOICE

Let me in. Quick, let me in.

The TWO YOUNG MEN *rush and open the door to admit their* FATHER. *He falls in their arms, breathing heavily and holding his hands to his bleeding head*

ALL

What is it? What has happened?

FATHER *merely groans*

DAUGHTER

A curse on these barbarians!

The SON-IN-LAW *gets his bandages and begins to tend to the* FATHER'S *wounds*

FATHER

Don't look so frightened. Aren't you used to this yet? Don't you know what it all means? Another *golus* has come upon us. The *golus* of Rome, the *golus* of Spain. And now the *golus* of the Nazis. But let us not forget what day this is. It is our Feast of Dedication.

His head bandaged, the FATHER *walks over to the Hanukkah Lamp and lights the candles, reciting*

FATHER

Blessed art thou, O Lord our God, King of the Universe, who hath preserved us alive and brought us to this season.

CURTAIN

SCENE VI

IN TEL AVIV

Curtain is down. From behind it comes the music of Hatikvah. *The curtain rises on a wide street.* SCHOOL CHILDREN *are marching in procession, carrying a huge Menorah lit with torches instead of candles. They chant first in Hebrew and then in English*

CHILDREN

Chanting in Hebrew

Tob lihyot, tob lihyot bearzenu,
Tob ledabber, tob ledabber bisefatenu,
Tob laharosh, tob laharosh admatenu,
Tob likzor, tob likzor tebuatenu,
Tob lashir, tob lashir et shirenu,
Tob lilmod, tob lilmod et toratenu.

Chanting in English

It is good to dwell in the land of Israel,
It is good to speak the tongue of Israel,
It is good to till the soil of Israel,
It is good to reap the harvest of Israel,
It is good to sing this song of Israel,
It is good to study the Torah of Israel.

The CHILDREN *move and stand back, and the procession of* HALUZOT *enters*

The CHILDREN *sing* Anashim 'Alizim
As the CHILDREN *sing, the* HALUZOT *dance*

THE DANCE OF THE HALUZOT

Music and singing of Stali **Boom**

Anashim 'alizim
Bema'agol mistobebim
Vehoshebim kamma yafeh!
Et ahubati ereh
Umi sherozeh lirkod itti
Ya'amod yafeh negdi, negdi.

Stali Boom, Stali Boom
Stali Boom tralalala
Stali Boom tralalala
Stali Boom tralalala
Umi sherozeh lirkod itti
Ya'amod yafeh negdi, negdi.

The dancers stand in a large circle. Rhythmically they hop toward the left, singing. A dancer enters the center of the circle and hops around to the right. At the chorus of the song, she crooks her finger at one of the others, summoning a partner. These two fold their hands across their chests. As the children sing *Stali Boom* they clap their hands.

Dancer on the outside dances forward and No. 2 goes toward outer part of the circle, turns, dances back past partner again. The third time *Stali Boom* is sung, they both meet in center, clap their hands on *umi* and link left arms and dance around until *ya'amod* is reached; then they clap their hands again, link right arms, and dance. The dancers link hands to form circle again, and the entire dance is repeated with new partners.

CURTAIN

EPILOGUE

IN PALESTINE

The curtain remains down for a minute, and then rises on the DANCERS. ANCIENT ISRAEL *suddenly appears with his staff and sack. He moves from child to child and watches the dancing. Suddenly he casts down his staff and throws his sack on the ground. He dances into the middle of the circle. In a few minutes the circle opens to reveal him without a beard. He has become* YOUNG ISRAEL. *He dances in the middle of the circle while they all clap hands and to the chanting of* 'Am Yisrael Hai *dance the Hora.*

> Israel lives eternal, 'Am yisrael hai
> Israel lives eternal, 'Am yisrael hai
> Israel lives eternal, 'Am yisrael hai.

THE HORA

Formation

Circle of children, with their hands on neighbor's shoulders.

Steps

Step left, step back with right foot, jump on both; kick right, jump on both; kick left. Repeat to entire song.

CURTAIN

VERSE

Hanukkah Lamp, copper, Moorish.
Museum, Jewish Theological Seminary of America.

Hanukkah Lamp, Salomon Collection, *Hebraica*, plate XXI.

FOR THE SABBATH OF HANUKKAH[1]

By Benjamin Cohen

A Tower of strength are the salvations of God,
They are wonders that pass our understanding.
He decreed good for Israel
And stilled the shouts of our oppressors,
He exacted requital for our blood
From the hand of the enemy who had done wickedly.
Therefore, day unto day,
And generation unto generation
Proclaim Thy faithfulness.
    My mouth shall speak Thy praises,
    Thy salvations all the day.

Mighty ones pursued us,
Until they defiled the holy house.
Upon the mountains they attacked us
On days of Sabbath and New Moon.
They forbade Thy people
To perform the rite of the Covenant—
Numberless were the martyrs,
For they rejoiced to do Thy commandments.
    My mouth shall speak Thy praises,
    Thy salvations all the day.

[1] The collection of religious poetry bearing the name *Ayeleth Ha-Shahar*, Star of the Morning, Mantua, 1612 and 1724, consists of additional prayers for various occasions used by the congregation of Mantua, Italy. It contains Hanukkah poems, folios 75–84 and 89–96 of the respective editions. The above is one of them, contained in the 1724 edition; it was written by Benjamin Cohen. This English version is by Solomon Solis-Cohen.

We sat in deepest darkness;
Strangers prevailed against us;
A mother died embracing her sons,
Heavy, heavy was the yoke of the tyrant.
But Thou didst recall Thy covenant with us,
Thou God and Worker of marvels,
And thou didst bring forth from captivity
The house of Thy dwelling which Thou lovest.
    My mouth shall speak Thy praises,
    Thy salvations all the day.

Thou didst stretch forth Thy strong right hand
Toward the house of Aaron whom Thou hadst set apart;
Thou didst lead them into Thy strong-hold.
Thy holy name didst Thou greatly magnify,
For them Thou didst surely guide
From of old, to overthrow Thine adversaries.
Thou didst pour Thy wrathful anger
Upon the enemy, in Thy jealousy.
    My mouth shall speak Thy praises,
    Thy salvations all the day.

The lamp of the commandment and the light of the Torah
Together lifted up our heads;
Light came to us
At this time in our holy house.
For Thee, O God, our soul was waiting.
Oil for the head Thou didst pour in plenty.
In majestic glory Thou didst shine
Through the miracles of Thy wonders.
    My mouth shall speak Thy praises,
    Thy salvations all the day.

Glorified and sanctified
Were Thy holy house and Thine altar,
And with psalmody and joyous song
They thanked and blessed Thee.
For Thou wilt not abandon Thy children,
But forever wilt Thou bestow on them the abundance
      of Thy loving-kindness.
Arise, O Lord, lift up Thine hands,
Forget not Thy treasured people.
    My mouth shall speak Thy praises,
    Thy salvations all the day.

The stone which the builders rejected
May it be exalted as from of old;
Thou, shepherd among the roses,
Smite the loins of my adversaries;
And in the midst of the City of Jerusalem
Be Thou strengthened in Thy might,
Thou and the ark of Thy strength,
Arise to Thy resting-place.
    My mouth shall speak Thy praises,
    Thy salvations all the day.

Benjamin is a ravening wolf,
May he feed forever in Thy sanctuary.
The eternal fire that consumes
Will yet burn for Thy offerings.
Between the shoulders of Thy soul's beloved
Thy house of prayer will be established.
There the priest at Thy command
Will kindle a light in Thy courts.
    My mouth shall speak Thy praises,
    Thy salvations all the day.

MACCABEAN BATTLE-SONG[1]

Solomon Solis-Cohen

To battle! To battle! Though few be our band,
While the hosts of the tyrant are countless as sand,
  Fear not! For they trust
  In the right arm of dust,
In shields that may shiver, in swords that may rust;
  But our arm of defence
  Is the arm of the Lord.
His Law is our shield, and His wrath is our sword;
The heroes that lead us are priests of His shrine,
And his glorious Name is our banner divine!

To battle! To battle! Ye proud heathen horde,
Among all the elim who is like to the Lord?
  A stone, from the sod
  Ye dig out: " 'tis a god!
Quake, earth, tremble, heaven, before his dread nod!"
  Aye, quake earth and skies;
  All ye peoples, be still;
Hark! the loud-rolling thunder! It voices His will
Who fashioned the storm cloud—who speaks not in vain,
And the Hammer of God rives Olympus in twain!

To battle! To battle! The cornets ring loud,
Speaking hope to the weak, speaking death to the proud.
  Lo! Jerubbaal's sword
  Unto Judah restored,

[1] *When Love Passed By and Other Verses*, Solomon Solis-Cohen. The Rosenbach Co., 1929, p. 33.

Flashes bright at our head as the flame of the Lord!
　　And woe to the foe
　　Whom its keen edge shall smite,
No safety remaineth for Javan, but flight;
No help from blind metal, no help from deaf stone—
The Lord God of Hosts reigns Eternal, Alone!

THE BATTLE OF EMMAUS

Solomon Solis-Cohen

Shout! ye redeemed of Israel, shout!
    A loud triumphant peal!
A ringing cry to shake the sky,
    And cause the mountains reel!
For, broken are the captive's chains,
    And shattered is the yoke;
The Hammer of the Lord of Hosts
    Hath dealt a mighty stroke!

As onward marched the Grecian host
    Earth shook beneath their tread;
Their banners that obscured the sun
    Ill-omened shadows spread;
And far and wide, on every side,
    As countless as the sand,
Their ranks . . . like locust settled down
    To devastate the land.

Prayerful a space, our soldiers stood,
    Then, Judah drew his sword—
Our hero-priest, fit chief to lead
    The armies of the Lord!—

"There is the foe! Let him that fears,
        Or is but newly wed,
Or waits his vine's first fruitage, turn;
        God's blessing on his head.

"But he with me whose spirit burns
        To free our sacred soil
From heathen stain; and with their slain
        Avenge the Temple's spoil—
Who for his country and his God,
        Dares brave the battle's fray—
Let him remain; and falter not
        At all their proud array.—

"As great was Pharaoh's army—
        Go seek it 'neath the wave!
As impious the Assyrian host—
        It found inglorious grave!
The Hand that wrote Belshazzar's doom,
        And laid proud Babel low,
This day is raised to strike for us—
        Who shall avert its blow!

"Not man-made gods of wood or brass
        Not shapes of senseless stone,
Ares like Marduk, Zeus like Bel,
        All shall be overthrown.
Now, men of Israel, for the lives
        Of those whom you hold dear—
For Law, for God, for Country—Charge!"
        Loud rang our answering cheer!

And swords flashed high, and rose the cry
　　"Who is like Thee, O Lord!"
As sudden, on the startled foe,
　　A storm of steel, we poured!

No lamb the Grecian warrior!
　　This, can the Persian tell.
No babe, the Syrian general,
　　This Egypt knoweth well.
But we were thinking of God's house,
　　By heathen bands defiled,
Of ravaged land and wasted home,
　　Of martyred wife and child.

And naught availed them all their skill
　　Or strength, or valor, then;
The Lord of Hosts inspired us,
　　And each man fought like ten!
Where Judah led, lay Grecian dead,
　　Like leaves before the storm;
The power of an hundred men
　　Was in his single arm!

They waver—break—they turn—they fly,
　　As swift as hinds their feet!
Well for the Greek his sacred games
　　Have made his limbs so fleet!
Of all the host, this morn, that marched
　　With banners streaming high,
Not one remains upon the field
　　Save those that cannot fly.

Oh, daughter of the Holy Mount,
    Break forth in joyful song;
Lift up thy head, thou that in bonds
    And tears, hast dwelt so long;
Thy God hath seen, hath pitied thee,
    Hath rent the tyrant's yoke.
The Hammer of the Lord of Hosts
    Hath dealt a mighty stroke.

LAMPS OF DEDICATION

Solomon Solis-Cohen

Shine, lamps of Dedication, shine,
Your hallowed radiance be the sign
That still there burns undimmed by years,
Not quenched, but fed by blood and tears,
In Israel's heart, clear, steadfast, bright,
The flame it caught from Sinai's height.

HANUKKAH HYMN

Louis Stern

Let our grateful anthems ring,
　　Joyous songs and gladsome lays,
To our God and Heavenly King,
　　Sing His glory! Sound His praise!
　　He who never sleepeth
　　Israel safely keepeth,
Hears their cry, from on high,
　　E'er when Judah weepeth.

Syria's mad and mighty host
　　Fiercely down upon us swept.
To destroy us was their boast;
Israel trembled, Judah wept!
　　But behold! salvation
　　God wrought for our nation,
Sending light, clear and bright,
　　'Midst our tribulation.

"Feast of Lights"—O glorious name!
　　Cast thy rays o'er land and seas;
Kindle in all hearts the flame
　　That inspired the Maccabees;
　　Heroes to be ever,
　　Cowards, traitors—never!
And to love God above,
　　Right and truth forever.

THE FEAST OF LIGHTS[1]

Emma Lazarus

Kindle the taper like the steadfast star
Ablaze on evening's forehead o'er the earth,
And add each night a lustre till afar
An eightfold splendor shine above thy hearth.
Clash, Israel, the cymbals, touch the lyre,
Blow the brass trumpet and the harsh-tongued horn;
Chant psalms of victory till the heart take fire,
The Maccabean spirit leap new-born.

Remember how from wintry dawn till night,
Such songs were sung in Zion, when again
On the high altar flamed the sacred light,
And, purified from every Syrian stain,
The foam-white walls with golden shields were hung,
With crowns and silken spoils, and at the shrine,
Stood, midst their conqueror-tribe, five chieftains sprung
From one heroic stock, one seed divine.

Five branches grown from Mattathias' stem,
The Blessed John, the keen-eyed Jonathan,
Simon the fair, the burst-of-Spring, the Gem,
Eleazar, Help of God; o'er all his clan
Judas the Lion-Prince, the Avenging Rod,
Towered in warrior-beauty, uncrowned king,
Armed with the breastplate and the sword of God,
Whose praise is: "He received the perishing."

---

[1] From *Poems of Emma Lazarus*, Houghton, Mifflin & Co., Boston, 1899.
Part of this poem has been set to music as *Kindle the Taper*. (See above, p. 78).

They who had camped within the mountain-pass,
Couched on the rock, and tented 'neath the sky,
Who saw from Mizpah's height the tangled grass
Choke the wide Temple-courts, the altar lie
Disfigured and polluted, who had flung
Their faces on the stones, and mourned aloud
And rent their garments, wailing with one tongue,
Crushed as a wind-swept bed of reeds is bowed.

Even they by one voice fired, one heart of flame,
Though broken reeds, had risen, and were men,
They rushed upon the spoiler and o'ercame,
Each arm for freedom had the strength of ten.
Now is their mourning into dancing turned,
Their sackcloth doffed for garments of delight,
Week-long the festive torches shall be burned,
Music and revelry wed day with night.

Still ours the dance, the feast, the glorious Psalm,
The mystic lights of emblem and the Word.
Where is our Judas? Where are our five-branched palm?
Where are the lion-warriors of the Lord?
Clash, Israel, the cymbals, touch the lyre,
Sound the brass trumpet and the harsh-tongued horn,
Chant hymns of victory till the heart take fire,
The Maccabean spirit leap new-born!

THE BANNER OF THE JEW[1]

Emma Lazarus

Wake, Israel, wake! Recall today
    The glorious Maccabean rage,
The sire heroic, hoary-gray
    His five-fold lion-lineage:
The Wise, the Elect, the Help-of-God,
The Burst-of-Spring, the Avenging Rod.[2]

From Mizpah's mountain-side they saw
    Jerusalem's empty streets, her shrine
Laid waste where Greeks profaned the Law,
    With idol and with pagan sign.
Mourners in tattered black were there,
With ashes sprinkled on their hair.

Then from the stony peak there rang
    A blast to ope the graves: down poured
The Maccabean clan, who sang
    Their battle-anthem to the Lord.
Five heroes lead, and following, see,
Ten thousand rush to victory!

Oh, for Jerusalem's trumpet now,
    To blow a blast of shattering power,
To wake the sleepers high and low,
    And rouse them to the urgent hour!
No band for vengeance—but to save,
A million naked swords should wave.

[1] From *Poems of Emma Lazarus*, Houghton, Mifflin & Co., Boston, 1899.
[2] The sons of Mattathias.

Oh, deem not dead that martial fire,
    Say not the mystic flame is spent!
With Moses' law and David's lyre,
    Your ancient strength remains unbent.
Let but an Ezra rise anew,
To lift the *Banner of the Jew!*

A rag, a mock at first—ere long,
    When men have bled and women wept,
To guard its precious folds from wrong,
    Even they who shrunk, even they who slept,
Shall leap to bless it and to save.
Strike! for the brave revere the brave!

FEAST OF DEDICATION[1]

Penina Moise

Great Arbiter of human fate,
    Whose glory ne'er decays,
To Thee alone we dedicate
    The song and soul of praise.

Thy presence Judah's host inspired,
    On danger's post to rush;
By Thee the Maccabee was fired,
    Idolatry to crush.

Amid the ruins of their land
    (In Salem's sad decline),
Stood forth a brave but scanty band
    To battle for their shrine.

In bitterness of soul they wept,
    Without the temple wall;
For weeds around its courts had crept,
    And foes its priests enthral.

Not long to vain regrets they yield,
    But for their cherished fane,
Nerved by true faith they take the field,
    And victory obtain.

[1] From *Poems by Penina Moise*, Charleston, S. C. Section of Council of Jewish Women. Nicholas G. Duffy, Printer, 1911.

But whose the power, whose the hand,
    Which thus to triumph led
That slender but heroic band,
    From which blasphemers fled?

'Twas Thine, O everlasting King
    And universal Lord!
Whose wonder still Thy servants sing,
    Whose mercies they record.

The priest of God his robe resumed,
    When Israel's warlike guide
The sanctuary's lamp refumed,
    Its altar purified.

Oh! thus shall Mercy's hand delight
    To cleanse the blemished heart,
Rekindle virtue's waning light,
    And peace and truth impart.

SOLDIERS

Elma Ehrlich Levinger

My father says the Maccabees
Were soldiers strong and fine,
Who battled for our Temple
In far-off Palestine.

They suffered cold and hunger
And wounds and death and shame;
They died on field, in prison,
To glorify God's name.

Now, too, we have our Maccabees,
Our soldiers strong and fine;
Who battle like true heroes
To give us Palestine.

Their swords are turned to ploughshares,
They fight the harvest's foes,
They sweat and toil until the dust
Has blossomed like the rose.

Halutzim, you are Maccabees,
You hold the battle-line;
Your ploughshares are the weapons
That give us Palestine!

BEFORE THE MENORAH[1]

ELMA EHRLICH LEVINGER

In the candle's rays I see
Lovely pictures beckoning me:
Judas with his shield and sword,
Pledged to battle for the Lord;
Eleazar, steadfast, strong,
'Mid the mocking heathen throng;
Hannah straight as candle's flame,
Sons who glorified her name—
Soldiers all, they smiled in pride,
Glad and unafraid they died—
God of Israel, may I be,
A soldier worthy them and Thee!

[1] *Poems for Young Judeans*, Young Judea, New York, 1925.

MATTATHIAS[1]

Elma Ehrlich Levinger

He struck the traitor to the earth,
  He raised his sword that all might see;
    His words rang like a trumpet blast:
  "All who are faithful, follow me!"
From near and far all Israel came;
  They rallied to his battle cry;
    They prayed unto the God of Peace,
  And for their Law went forth to die—
To die—and yet today they live;
  Far down the centuries flaming see
    That beacon-sword! Hear that strong cry:
  "All who are faithful, follow me!"

[1] *Poems for Young Judeans*, Young Judea, New York, 1925.

BLESSINGS FOR HANUKKAH

Jessie E. Sampter

Blessed art Thou, O God our Lord,
Who made us holy with His word,
And told us on this feast of light
To light one candle more each night.

(Because when foes about us pressed
    To crush us all with death or shame,
The Lord His priests with courage blest
To strike and give His people rest
And in the House that He loved best
    Relight our everlasting flame.)

Blest art Thou, the whole world's King,
Who did so wonderful a thing
For our own fathers true and bold
At this same time in days of old!

MY HANUKKAH CANDLES[1]

PHILIP M. RASKIN

Eight little candles,
    All in a line;
Eight little candles
    Glitter and shine.

Eight little candles—
    Each little flame,
Whispers a legend
    Of honor and fame.

Eight little candles
    Bashfully hide
The soul of a people,
    Its hope and its pride . . .

Eight little candles,
    Sparklets of gold,
Stories of battles,
    And heroes of old.

Heroes undaunted,
    And noble, and true;
Heroes who knew
    How to dare and to do;

[1] *Songs of a Wanderer*, by Philip M. Raskin, Jewish Publication Society, 1917, pp. 169–70.

Heroes who taught
    The ages to be
That man can be brave,
    And that man should be free . . .

Eight little candles,
    Look at them well,
Floods could not quench them,
    Tempests not quell.

Modest and frail
    Is their light—yet it cheers
A people in exile
    Two thousand years . . .

Eight little candles—
    Their guttering gleams
Speak to my heart
    In a language of dreams.

Light to my eye
    Is their smile and their cheer,
Sweet to my ear
    Is their whisper to hear.

"Courage, but courage,
    Maccabee's brave son,
Fight for light—
    And the battle is won."

HANUKKAH LIGHTS[1]

Morris Rosenfeld

Translated from the Yiddish

By Helena Frank

I

Little candles glistening,
Telling all those listening
Legends manifold.
Many a little story,
Tales of blood and glory,
Of the days of old.

As I watch you flicker,
As I list you bicker,
Speak the ancient dreams:
"Jew, you also took the field,
Jew, you made the foeman yield."
God, how strange it seems!

Once you knew on what you stood,
Wore the crown of nationhood,
Ruled among the rest.

[1] *Apples and Honey*, edited by Nina Salaman. Published by Doubleday, Page & Co. for Bernard G. Richards Company, 1922.

"Jew, you had a land, one time,
And an armed hand, one time—"
How it stirs the breast!

Little flickering glories,
All your little stories
Wake the sleeping pain.
In my heart it stirred and cried,
Asks, and will not be denied:
"Shall this be again?"

II

Not always have we been, as now,
A nation given to moans and sighing.
We too made would-be conquerors bow,
And sent the astonished foeman flying!

We too have rushed to face the fray,
For our belief the battle braved,
And through the swords have fought our way,
And high the flag of victory waved.

But generations come and go,
And suns have risen and set in tears,
And we are feeble now and slow,
Foregone—the might of ancient years!

The courage of another age
Is lost amid oppression dire;
Yet in our blood the heritage
Of olden Maccabaean fire.

The nations round with cruel flail
Have threshed us—yet we have not blenched.
The fire within can never fail,
In seas of blood it burns unquenched.

Oh, great and terrible our fall!
And all, except our dream, is gone.
We're weak as flies upon the wall,
But still the dream, the dream lives on!

THE MENORAH[1]

Miriam Del Banco

In the Temple softly, clearly burning,
Bathing all in floods of light divine,
Arch and post to gilded portal turning,
Doth the light of the Menorah shine.

Seven branches, quaint and queer, it beareth,
Tipped with flame and curving gracefully,
And the buds and leaves and flowers it weareth,
Are like those upon the almond tree.

Trees like this with golden branches seven,
Gild each tiny bud and leaflet frail,
Children picture in their dreams of heaven,
Or the wonders of some fairy tale.

Oil as pure and clear as crystal seeming
Feeds the flame so beautiful and bright,
Thus do thoughts of true and noble meaning
Blossom out in words of glowing light.

Holy lamp! Symbolic of our nation's
Earliest activity and strife,
Of its struggles, of its aspirations
To a purer and a better life.

[1] From *Song Service for The Feast of Lights*, Henry Berkowitz, arranged by
I. S. Moses.

Thou dost speak of God—His Revelation;
For the light of knowledge so divine,
So immortal, is His emanation—
Leads to Him and from His truth doth shine.

And as all thy branches in their twining
Toward the seventh, central light do burn,
And as this itself, in splendor shining,
To the Holy Shrine doth ever turn;

As each day that swiftly passes o'er us,
Leads unto the day that God hath blessed,
As the toil and care we see before us
End, with its approach, in peace and rest;

So should every act, each new endeavor—
The result of every passing hour,
Echo back, forever and forever,
Praise to God, His goodness and His power!

Light is knowledge and to spread its glory
Far as pen can reach or tongue can tell,
Rays of truth from science, art, or story,
Is the blessed task of Israel!

Burn thou brightly, light of the Menorah!
Let thy gleams through every shadow shine!
Cast thy loving glances on the Torah,—
Gild, illuminate its truth divine.

THE CALL[1]

H. SNOWMAN

Victor of God, O thou whose lamp of fame,
Fed with the fire of immortality
Doth swing, triumphant, 'cross the glooming sea
Of time! Preserver of thy country's name!
Judas, whose heart and arm were as a flame
To burn and burst the bands of slavery,
And rage about the witching upas tree
Of Grecian glamour and of Grecian shame!
Soul of th' undying dead! Arise and hear
The troubled cry of Israel that comes
And quivers o'er his fathers' ancient tombs,
And perishes in night of doubt and fear!
While East and West voice self-shaped destinies;
Come, great Deliverer, arise, arise!

[1] From *Poems for Young Judeans*, Young Judea, New York, 1925.

HAIL THE MACCABEES[1]

ISRAEL GOLDBERG

Hear Judea's mountains ringing,
    Hail the Maccabees!
Hosts from cleft and cave upspringing,
    Hail the Maccabees!
Shining shields and spear-heads glancing,
See the lion brood advancing.
    Hail the Maccabees!
    Hail the Maccabees!

Wild the battle din is beating,
    Hail the Maccabees!
See the tyrant hordes retreating,
    Hail the Maccabees!
Loud shall rave the tyrant-weakling,
Mad Antiochus, the Greekling.
    Hail the Maccabees!
    Hail the Maccabees!

See the bright procession wending,
    Hail the Maccabees!
Hear the songs of praise ascending,
    Hail the Maccabees!
Holy—great the dedication
Of a liberated nation:
    Hail the Maccabees!
    Hail the Maccabees!

[1] *Poems for Young Judeans*, Young Judea, New York, 1925.

HASMONEAN LIGHTS[1]

J. FICHMAN

Pure is the oil I take
My festal lights to kindle,
Lights of holiness,
Tiny lights,
Lights of God,
Reminders
Of the miracle of the Hasmoneans.

Rage winds,
Fall snows,
My wicks are aflame!
Away, evil winds,
A drop of oil remains—
My lamp still burns—
Lights of God,
Lights of the Hasmoneans.

[1] A Hebrew poem "*Nerot Hanukkah.*" From *A Hanukkah Evening*, Keren Kayemeth, Jerusalem, Jewish National Fund Publication.

HANUKKAH[1]

Cecilia G. Gerson

The hand of Time moves o'er the dial,
    And guides the seasons through the year;
It drives the sorrow from our hearts—
    Behold—the Feast of Lights is here!

The Feast of Lights—old mem'ries stir,
    And pride within our breast soars high,
We live again in ancient days,
    When Judah's glory was the cry.

We see the Maccabees of old
    Bow low within the house of God;
Where Syrian hands defiled the halls,
    Where Israel's patriarchs had trod.

Now light we tapers for their deeds;
    Awak'ning in each heart a prayer,
That we may like the Maccabees
    The glory and the valor share.

The Feast of Lights—a time when hope
    Throws off the yoke of sorrow's rod,
To wing its way above the flames
    That leap to glory and to God!

[1]*The Jewish Exponent*, April 17, 1914.

PROSE

THE MENORAH[1]

Theodor Herzl

DEEP in his soul he began to feel the need of being a Jew. His circumstances were not unsatisfactory; he enjoyed an ample income and a profession that permitted him to do whatever his heart desired. For he was an artist. His Jewish origin and the faith of his fathers had long since ceased to trouble him, when suddenly the old hatred came to the surface again in a new mob-cry. With many others he believed that this flood would shortly subside. But there was no change for the better; in fact, things went from bad to worse; and every blow, even though not aimed directly at him, struck him with fresh pain, till little by little his soul became one bleeding wound. These sorrows, buried deep in his heart and silenced there, evoked thoughts of their origin and of his Judaism, and now he did something he could not perhaps have done in the old days because he was then so alien to it—he began to love this Judaism with an intense fervor. Although in his own eyes he could not, at first, clearly justify this new yearning, it became so powerful at length that it crystallized from vague emotions into a definite idea which he must needs express. It was the conviction that there was only one solution for this *Judennot*—the return to Judaism.

When this came to the knowledge of his closest friends, similarly situated though they were, they shook their heads gravely and even feared for his reason. For how could that be a remedy which merely sharpened and intensified the evil? It seemed to him, on the other hand, that their moral distress was so acute because the Jew of to-day had lost the poise which was his father's

[1] Translated from the German by Bessie London Pouzzner, *The Menorah Journal*, I (1915), pp. 264–67.

very being. They ridiculed him for this when his back was turned—many even laughed openly in his face; yet he did not allow himself to be misled by the banalities of these people whose acuteness of judgment had never before inspired his respect, and he bore their witticisms and their sneers with equal indifference. And since, in all other respects, he acted like a man in his senses, they suffered him gradually to indulge in his infatuation, which a number of them soon began to call by a harsher term than· *idée fixe*.

He continued, however, with characteristic persistence, to develop one idea after another from his fundamental conviction. At this time he was profoundly moved by several instances of apostasy, though his pride would not permit him to betray it. As a man and as an artist of the modern school, he had, of course, acquired many non-Jewish habits and his study of the cultures of successive civilizations had left an indelible impress upon him. How was this to be reconciled with his return to Judaism? Often doubts assailed him as to the soundness of his guiding thought, his *idée maîtresse*, as a French thinker calls it. Perhaps this generation, having grown up under the influence of alien cultures, was no longer capable of that return which he had perceived to be their redemption. But the new generation would be capable of it, if it were only given the right direction early enough. He resolved, therefore, that his own children, at least, should be shown the proper path. They should be trained as Jews in their own home.

Hitherto he had permitted to pass by unobserved the holiday which the wonderful apparition of the Maccabees had illumined for thousands of years with the glow of miniature lights. Now, however, he made this holiday an opportunity to prepare something beautiful which should be forever commemorated in the minds of his children. In their young souls should be implanted

early a steadfast devotion to their ancient people. He bought
a Menorah, and when he held this nine-branched candlestick
in his hands for the first time, a strange mood came over him.
In his father's house also, the lights had once burned in his
youth, now far away, and the recollection gave him a sad and
tender feeling for home. The tradition was neither cold nor dead,
—thus it had passed through the ages, one light kindling another.
Moreover, the ancient form of the Menorah had excited his
interest. When was the primitive structure of this candlestick
fashioned? Clearly the design was suggested by the tree—in
the center the sturdy trunk, on right and left four branches, one
below the other, in one plane, and all of equal height. A later
symbolism brought with it the ninth branch, which projects in
front and functions as a servant. What mystery had the generations which followed one another read into this form of art, at
once so simple and natural? And our artist wondered to himself
if it were not possible to animate again the withered form of
the Menorah, to water its roots, as one would a tree. The mere
sound of the name, which he now pronounced every evening to
his children, gave him great pleasure. There was a lovable ring
to the word when it came from the lips of little children.

On the first night the candle was lit and the origin of the
holiday explained. The wonderful incident of the lights that
strangely remained burning so long, the story of the return from
the Babylonian exile, the second Temple, the Maccabees—our
friend told his children all he knew. It was not very much, to
be sure, but it served. When the second candle was lit, they
repeated what he had told them, and though it had all been
learned from him, it seemed to him quite new and beautiful.
In the days that followed he waited keenly for the evenings,
which became ever brighter. Candle after candle stood in the
Menorah, and the father mused on the little candles with his

children, till at length his reflections became too deep to be uttered before them.

When he had resolved to return to his people and to make open acknowledgment of his return, he had only thought he would be doing the honorable and rational thing. But he had never dreamed that he would find in it a gratification of his yearning for the beautiful. Yet nothing less was his good fortune. The Menorah with its many lights became a thing of beauty to inspire lofty thought. So, with his practiced hand, he drew a plan for a Menorah to present to his children the following year. He made free use of the motif of the right branching arms projecting right and left in one plane from the central stem. He did not hold himself bound by the rigid traditional form, but created directly from nature, unconcerned by other symbolisms also seeking expression. He was on the search for living beauty. Yet, though he gave the withered branch new life, he conformed to the law, to the gentle·dignity of its being. It was a tree with slender branches; its ends were moulded into flower calyxes which would hold the lights.

The week passed with this absorbing labor. Then came the eighth day, when the whole row burns, even the faithful ninth, the servant, which on other nights is used only for the lighting of the others. A great splendor streamed from the Menorah. The children's eyes glistened. But for our friend all this was the symbol of the enkindling of a nation. When there is but one light, all is still dark, and the solitary light looks melancholy. Soon it finds one companion, then another, and another. The darkness must retreat. The light comes first to the young and the poor—then others join them who love Justice, Truth, Liberty, Progress, Humanity, and Beauty. When all the candles burn, then we must all stand and rejoice over the achievements. And no office can be more blessed than that of a Servant of the Light.

THE MARTYRED MOTHER[1]

GRACE AGUILAR

DURING the persecution under Antiochus Epiphanes, the sufferings of the women of Israel must have been as fearful as their constancy and fidelity were powerful proofs of the perfect adaptation of the Law of the Eternal to their temporal and spiritual wants. Never could a religion which made them soul-less slaves have become so dear, so part of their very hearts, that it was easier to endure torture, and slavery, and death, rather than depart from it themselves, or refuse its privileges to their infant sons. Eighty thousand persons, men, women and children, slain in the forcible entrance of Antiochus within Jerusalem, and forty thousand of both sexes sold into slavery was the horrible preface to the misery which followed. Every observance of the law, from the keeping of the Sabbath and the covenant of Abraham, to the minutest form, was made a capital offence. Yet, in spite of the scenes of horror so continually recurring, the very relation of which must now make every female heart shrink and quiver—yet were there female martyrs baring their breast to the murderous knife, rather than bow down to the idol, or touch forbidden food. Women, young, meek, tender, performed with their own hands the Covenant of Abraham upon their sons, because none else would so dare the tyrant's wrath; and with their infants (for whose immortal souls they had thus incurred the rage of man) suspended around their necks, received death by being flung from the battlements of the Temple into the deep vale below; others were hung, and

---

[1] *Women of Israel*, vol. II, by Grace Aguilar, R. Groombridge, London, 1845.

cruelties too awful to relate practiced upon others. Yet no
woman's spirit failed; and what must have been their attach-
ment to their holy religion, what their sense of its responsibility,
and its immortal reward, what their horror of abandoning it
themselves and cutting off their sons from its sainted privileges,
to incur martyrdoms like these? It is useless to argue that
persecution always creates martyrs, as opposition kindles constancy. The religion degrading or brutalizing woman never yet
had martyrs.

Where, in the vast tomes of history, sacred or profane, shall
we find a deed more heroic, a fortitude more sublime, than is
recorded of Hannah, the Hebrew mother, during the persecution
of Antiochus?

Great emergencies will often create great characters; but in
the narrative which we have been considering, we read something more in the character of the Hebrew mother than even
the heroism which she displayed. By her close connection with
her sons, in being brought before the tyrant, and condemned
to share their fate, it is clear that though a woman in Israel,
her influence must have been supposed of some consequence.
That her sons owed their all to her, even to their education,
and that her influence on them was very great, we read alike in
her own words, and in the appeal of the king to her, to save by
her exhortations her youngest born. And in the calm courage,
the noble words of each of her sons, we learn the education she
had given. They had probably been amongst the valiant, though
unsuccessful defenders of their land; amongst the faithful few,
who, in the very face of the persecutor, dared to obey the law
of Moses, and refused every effort to turn them from their God.
Would this patriotism, this devotedness, have come at the
moment needed, had it not been taught, infused from earliest
boyhood—by example as well as precept? A mother in Israel

could be herself no warrior, but she could raise up warriors—
she could be no priest, but she could create priests—she could
not face the battle's front, or drive the idolatrous invader from
God's Holy Land—she could not stem the torrent of persecution, and of torture; but she could raise up those who would
seek the one, and, by unshrinking death, bear witness to the
fruitless efforts of the other; and it was these things this heroic
mother did. She had trained up her boys in that faithfulness,
that constancy, which could only spring from virtue.

.   .   .

That mother's lessons may still be to us as guidance—may
teach us how we should instruct our children, so as to provide
them against the arrows of misfortune, which, ere life close,
may assail them, either through bodily affliction or mental woe.
Religion, real spiritual religion, *will not* find resting in the human
heart unless infused—unless made the first great object in childhood; not to affect with gloom, but inexpressibly to deepen the
enjoyment and hilarity of youth. Affliction may do the work
for us in riper years, and bring the soul to its God—but Oh! it
is a fearful thing, when we wait for affliction to teach us our God
—when sorrow must be sent to bring us to Him.

MESSENGERS AT MODIN[1]

EMILY SOLIS-COHEN, JR.

NOW, all this time the officers of the king went throughout
the land, and set up groves and chapels of idols, and
builded idol-altars in all the cities of Judah. So on a day they
came to Modin.

On the morning following the arrival of the Greeks, a reluc-
tant crowd gathered in the market place, for such was the order
of Apelles, the king's captain, and they feared to risk his
displeasure.

A heap of mud and stones had been thrown up on a slight
elevation to serve as an altar to Zeus, whose image looked
down on it. The Greeks were making ready for the sacrifice,
and the Jews watched the preparations with sullen curiosity.

At the furthest edge of the throng stood the old men, as if
in fear of defilement. Few words fell from their stern-set lips.
Their eyes, filled with defiant scorn for the Greeks, softened to
pitying reproach as they rested on the children edging nearer
and nearer to the altar. The little ones seemed to feel the dis-
approval. They paused, and looked at one another in questioning
alarm. The daring, after the first hesitation, advanced in their
play closer to the strangers, upon whom their round eyes rested
in curious surprise; but if a soldier stopped his work to smile
at them, they fled laughing in mock fear to the shelter of their
mothers' skirts, whence their fascinated gaze peered back at
the men in armor.

---

[1] From "The Sacrifice at Modin" in *David the Giant Killer and Other Tales
of Grandma Lopez*, by Emily Solis-Cohen, Jr. Philadelphia. The Jewish
Publication Society of America, 1908.

"Look, look!" suddenly piped a childish treble. "Mother, Grandfather, see! They're sweeping the ground before the stones with myrtle boughs."

"God speed the day that sweeps them from the land!"

The crowd turned to the speaker in half-deprecating admiration. With head thrown back and threatening arm uplifted stood the white-haired man. All the agony of tortured pride so long pent up in his torn heart burned in his eyes. Only for a moment the flame smoldered, then his arm dropped inert to his side. Silence again held sway.

Not so was it among the younger men. At last indignant tongues were loosed. Stories of cruel persecutions sped from angry lip to lip. More tightly did wan-faced mothers clasp the trusting arms about their necks, at the thought of those other mothers hurled from the battlements, their dead babes in their embrace. Husbands, white to the lips, threw protecting arms about wives, as the tale was repeated of the brave women who went to the torture first, that the fainting hearts of men might be made strong. Sons clenched their eager hands, and their pleading gaze seemed to beg permission to strike, ere the fate of Eleazar should be that of their own sires. For that dauntless old man had suffered death by torment rather than save his life by making mock of the holy laws of God, in pretending to eat the flesh of swine . . .

There was a stir in the throng, and a travel-stained man clad in sackcloth stood in the midst of them.

"Woe. woe, woe!" broke from his ashen lips.

None questioned him, for fear of his reply.

The Greeks looked up from their toil.

He caught the look. He raised imploring hands to heaven. "How long, O Lord, how long!"

"Vengeance is Mine, saith the Lord, I will requite," came the calm tones of Mattathias.

"Vengeance!" He caught the word almost before it was uttered. "Vengeance for the mother and her seven sons!"

The mother and her seven sons!

What new horror was this? An appalling stillness fell over the place. Children ceased to play; babes whimpered in indefinable fear. The messenger of ill tidings spoke:

"A woman with her seven lads was taken before the king. The flesh of swine was set before them. They were bidden eat. But one of them that spake first said: 'What wouldst thou ask or learn of us? We are ready to die rather than trangress the law of our fathers.' In a rage the king had pans and caldron heated."

A groan swept the crowd. No need of words to paint the death-agony of that boy.

"The others—what of them?"

"They exhorted one another and the mother to die manfully, comforting themselves, 'The Lord God looketh upon us.' "

"I almost doubt it," sobbed a woman's voice.

"Nay, say not so. When the first was dead, they brought the second, and asked him, 'Wilt thou eat before thou art punished throughout every member of thy body?' "

"No!" The swaying mob took the answer from the speaker's mouth.

"When he was at the last gasp, he cried unto the king, 'Thou, like a fury, takest us out of this present life, but the King of the world shall raise us up, who have died for His laws, to everlasting life.' So they all met death with hearts full of trust. And the mother was brave above them all, for she held back her tears and ever encouraged them to die.

"Now, the seventh son was so fair to look upon, that the heart of the king relented, and he said, 'Do thou but taste of this meat, and I, the king of kings and lord of lords, will make thee rich with untold wealth.' The heart of the mother stopped an instant."

"How could she doubt him, her son?" exclaimed a woman, with a fond glance at the comely lad at her side.

"Upon his refusal, the king said: 'Thy brothers have paid the penalty of disobedience. An thou doest my command, I shall take thee for the king's friend, and give into thy hand great matters.' "

The crowd could almost see the reassuring look the lad gave his anxious mother, as the messenger repeated his reply: " 'I will not obey the king's commandment, but I will obey the commandment of the law that the Lord gave our fathers by the hand of Moses.' "

A sigh of relief went up from the breasts of the old men, and the young men straightened proudly.

"Then Antiochus called the woman near, and bade her counsel her son to take pity upon her and save his life."

"She bade him remain firm," came a mother's exultant cry.

"Yea. She said unto him: 'Verily, my son, have pity on me who bare thee, and nourished thee, and brought thee up unto this age. I beseech thee, my son, look upon the heaven and upon the earth and all that is therein, and consider that God made them of things that were not. And so mankind was made likewise. Fear not, then, this tormentor, but, being worthy of thy brethren, take thy death that I may receive thee again in mercy with thy brethren.' "

"With women like that in Israel," cried Judah, "shall we men stand by in craven fear and content ourselves by saying that God has forsaken His people?"

A wild murmur of protest swept through the crowd, while the old men shook their heads, and muttered imprecations in their beards, and here and there rose cries of "Vengeance! Vengeance!"

The Greeks caught the sounds, and perceived the angry gestures. "Shall we not order yon babbler from the place?" said the lieutenant. "Meseems he counsels mutiny."

"What!" chided their leader, "are ye Greeks, and afraid of words?"

So the torrent of passionate speech poured on.

"Thus said the lad unto Antiochus: 'Thou, O godless man, of all others most wicked, be not lifted up without a cause, nor puffed up with uncertain hopes, lifting up thy hand against the servants of God. For our brethren who have suffered a short pain are dead under God's covenant of everlasting life, but thou, through the judgment of God, shalt receive a just punishment for thy pride.' "

"Aye, and right speedily!" breathed the men who heard.

Again were the Greeks alarmed. "We like not the look of that mob," said the spokesman. "We would that our Lord Apelles sacrificed at once, that we may view the omens."

"Ye are Greek women, not Greeks," taunted Apelles.

With broken voice the messenger of woe spoke on, "Last of all, after the sons, the mother died."

An anguished sob bowed the throng, but not a word was spoken. Hands groped for missing weapons.

THE HANUKKAH LIGHTS[1]

EVERYBODY loved the Hanukkah lights. Daddy loved them. He said a *berakah*, a "Thank you God for them," and Mother and Daniel said, "Amen."

The *Shammash* candle—you know, the candle Daddy lights the other candles with—it loved the Hanukkah lights, too. It kissed them with its flame. It sang to them.

Rise on tip toe,
Lift your light
Up and up and up!
Flicker, flicker,
Shine and shine,
It's Hanukkah tonight.

Mother sang songs about the Hanukkah lights. Baby Judith clapped her hands to show she loved them, too.

Even the wind loved the shining little flames. It crept in through a crack in the window. It called to each of them.

Sway and dance,
Dance, little light;
Up and up and up!
Whirl and flicker,
Flicker and whirl:
It's Hanukkah tonight.

And the lights rose on tiptoe and swayed and danced.

Once a light laughed too, a tiny sputtery laugh. It laughed until it cried. Big wax tears slid down its cheek, and Daniel

[1] From *What Danny Did*, by Sadie Rose Weilerstein, Bloch Pub. Co., 1932, p. 53.

293

cried, "Quick, Daddy! Shut the window tight, or the candle
will cry itself away."

Then Daniel, too, sang a little song to the lights. He made
it up out of his own head, but Mother and Daddy helped.

> Hanukkah light, we love you so,
> Do be careful, or out you'll go.
> > Slow and steady,
> > Steady and slow!
> We're not ready to let you go.
> Tomorrow I'll sit and watch your brother,
> And next to him there'll be another.
> Then there'll be three, four, five, six, seven.
> I wish that there might be eleven;
> Last, eight bright candles in a row.
> Hanukkah lights, I love you so.

THE RESCUE OF THE SAGE[1]

Isaac Mayer Wise

"AWAKE, awake! Judah, my beloved son! Again the sun rises over the mountains of Israel, and the daughter of Zion still lies in chains." So Miriam, the wife of Mattathias, woke all her sons every morning with the rising of the sun. Judah rose and beating his breast with his right hand he invoked the Deity to hear his vow. "If I forget thee, O Jerusalem, may my right hand forget me," said he. "Here I again vow not to taste of the cup of joy until shame and subjection be banished from the house of Israel." Then he clasped his sword and swung it over his head. "Again I consecrate this sword to the liberty and independence of my people! . . ."

The hoary priest Mattathias and his five sons repeated this vow every morning even after Antiochus Epiphanes, the despot of Syria, attempted to exterminate the religion and nationality of Israel, and committed the most intolerable atrocities to achieve a complete victory over the brave and bold defenders of Israel's heritage.

. . .

The Tower of the Furnaces at the western extremity of the city, only one hundred yards distant from Golgotha, was the prison of Jose ben Joezer. The heavy gates of that prison were opened, the light of the torches fell into the cell which the old prince occupied. Apollonius and Menelaus entered. Alcymos with his warriors guarded the door. Jose rose from his couch. His countenance was calm, his looks were bright, his attitude

[1] From Chapters I and VI of *The First of the Maccabees, a Historical Novel,* by Rev. Dr. I. M. Wise.

straight and firm "In the name of God I receive you," he said. "We came in the name of Jupiter and the rest of the immortal gods," said Apollonius, "to communicate to you the will of our illustrious master, Antiochus Epiphanes, king of all Syria and Persia, the favorite of the gods and especially of Mars and Venus."

Jose made no reply and Apollonius continued. "Your cause was laid before our illustrious master and after consultation with the gods, prayer and sacrifice, it was revealed to him, that you, Jose ben Joezer of Zeredah, formerly prince of the Sanhedrin of Jerusalem, are guilty of blasphemy against the immortal gods, and of high treason against your king. Therefore you shall be beheaded this night, that your blood appease the offended deities."

"To what purpose so many words?" Jose asked, calmly, not a feature of his countenance being the least changed. "I am prepared to die for the sacred cause of my God and my people."

"If your God is so mighty, why does He not help His devout servant?" Apollonius asked scornfully.

"He has helped and He will help, for He is a God of truth and mercy," said Jose solemnly. "He never forsakes Israel entirely. You may stride over our corpses, or wade in our blood to short-lived victory; but the day of revenge and recompense will come, Israel will be redeemed and its sacred cause will be triumphant; for their redeemer is strong, the Lord of Hosts is His name. As for me, I am old and gray, ripe for death.—A few days sooner or later, in this or that manner, is immaterial to me. It is material to me that I seal the truth of my people with my blood, and this blood will inspire many a heart in Israel to live and die for the sacred cause of my people."

"I say you are a hoary and obstinate criminal who drags his own people into nameless misery," said Apollonius. "The blood that will be shed, the tears that will flow, and the affliction that will befall the surviving, fall hot and burning on your head.

For if you would yield to the king's command, full pardon would be granted you, and my gracious king nominates you priest of Apollo. This would certainly convince many a stubborn mind that it is time to part with the old prejudices, the inveterate superstitions, the obstinacy and hardness of heart characterizing your people. Thus many a precious life would be saved, many a scene of horror spared, and many a happy year won."

"At the expense of truth, divine truth, manliness, justice and liberty? No! Never!" Jose exclaimed, with youthful fire. "Let our blood crimson the ruin of our destroyed cities and the soil of our holy land; let our sucklings be slaughtered on the bosoms of their helpless mothers, and the shrieks of horror and woe silence the roar of the foaming breakers dashing against our rocks—yet the surviving sons of Israel shall bravely rally around the banner of the Lord of Hosts; yet there shall be myriads in Israel whose knees were not bent before a lie, who submitted not to cruel despotism. I will set them the example that death is not the greatest evil; slavery is. And the lowest slave is he who sacrifices truth, justice, and liberty, because his life is in jeopardy. Jose ben Joezer knows how to die contented when he can no longer live a free man, a son of Israel."

Both men looked amazed upon the old Hebrew, and it was a good while ere they could speak again. Then Menelaus said in a subdued tone: "Jose ben Joezer, if you believe one man of those who oppose the will of the king will be spared, you are grievously mistaken. The king determined firmly upon exterminating either our race or our religion, laws and nationality, and the king's power is immense, thrice sufficient to uproot our mountains, and slay every living creature in this country. Why should we all die, and no scion and no trace be left of Israel? God gave us laws to live and not to die with. If it is His will that we should obey them, He will again perform miracles for us, as in days of yore. But if dead we are, all of us, every hope is gone forever.—'Not the dead will praise the Lord, nor all those who descend to silence.' Let us yield and live, and may God in future do as is His will."

"Whoever yields is dead, and whoever dies a man, lives. The wicked are dead while they yet appear to live, and the righteous live while they appear to slumber in the embrace of death," said Jose, solemnly.—"Hear me, man of cowardish peace! I despise the hypocrite and the coward, infinitely more than the wicked man and the violent man. If it pleases God to transport us all from the earthly to the heavenly Jerusalem, we will worship Him in the everlasting temple of heavenly fire, where Seraphim and Cherubim sing His praise, and no high priest is guilty of apostasy. But the blood of a slain nation will cry aloud to the ear of humanity. When the clouds of violence and prejudice will be dispersed, nations will come, open our graves, examine our wounds, inquire into the cause of our death, and bless our bones. Truth will resurrect from our graves as the vapor rises from the sea, to refresh the nations with the heavenly shower of divine grace, and Israel will live in the grateful hearts of redeemed nations. Every blade of grass that grows on our graves will be a trumpet of resurrection to suffering humanity. But the wicked will perish and their names will be a curse and an abomination. We live and die for sacred truth, for Israel and all nations, all the children of God. Why do you hesitate? Why do you waste words? I am prepared to die with my God and my faith. I go home. Call your executioners; I am ready for them."

Jose observed an obstinate silence notwithstanding the promises and threats of Apollonius and Menelaus. They saw that words were wasted in vain; Apollonius called Alcymos and delivered the prisoner to his care. The back door of the tower was opened and Jose was led forth to Golgotha to be beheaded. It was a dark and stormy night, not a star was visible in the skies. The men, to prevent excitement, proceeded in the dark to execute a murderous king's edict. Alcymos went by the side of Jose and scorned his foolish confidence in God. "It is too dark tonight," he sneered, "your old God cannot see you. The young gods of Greece and Syria can see better. You had better call on them. They might help you yet."

"The everlasting God will punish thee for this blaspheming," said Jose. Alcymos continued teasing and insulting the old man, and disturbing him in his last prayers. Meanwhile the foot of Golgotha was reached. Jose could not walk as fast as his guards, and Alcymos urged, "Go faster, old sinner, time enough for you to rest up there."

Jose obeyed without a murmur. Faster he proceeded to the scaffold, and Alcymos scorned him again. "If you go so fast, your God cannot reach you; He is old and stiff."

At this moment two strong arms seized the amazed Alcymos and before he could think of resistance he was laid on the ground, a man knelt upon him, and holding the point of a dagger over his heart, threatened: "One sound and I will make an end of thy wicked life." Jose saw with amazement that all the Syrian soldiers surrounding him were suddenly seized, disarmed, and tied together before they had time to make use of their arms. It was the work of a moment. Not the least noise was made. The patriots, favored by the darkness of the night and the numerous Palm trees, lay in wait on both sides of the road, and suddenly and unexpectedly fell on Alcymos and his men, disarmed them and tied them together.

"You are rescued, my glorious prince," Jonathan exclaimed, joyfully, "and all the armies of Syria shall not wrest you from our hands.—Mount your asses," he commanded his men. "Drive

the captives before you as fast as possible. Keep one stadion
from the city and follow me to Mizpah. We must reach Mizpah
before they suspect anything in Jerusalem. We are safe in
Mizpah."

An ass was brought to Jose; he mounted, and the party hastily
proceeded. "It is Jonathan!" Alcymos exclaimed. "Be dumb,
or thou art a dead man!" Jonathan commanded, and silence was
restored. Jose clasped the hand of Jonathan, and a little louder
than a whisper he exclaimed: "May God bless thee, noble
Asmonean."

> "Arms, arms! he cries: the sword, and shield prepare,
> And send the willing chief, renewed to war:
> This is no mortal work, no cure of mine,
> Nor art's effect, but done by hands divine."
>
> Virgil, Aen. XII.

THE LIGHT THAT NEVER FAILED[1]

Elma Ehrlich Levinger

"FATHER," pleaded Bennie, "please let me light it just once."
Mr. Roth shook his head. "Not today, Bennie. We have
no candles small enough for the menorah; besides, you must not
light the candles until the first night of Hanukkah."

Bennie pouted a little. When one is a boy of five, living on a
farm three miles away from his nearest playmate, it is hard
to wait patiently for a new privilege. And until this year Bennie's
father had not considered him old enough to light the Hanukkah lights and say the blessing. "How long must I wait till
Hanukkah?" he asked with an impatient wriggle, as Mr. Roth
replaced the tin menorah he had shown him on the top shelf
of the cupboard.

"Just two weeks," Mr. Roth consoled his son. "Suppose we
begin to learn the blessing now?"

Bennie nodded eagerly and a few moments later his mother,
entering the kitchen, smiled to hear him repeating: "*Boruch
atto—boruch atto—boruch atto Adonoi*—and what's the next word,
papa?" She put away the jar of butter she had brought up
from the cellar, and stood for a moment behind Bennie's chair,
her hand resting on his curly head.

"He learns easily, doesn't he?" she said a little wistfully.
"When he is a little older perhaps he can go to Hebrew school
like his cousins in New York." She sighed, her eyes wandering
through the window over the vast white fields. "It is lonely
out here, away from all Jews," she murmured half to herself.

[1] From *Jewish Holyday Stories*, Bloch Publishing Co., Inc., New York, 1932.

Her husband nodded, for he understood how she missed her family and all the neighbors in the crowded Jewish quarter where she had lived until her marriage. He realized, too, how hard she found her many farm duties, how easily she became tired these days, when the heavy snowdrifts seemed to shut them off from the outer world and even the postman failed to appear down the unbroken road, bringing their daily Jewish paper and an occasional letter in his bag. But Morris Roth feared to return to the city, for the doctor had warned him that he would never be well so long as he worked in a crowded tailor shop. His brother had lent him enough money to travel west to take up a claim in Dakota; if he lived on the land just a little longer, the government would give it to him for his own, and there would be a secure home for Bennie and his mother. He had learned to love his new free life in the great out-of-doors; he felt he could not bear to go back to the city again; but he grew worried when he noticed how pale and thin his wife had grown, how often she spoke longingly of home. "When I have a little more saved, I will send her back for a visit," he told himself. "Perhaps she can take Bennie with her. If only her cough would be better and she would not get so tired!"

On this bleak December afternoon, Mr. Roth renewed the same old promise to himself as he taught Bennie the blessing for the Hanukkah lights. And yet that evening, as his wife moved about the little kitchen putting the supper dishes away, there was such a fine color in her cheeks and her eyes were so bright that Mr. Roth felt he had been needlessly anxious. But a week later she complained of pains in her chest and throat, and when Bennie wriggled because she dressed him so slowly, she allowed him to finish buttoning his shoes for himself. Bennie was thunder-struck; he was so used to having his mother pet and spoil him that now he just sat on the edge of the bed with his mouth wide-open, too astonished even to protest when his mother lay back on the pillows and said she was too tired to dress him. When Mr. Roth came in from milking, she tried to laugh away her faintness, but he was badly frightened. He dressed Bennie as well as he could and awkwardly set the table for breakfast and heated some coffee. He would not allow Mrs. Roth to get up again, although he promised not to go for the doctor if she felt any better the next day.

The next morning Mrs. Roth tried to drag herself about the house, but by noon she was back in bed again, looking so white and weak that even Bennie was frightened. He stood watching his father with great round eyes as Mr. Roth pulled on his heavy boots and sweater, and moved nervously about the kitchen preparing for a trip to town ten miles away. Bennie went to the window and scratched a little hole in the frosted pane.

"Papa," he announced, "you can't go to town today. There aren't any roads. Its all white and smooth just like a table cloth."

Mr. Roth's lips tightened. "I've got to make a road, Bennie boy," he said simply. "I'll take a shovel along and dig my way through." He followed Bennie to the window and looked from the white prairies to the grey clouds overhead with troubled eyes. "If the blizzard only holds off a little while longer," he muttered more to himself than to Bennie, "I'll get the doctor back here. But if we're held up in the snow—"

"Is mama very sick?" Bennie asked him.

"I'm afraid so." His father pulled on his heavy fur mittens. "So you must be a very good boy and take care of her until I get back. Don't worry her, and if she doesn't want to talk to you, just let her rest. I'll bring you some candy from town and," with sudden inspiration, "if you're a good boy all afternoon, I'll let you light the candles and say the blessing tonight."

Bennie clapped his hands gleefully. "Tonight's Hanukkah, tonight's Hanukkah," he chanted shrilly. *"Boruch atto Adonoi* —please hear me say the blessing before you go, papa." But his father kissed him hastily and started for the door. "Tonight, when you light the candles," he promised. "But now I must go for the doctor right away."

Feeling strangely frightened, although he hardly knew why, Bennie followed his father to the bedroom, where his mother lay tossing upon the bed. Her face was flushed and she threw her head about on the pillow. But she tried to smile when she saw that Bennie drew back afraid.

"It's just my throat," she managed to whisper. "I don't seem able to breathe. But I'll get along all right till you come back," she ended bravely. "Just leave something on the table for Bennie's supper. And, Bennie, please don't come in and bother mama for a little while. Play out in the kitchen and let her sleep."

A few moments later Bennie stood in the middle of the kitchen, feeling very much alone. The rapidly rising wind howled and blustered, until the frail little house seemed to shake before it; then the howling would cease for a moment and all would grow so quiet that it seemed as though he were the only living person in the world. The little fellow wanted to run to his mother, as he always did, for comfort; then he remembered that he was a big boy now, big enough to take care of mother and the farm, when father was away. He squared his shoulders resolutely, as he went to the cupboard for his box of toys.

There were only a few playthings; the tin soldiers his Aunt Minna had sent him for his birthday, a rubber ball which had refused to bounce properly after he had pricked it with a pin, a box of dominoes, excellent for building forts for his soldiers, and several picture books. For a while he amused himself turning the pages and murmuring the stories his mother had told him so often that he knew them by heart. There were Golden-Locks in a little blue dress and red Sunbonnet driven home by three angry bears; on the next page Cinderella rode to the ball behind six prancing white horses, and here was Jack climbing the beanstalk which grew beside his mother's cottage door. Best of all were the pictures in the largest story book, pictures of a little boy named Joseph, with a kind father and wicked brothers, who stole his pretty coat and threw him into a cave. Bennie studied the pictures with satisfaction, especially the one of Joseph sitting in a big chair with a great many people fanning him or bowing before him. But soon he found that it was growing too dark to see the pictures distinctly; the short December day had deepened into twilight and the room was gray with misty lights, while the great stove in the corner cast queer flickering shadows on the walls.

The boy walked to the window to raise the blinds and again scratched a deep hole in the frosty pane. It was snowing hard, great, white flakes that whirled and danced like bits of torn paper. Bennie shivered a little as he hoped his father would be home soon; he knew Daddy was a big, strong man, but it was not good to think of him out there in the darkness. He wondered what time it was, anyhow. There was a clock in the bedroom, and if mother was awake she would be glad to tell, he reasoned. He stole softly to her bed. In the uncertain light he could see that her eyes were closed; she seemed to be asleep, but she made queer sounds like some one crying and her breast rose and fell jerkily beneath the blankets.

Bennie tiptoed back into the kitchen, curled himself up on the sofa and wondered what to do next. He had been taught not to be afraid of the dark, but he did not want to go on looking at his picture books and playing with his soldiers. Besides, he was beginning to feel hungry, and he was sure he wouldn't enjoy the supper of bread and milk and pie father had left on the table, if he had to eat it in the dark. But ever since he could remember, both father and mother had forbidden him to light the lamps. He wondered whether they would care tonight, when he was such a big boy, old enough to light the Hanukkah candles.

Suddenly he jumped to his feet. Hadn't father said, just before he left, that tonight was Hannukah! Then he must light his candles right away, for hadn't father explained to him, while learning the blessing, that he must kindle the first yellow taper and say the strange Hebrew words just as soon as it got dark on the first night of Hanukkah? Bennie didn't understand just why he wasn't allowed to light the lamps, but would be permitted to light the Hanukkah candles; nor did he consider how worried his parents would be to have him striking matches unless they stood near to watch him. It was enough for him that it was Hanukkah at last and that he knew the difficult blessing, every word of it. Why, he wouldn't have to awaken poor mother to help him, which relieved him a good deal, as he felt somehow that she would get well quicker if she were allowed to sleep as long as she pleased. But how could he reach the menorah father had put away on the very top shelf, next to the candlesticks for *Shabbas*? Bennie was not easily daunted. Even if he couldn't use the menorah the first night, he was determined not to be cheated out of lighting the very first candle tonight. He couldn't reach the box of little yellow tapers that father had put away with the menorah, but on the lowest shelf he found just what he wanted—an old tin candlestick with a half-burned candle which mother sometimes used when she went down into the cellar, and didn't care to bother with a lamp.

Mrs. Roth always kept the box of matches well out of the reach of Bennie's active fingers, so he didn't trouble himself to look for them. Taking the candle he opened the stove door and thrust it into the flames. Walking very carefully, for he felt mother might consider what he was doing almost as naughty as playing with fire, he put the candle back into the holder and set it upon the window sill. Then, standing very straight, he slowly repeated the Hebrew benediction: *"Boruch atto Adonoi Elohenu Melech ho-olom asher kiddeshonu bemitzvosov vetsivonu lehadlik ner shel Hanukkoh."*

Sitting on the floor in the warm patch of light cast by the stove, Bennie ate his supper, looking proudly all the while at his candle, burning fine and straight in the window. When the dishes were all empty, he went to the window pane and amused himself by scraping off the frost with the kitchen knife. He wanted to see his candle throwing a pretty ribbon of light on the snow; he knew it would look nice, for he remembered how pretty the lamp in the kitchen window had appeared to him one night when they had come from town and had seen it shining as they drove up the hill. He wanted his candle to shine a long ways—just like a lamp—and, bringing out an old lantern which his father had once given him to play with, he set the light within it and again placed it before the carefully scraped pane. Then he sat down on the window sill, watching the snow flurries and wishing for father to come home.

Father came at last, bringing with him a tall, bearded man who carried a little black satchel and hurried into mother's room without saying a word. Father went after him and for a long time Bennie sat trembling beside his Hanukkah light, wondering what it was all about. After a very little while, although it seemed to Bennie that he had waited all night, father came back into the kitchen and took the little fellow in his arms. Bennie saw that he was crying and it frightened him, for he had never seen his father cry before.

"Is mama very sick?" he asked.

"The doctor says she will get well," answered Mr. Roth, and his voice trembled. "You can't understand it all, Bennie boy, but there was something bad in her throat," and he added something about diphtheria, which meant nothing to Bennie, who just considered it one of the big words grown-up people were always using to confuse him. "But the doctor has just burned it all out and she will get well. Only if we hadn't come in time—" He stopped and shuddered. "Bennie, if you hadn't put your light in the window we might have been an hour later getting here and then the doctor says it would have been too late. Our lanterns went out at the top of the hill and the snow was so blinding that we might have floundered about half the night before we found the house. But your little candle helped us find the way."

"I said the blessing all right," Bennie told his father, "but was it all right not to use the regular menorah and a yellow candle?" he ended anxiously.

"You did just the right thing," his father assured him.

But Bennie was not satisfied. "Please, papa," he pleaded, "please get down the yellow candle and let me light it and say the Hebrew for you. Please!"

Smiling a little uncertainly, Mr. Roth brought down the tin menorah and the box of yellow tapers. He gave Bennie one for the *Shammash*, explaining that it was to light the others, and watched him with the same twisted smile as the child adjusted and lit the first candle. "*Boruch atto Adonoi*," began Bennie proudly, and he wondered why his father hid his face in his hands and started to cry all over again.

PART III

FOR THE YOUNG

INTRODUCTION

The covers of The Hanukkah Book have been spread apart
to admit stories for the little ones — for children in the nursery,
for children growing into their teens, for all who like to hear
Mother read tales from the long ago.

These stories have been written especially for this Book.

Two of them set forth the simple and eternal truth of
Hanukkah, the truth which, generation after generation, en-
kindles in Israel's children the resolve not to depart from the
way of their fathers, "either to the right hand or to the left."
Perhaps Mother will sketch in the historical background to
enhance these tales of the Maccabees.

A SONG OF ALWAYS

Efraim Rosenzweig

The Temple is clean,
    The lamp burns bright;
Judah the leader,
    Has started the light.

The sun shines by day,
    And dark is the night;
But always and always
    The lamp burns bright.

RUTH SHINES THE MENORAH[1]

Sadie R. Weilerstein

HANUKKAH was coming. Ruthie climbed on a chair and took the Menorah down from the shelf. The Menorah was like a little tree, a golden tree with golden branches. There were one, two, three, four, five, six, seven, eight branches and a high-up branch besides.

"I will clean the Menorah; I will make it shining bright," Ruthie said. She got a woolly cloth. "First I will clean the high-up branch. It is for the *Shammash* candle."

> Rub, rub, rub!
> You will light the others.
> Rub, rub, rub!
> All the candles brothers.

Next she shined the first little branch. "You are for the first Hanukkah light," she said.

Rub, rub, rub! She shined the second branch. "We will need *two* branches on the second night," she said. "We will need the first branch and we will need you."

She rubbed the third branch and the fourth the fifth and the sixth and the seventh and the eighth. Then off she went to Mother.

"See, Mother," said Ruth. "The Menorah is all ready for the Hanukkah candles."

[1] For the pre-school child.

"How bright you have made it," said Mother. "It is like a mirror. Look inside it, Ruthie."

Ruth looked into the Menorah and what do you suppose she saw? She saw a little girl. The little girl looked up at her. Her teeth were white and her eyes were crinkly. She was laughing.

"I wonder what the little girl's name is?" said Mother.

"Her name is Ruthie," laughed Ruth. "She is laughing because Hanukkah is coming. She thinks Hanukkah is a *good* holiday. She is going to light the first Hanukkah light tonight."

DREIDEL SONG

Efraim Rosenzweig

Twirl about, dance about,
 Spin, spin, spin!
Turn, Dreidel, turn —
 Time to begin!

Soon it is Hanukkah —
 Fast, Dreidel, fast!
For you will lie still
 When Hanukkah's past.

HOW RUTH COUNTED THE HANUKKAH CANDLES[1]

Sadie R. Weilerstein

ONCE there was a little girl whose name was Ruth. "You are a big girl now," her Daddy said. "You are four years old and can count to ten. Do you think you are big enough to take care of the Hanukkah candles?"

"All by myself?" asked Ruthie.

"All by yourself," said Daddy.

He put the box of little yellow candles in Ruth's hand. How proud Ruth was! She took such good care of the Hanukkah candles. Each night she counted out the proper number and put them into the Menorah. She *never* made a mistake.

On the first night she counted 1,	i and the *Shammash*
On the second night she counted 1, 2,	ii "
On the third night she counted 1, 2, 3,	iii "
On the fourth night she counted 1, 2, 3, 4,	iiii "
On the fifth night she counted 1, 2, 3, 4, 5,	iiiii "
On the sixth night she counted 1, 2, 3, 4, 5, 6,	iiiiii "
On the seventh night she counted 1, 2, 3, 4, 5, 6, 7,	iiiiiii "
On the eighth night she counted 1, 2, 3, 4, 5, 6, 7, 8,	iiiiiiii "

But she didn't count 1, 2, 3, 4, 5, 6, 7, 8, 9, and the *Shammash*.

She didn't count 1, 2, 3, 4, 5, 6, 7, 8, 9, 10, and the *Shammash*.

I wonder whether you can guess why.

---

[1] The following story is to be told with paper and pencil in hand. Draw the candles as you count. Let your little listener help you with the counting.

HOW RUTH WENT OUT AT NIGHT —
ON HANUKKAH

Sadie R. Weilerstein

RUTH sat looking at the little Hanukkah light in the window. It blinked and winked. It danced and twinkled.

"D'ling!" went the bell. Aunt Ann was at the door.

"Happy Hanukkah, Aunt Ann," said Ruthie. "Did you see our little Hanukkah light in the window?"

"Of course I saw your Hanukkah light," said Aunt Ann.

> Through the darkness,
> Through the night,
> It sent its little
> Dancing light.

"Oh," said Ruthie, "I wish I could see my little candle shining in the dark."

"Perhaps you can," said Mother. The next minute Ruth was bundled up in her snow suit and muffler and galoshes, and she and Mother were out-of-doors — at *night* — in the *darkness*.

"Crunch, crunch, crunch!" went the snow under their feet. They threw back their heads and looked up. There was their little Hanukkah light shining in the window.

How bright it looked in the darkness. Ruthie would never have believed that her light could shine so bright. Her eyes danced when she saw it. She smiled up at the little Hanukkah light and the light smiled down at her.

Then — crunch, crunch, crunch! Down the street went Mother and Ruth to Joan's house. There was a little Hanukkah light shining in Joan's window.

Mother and Ruth sang a song to it.

> Little light,
> Twinkling bright,
> Joan kindled you tonight!

Crunch, crunch, crunch! They were at Edward's house and there was Edward's Hanukkah light in the window. So they sang to Edward's light.

> Little light,
> Twinkling bright,
> Edward kindled you tonight.

They sang to Hedvah's light, too, and to Lorna's. Then crunch, crunch, crunch, down the street and around the corner they went, and they were home again.

Their Hanukkah light was waiting for them in the darkness. It winked and blinked. It danced and twinkled. It was *so* glad to see Ruth back again.

"See," said Mother. "Your Hanukkah light has made a path for you. It wants you to come home."

Ruthie looked down. There was a golden path across the snow, a little path of light.

"I'm coming, little Hanukkah light," Ruth called. And she danced down the little golden path to her door.

A HANUKKAH STORY[1]

SADIE R. WEILERSTEIN

MOTHER looked at the little Hanukkah light in the window. It reached up and up. "I am thinking of another little light," she said. "The Hanukkah light reminded me. I am thinking of a little light and of a foolish king and of a brave man. The foolish king's name was Antiochus. The brave man's name was Judah Maccabee. And the name of the little light was the *Ner Tamid*.

It all happened a long time ago in a far away land, in the Jewish land, in Palestine.

In the heart of Palestine was a high-up hill. On the high-up hill was a beautiful city. It was Jerusalem. In Jerusalem was God's Temple. In the Temple was a light. It wasn't a candle. It was an oil light. It was the *Ner Tamid*.

The light burned all day and all night. It burned *every* day and *every* night. It never went out. It was The Light-That-Burns-Forever.

The people looked at the light. It burned steady, steady. They said, "The light burns always and always, and God loves us always and always."

They looked at the light. It was warm and bright. They said, "The light burns always and always, and we love God always and always."

[1] For children of five and six.

320

They looked at the light. It reached up and up. "We must be brave and true and loving," they said. "God *wants* us to be brave and true and loving."

They were glad because of the light. They sang:

> The little oil lamp sheds its light;
> It burns all day; it burns all night.
> The light will never go out — never!
> It is the Light-That-Burns-Forever.

But a foolish king came from another land. (You remember, his name was Antiochus.) He was foolish and he was wicked.

"I will go up to Jerusalem," he said, "and Poof! I will put out the Light-That-Burns-Forever."

"Aren't you afraid of God?" the people asked him.

"Afraid of God?" The wicked king laughed. "I have soldiers," he said — "hundreds and hundreds and hundreds of soldiers. I have horsemen. I have fighting elephants. I am not afraid of anyone."

So — march, march, march!

The soldiers of the foolish king went up to Jerusalem.

Tramp! Tramp! Tramp! They were at the gates of the Temple. They were *in* the Temple.

And there the soldiers of that wicked, foolish king — *put out the Light-That-Burns-Forever.*

"Now the Temple is not God's Temple anymore," said the king. "It is *my* Temple. It is *my* Jerusalem. It is *my* Palestine.

He sent messengers to all the Jewish people. "You must stop praying to God," he said. "Bow down to me and my statue."

But the foolish king didn't know about Judah Maccabee. Judah Maccabee was a strong, brave Jew. He was brave as a lion. He was strong as a giant. And he loved God.

"Foolish king!" he cried. "We will not bow down to you and to your statue. We are few and you are many. But God will help us. God is stronger than all the kings and all the soldiers in the world."

Then Judah Maccabee took his sword and shield and rushed down on the soldiers of the wicked king. All the Jews who loved God followed him.

They drove the soldiers out of the Temple — out of Jerusalem — out of Palestine. It was the end of the wicked king.

Then Judah and the people went back to the Temple and lit the Ever-Burning Light again.

> The little oil lamp sheds its light;
> It burns all day; it burns all night!
> The light will never go out — never!
> It is God's Light-That-Burns-Forever.

THE BRAVE RIDER

Efraim Rosenzweig

Up-a-hill, down-a-hill,
    Gallop and trot!
Here comes a brave rider;
    What has he brought?

Judah the Maccabee
    Fearless and bold;
Behind him an army
    Of young men and old.

All of them happy,
    All of them brave,
Because they are fighting
    Their Torah to save.

THE EVER-BURNING LIGHT THAT WENT OUT
AND WAS LIT AGAIN[1]

Sadie R. Weilerstein

LONG, long ago there was a beautiful Temple in Jerusalem. It was more beautiful than any Temple you ever saw. In those days it was the only Temple the Jews had in all the world.

All the Jewish people came to Jerusalem to visit the Temple. They came from the cities and the farms and villages. They came singing and glad. They brought gifts with them, fruit and grain and oil, and doves and goats and little lambs. They gave the gifts to the Priests, the *Kohanim.*

The Priests were the ones who took care of the Temple, they and their helpers the Levites. They kept the Temple clean and shining. They sang beautiful songs and prayers to God. They took care of the Ever-Burning Light, the *Ner Tamid.* Never, never did they let the light go out. There were no candles in those days, only oil lamps. The Ever-Burning Light had a bowl. The bowl was filled with oil and the oil made the light burn. But the Priests didn't use *any* kind of oil. No, they used special oil, pure, clean, olive oil. They pressed it out of big ripe olives, and poured it into jars and sealed it tight, and put the mark of the High Priest on it. And that was the only oil they ever used for the Ever-Burning Light.

The Jews loved Palestine. It was their home. They loved their beautiful Temple. They loved the *Ner Tamid*, the Ever-Burning Light that made them think of God.

[1] For children of seven to ten.

But a sad thing happened. A wicked king came from another land. His name was Antiochus the Syrian. Antiochus had many soldiers. He took the Temple away from the Jewish people. He put out the Ever-Burning Light. He brought pigs into the Temple. He set up a statue and said, "This is your god. Bow down to it."

The people were very sad, but they said, "We can still light our Sabbath lights. We can read the *Sefer Torah* and pray to God in our homes. We can be good Jews."

But the wicked king said, "I will not let you light your Sabbath lights. I will not let you pray. Bow down to my statue. Eat the flesh of pigs. You must stop being Jews."

There was an old man named Eleazar. The soldiers took hold of him and put pig's flesh in his mouth. But the brave Eleazar spat it out. "I would rather die" he said, "than break God's law." Those cruel soldiers beat him and beat him, but still he would not obey the wicked king. And so he died.

There was a brave mother named Hannah. She had seven sons. The soldiers dragged them all before the king. "Eat pig's flesh. Bow down to this statue," said the king. But not one of the seven sons obeyed, not even the youngest. So they, too, died.

And still, the people said, "We will not stop being Jews."

Many of them ran away and hid. They ran to the forest. They hid in caves — fathers and mothers, boys and girls and little babies. It was very sad. They were lonely for their homes. They longed for their beautiful Temple.

Then suddenly a wonderful thing happened. In a little village in the hills there lived a brave old man, Mattathias, a Priest. Mattathias had five strong sons, each one as brave as he. They were John, Simon, Judah, Eleazar and Jonathan.

Judah was the strongest and the bravest of them all. They called him Maccabee, the Hammer.

Mattathias and his sons loved God. They loved the Temple. They loved the Torah. They loved the Jewish people. But they didn't hide from the wicked king. No, they did something very different.

It happened that the king sent his soldiers to Modin, the village where Mattathias lived. The soldiers set up a statue in the center of the market. They called the people to bow down before it. Mattathias was there. His five sons stood about him.

The king's officer spoke to him.

"You are a great man," he said, "and a ruler in this city. You are strong with sons and brothers. Come, be the first. Bow down to this statue. Obey the king. Then you and your children will be the king's friends and he will give you gold and silver and many gifts."

Mattathias answered in a loud voice. "God forbid that we should give up God's law. We will not listen to the king's words. We will not go from our religion either to the right or to the left."

But there was a Jew in the crowd who was not so true and brave as Mattathias. He was a coward. "It would be nice to have silver and gold and presents from the king," he thought. "Besides, if I don't bow down to the statue the soldiers may kill me."

So, just as Mattathias finished speaking, he stepped up and said, "I will bow down and obey the king."

Then Mattathias rose up and struck down the cowardly Jew. He struck down the officers of the wicked king. He tore down the statue. He cried out in a loud voice, "Who is for God's Law, follow me."

Then he and his sons fled to the mountains. "We will fight the wicked Antiochus, they cried. "We will drive him out of our land, and take back our holy Temple."

Other men followed them. They came from the villages and the cities. They came from their caves and hiding places — Jewish fathers and brothers and sons, all those who loved God.

Judah Maccabee was made their leader. He was fierce and strong as a lion. His shield was like a giant's.

The wicked Antiochus sent his soldiers against him. He sent thousands and thousands of soldiers — soldiers on foot and soldiers on chariots. He sent huge fighting elephants.

But Judah Maccabee and his men were not afraid of the wicked king or his soldiers. They prayed to God to help them. They fought bravely and fiercely. The soldiers of the wicked king trembled when they saw them. Their strength went out of their hands. They threw down their swords and ran away.

How happy the mothers and the old people and the little children were when they heard the good news. They came out of their hiding places and went back to their homes. They lit their Sabbath lights and prayed to God and read the *Sefer Torah*. They were safe.

Then Judah and his brothers said, "Let us go up to our holy Temple and make it clean again." So up to Jerusalem they went. How changed the Temple was! Weeds and wild bushes grew in the court yard. Pigs ran about the grounds. There was filth and dirt everywhere. The Ever-Burning Light was out. The people wept when they saw it.

Judah called the *Kohanim*. "Cleanse the Temple," he said. "Make it pure and clean again." The helpers of the *Kohanim* drove out the squealing pigs. They scoured and scrubbed and scrubbed and scoured. They made new bowls of gold and silver.

They burned sweet-smelling spices. The Temple was filled with the sweetness. And now it was time to light the Ever-Burning Light. All the people stood about and waited.

"Fetch pure oil!" said the Priests.

But there was no pure oil to be found. The wicked king had spoiled it all.

Suddenly a voice was heard. Perhaps it was the voice of the little son of one of the Priests.

"Here is oil," said the voice. "I hunted everywhere, in every nook and corner, and I found this little jar. See, the High Priest's seal is not broken.

The High Priest took the jar in his hand and looked at it. "God be thanked," he said. "It is true. The seal is not broken."

"But it is such a little jar!" someone cried. "There is no use lighting it. It will only last one day."

"Nay," said the Priest. "We *will* light it. We must trust in God."

He broke the seal of the little jar. He poured the oil into the lamp and kindled it. The Ever-Burning Light was lit again.

AND IT DIDN'T GO OUT!

It didn't go out the next day, or the next, or the next. That little jar of oil burned eight whole days, and by that time the Priests had pressed fresh new oil from new olives.

All the people came to see the wonderful sight.

"It is a miracle! A miracle!" they cried. *Nes gadol hayah po*: "A great wonder has happened here."

They waved branches and sang songs of thanks to God and were glad. It was the first Hanukkah.

Ever since that day, when Hanukkah time comes around, we light our Hanukkah lights, thank God and are glad.

HANUKKAH AT VALLEY FORGE

(A Tale of the Might-Have-Been)

EMILY SOLIS-COHEN, JR.

1777.

IN TWO days it would be Hanukkah. It was the second year without Father. Father had joined the Continentals as soon as the first shot was fired. But now he was near. Near enough to come home . . . only the Redcoats were in the city . . . all over it . . . and a furlough would be of no use. But to be so near and not even have a lamp . . . Judah was grieved!

And he was to be bar-mitzvah too! On Sabbath Hanukkah. How he would miss Father. Luckily they had begun to study long, long ago before the fighting began. So Father knew that he would read well. And he had been reading daily to grandfather. It was fine at least once in a man's life to read the *sefer* . . . the *haftarah* too. That wouldn't be new. He had read one, once, when he was a little boy, about nine. It would be fun celebrating Hanukkah and reading while the Redcoats were here. Almost like throwing defiance right in their teeth . . . and in the teeth of the tyrant, George too. No matter if King George wasn't just like Antiochus — forbidding them to read *torah*, and killing swine on the altar. He was a tyrant anyhow! As Patrick Henry had said, "He'd better profit by example."

And if the War wasn't soon won King George would have him, Judah, to reckon with. His name wasn't Judah for nothing. When he was a mere baby and didn't know what it was all about, Father held him up to look at the Lights, and Mother took his little fingers and drew them around the lion on the base of the lamp. "Lion! Judah! Lion! Judah!" they'd say. They kept it up, over and over, even when he was old enough to know what they meant.

His chest swelled. He was indeed a Lion — and a Maccabee! Too bad he couldn't be a drummer boy. Some of the lads had run away to the Army, but he wouldn't. His mother needed him. He was all she had. The man of the house now . . .

Suddenly, a strange thought. Maybe he could do it. It would only take a day. Valley Forge wasn't so very far from Philadelphia. But then Hanukkah fell this year the same day as Christmas. It would not be well to reach camp then. He would wait until the latter days of the Hanukkah week. He would leave a note so Mother wouldn't worry too much. Tell her he had an important errand to do. It was important, even if it was his own errand. To take a lamp to Father . . . so all the Jewish soldiers could enjoy Hanukkah. Some were farther from home than Father, too. It might be hard getting by the British soldiers, but he'd slip through where they weren't looking. If he carried the lamp right out boldly, in full sight, they'd think he was going visiting somewhere. The soldiers were all right. They didn't bother people for nothing.

He'd get up early Monday and start off. He'd be there in time for the fifth light.

But now he must read his *haftarah*, practice it again and again.

Strange, that feeling that Father was in the room, reading with him!

*   *   *

In the encampment at Valley Forge, Judah's father was on sentry duty. It had been bitter cold ever since they had arrived. The British were warm and snug in Philadelphia. But not for long . . . They'd be driven out!

He paced his post; the rags around his feet hardly kept them dry. Under his breath he was chanting Judah's *haftarah*. How he had missed being there. Two days since the bar-mitzvah. They would be lighting the fifth candle tonight. "These lights we light because of the miracles, mighty deeds . . ."

Miracles and mighty deeds. They needed them now! His mind went back to the service that Sabbath. He had been there in his dream — watching the few of the congregation left in the city as they assembled for service. Hardly a *minyan*. Then his wife and Judah came. He mounted the steps back of them. She had turned and spoken to her son. "Just remember, dear, Father will be with us . . . in spirit."

He had followed the boy in . . . and stood back of the Reader . . . against the wall. No one saw him, unless Judah. The boy looked over as if he were watching his lips form the hardest of the words . . . as he used to when they studied together.

Suddenly he was startled out of his revery. Shadows of men approaching. Feet crunching on the snow. Halt! It was their own men, carrying a bundle, wrapped in one of their torn coats.

"A boy, sentry. Found him on a snow drift. Taking him to the nearest cabin."

As they were about to pass, the lips of the child stirred, "The lamp. Where is my lamp?"

Judah's voice! The father's heart skipped a beat. Was aught wrong with the boy's mother? He heard the little voice again, "Lamp. Lamp." He smiled. Just like Judah! He must have come all the way to bring his father the menorah.

He explained to the men. One said that he'd see if the officer of the day would allow an exchange of sentries. If so he'd come back, and the father could be released. If not he'd find his boy safe enough when his watch was over.

The soldiers moved off. They were not so far away when they halted again. Officers! General Washington himself making the rounds. They told the General of finding the small boy, pressed deep in a snow drift . . . told of the father on sentry duty . . . told of the lamp — of Hanukkah — Hanukkah —

Washington nodded. "It's not good practice, but I will order the exchange. The officer will understand. So it's here — , the Feast of the Maccabees."

Washington nodded to the officers and they followed him into the cabin.

Before long Judah was sitting up. Not much later his father came in with the Lamp which had been found, one branch sticking out of a snow drift.

Judah threw himself in his father's arms, and in one breath told him that he wanted all the Jews in the camp to celebrate Hanukkah. And so he had brought his lamp, the one grandfather had given him for bar-mitzvah. Mother's was still at home . . . Maybe father would have time to hear him read his *haftarah*. He had read it without a mistake.

The father glanced at General Washington, as if to apologize for his son, but the General nodded comprehendingly. "Stay and hear him read, man. We are all Maccabees here. This boy too."

Judah was not abashed. He addressed the General, "So you know about it, sir? How Judah drove the tyrant from the land and cleansed the Temple. And how the Maccabees threw down the idol."

Washington interrupted, " 'Who is for the Lord — to me!' cried Mattathias, the priest. Yes, my boy, we have a Temple to cleanse also — the Temple of Liberty. Some day we shall rekindle its lamp — the light of Freedom . . . You wish to read to your father, and we must be about our duty." The Commander-in-Chief withdrew. Judah and his father were alone . . .

1788.

The War had been won. Independence was attained. The Temple of Liberty had been cleansed, and the Thirteen States had built a new Roof. That's what folks were calling the Constitution. General Washington had refused a crown. He had been elected President. He was now in Philadelphia . . .

.   .   .

His Excellency, the President, was receiving a delegation from the Hebrew Congregation. They were come to present him with an Address on behalf of the Congregations in the Republic.

Manuel Josephson began to read:

Sir:

It is reserved for you to unite in affection for your Character and Person, every political and religious denomination of men; and in this will the Hebrew Congregations yield to no class of their fellow Citizens.

The wonders which the Lord of Hosts hath worked in the days of our Forefathers, have taught us to observe the greatness of His wisdom and His might throughout the events of the late glorious revolution, and while we humble ourselves at His footstool in thanksgiving and praise for the blessing of His deliverance, we acknowledge you the leader of the American Armies as His chosen and beloved servant. But not to your sword alone is our present happiness to be ascribed, that indeed opened the way to the reign of Freedom, but never was it perfectly secure, till your hand gave birth to the Federal Constitution, and you renounced the joys of retirement to seal by your administration in Peace, what you had achieved in war . . .

Something stirred in Washington's memory. He glanced at a tall lad standing at attention beside the reader. Now he remembered. Valley Forge! He smiled at the youth. Judah smiled back. No need for speech. Each read the other's thoughts.

PART IV

COMMEMORATION OF HANUKKAH

INTRODUCTION

During the week of Hanukkah it is customary to commemorate the festival by parties in the home and entertainments in the school and in the various communal organizations.

This volume has been designed to furnish material for the different types of commemorative exercises.

In this third section of the book there has been collected a series of programs which can be adapted in whole or in part to home or public celebrations. To make these programs of practical use, suggestions as to their production have been made, the duration of each unit has been approximated and combinations of the various units into single programs have been furnished as models.

The foregoing portions of this volume contain essays, plays, stories, poems, and music which may be used in the programs or from which material may be derived. The pagination of references listed in the program-outlines, or the text, is that of this volume.

Hanukkah Lamp, Salomon Collection, *Hebraica*, plate XVII.

Hanukkah Lamp, silver-gilded, in form of an Ark,
doors can be opened, Italian.
Museum, Jewish Theological Seminary of America.

SERVICE FOR HANUKKAH

SERVICE FOR HANUKKAH

בָּרוּךְ אַתָּה יְיָ אֱלֹהֵינוּ מֶלֶךְ הָעוֹלָם,

אֲשֶׁר קִדְּשָׁנוּ בְּמִצְוֹתָיו וְצִוָּנוּ

לְהַדְלִיק נֵר שֶׁל חֲנֻכָּה

בָּרוּךְ אַתָּה יְיָ אֱלֹהֵינוּ מֶלֶךְ הָעוֹלָם

שֶׁעָשָׂה נִסִּים לַאֲבוֹתֵינוּ

בַּיָּמִים הָהֵם וּבַזְּמַן הַזֶּה

בָּרוּךְ אַתָּה יְיָ אֱלֹהֵינוּ מֶלֶךְ הָעוֹלָם

שֶׁהֶחֱיָנוּ וְקִיְּמָנוּ וְהִגִּיעָנוּ לַזְּמַן הַזֶּה.

הַנֵּרוֹת הַלָּלוּ [וְאָנוּ] אֲנַחְנוּ מַדְלִיקִין[וֹם] עַל הַנִּסִּים [וְעַל הַפֻּרְקָן] וְעַל הַגְּבוּרוֹת] וְעַל הַתְּשׁוּעוֹת וְעַל הַנִּפְלָאוֹת [וְעַל הַנֶּחָמוֹת] שֶׁעָשִׂיתָ לַאֲבוֹתֵינוּ [בַּיָּמִים הָהֵם וּבַזְּמַן הַזֶּה] עַל־יְדֵי כֹּהֲנֶיךָ הַקְּדוֹשִׁים; וְכָל־ שְׁמוֹנַת יְמֵי חֲנֻכָּה הַנֵּרוֹת הַלָּלוּ קֹדֶשׁ [וְהֵם] וְאֵין לָנוּ רְשׁוּת לְהִשְׁתַּמֵּשׁ בָּהֶם, אֶלָּא לִרְאוֹתָם בִּלְבָד, כְּדֵי לְהוֹדוֹת לְשִׁמְךָ עַל־נִסֶּיךָ וְעַל יְשׁוּעָתָךְ [וִישׁוּעוֹתֶיךָ] וְעַל־נִפְלְאוֹתֶיךָ.

SERVICE[1]

The Feast of Dedication lasts eight days. On the first eve-
ning a light is kindled, the number of lights being increased
by one on each consecutive evening. The Hanukkal. lights
should be kindled as soon as possible after nightfall.

On Friday the lights are kindled before the
beginning of the Sabbath.

Before kindling the lights the following Blessings are said:

Blessed art Thou, O Lord our God, King of the universe,
who hast sanctified us by Thy commandments, and commanded
us to kindle the light of Hanukkah.

Blessed art Thou, O Lord our God, King of the universe,
who wroughtest miracles for our fathers in days of old, at this
season.

The following Blessing is said on the first evening only:

Blessed art Thou, O Lord our God, King of the universe,
who hast kept us in life, and hast preserved us, and enabled us
to reach this season.

After kindling the lights, the following is said:

We kindle these lights on account of the miracles [redemp-
tions, mighty deeds], the deliverances and the wonders [and
consolations] which Thou didst work for our fathers [in those
days and at this season], by means of Thy holy priests. During
all the eight days of Hanukkah these lights are sacred, neither
is it permitted us to make any profane use of them; but we are
only to look at them, in order that we may give thanks unto
Thy name for Thy miracles, Thy deliverances and Thy wonders.

[1] The brackets indicate the changes in the Sephardic ritual.

סדר חנוכה[1]

In the home the following Hymn is chanted:—

לְךָ נָאֶה לְשַׁבֵּחַ.	מָעוֹז צוּר יְשׁוּעָתִי.
וְשָׁם תּוֹדָה נְזַבֵּחַ.	תִּכּוֹן בֵּית תְּפִלָּתִי.
מִצָּר הַמְנַבֵּחַ.	לְעֵת תָּכִין מַטְבֵּחַ.
בְּשִׁיר מִזְמוֹר.	אָז אֶגְמוֹר.

חֲנֻכַּת הַמִּזְבֵּחַ.

בְּיָגוֹן כֹּחִי כָלָה.	רָעוֹת שָׂבְעָה נַפְשִׁי.
בְּשִׁעְבּוּד מַלְכוּת עֶגְלָה.	חַיַּי מֵרְרוּ בְקֹשִׁי.
הוֹצִיא אֶת־הַסְּגֻלָּה.	וּבְיָדוֹ הַגְּדוֹלָה.
וְכָל־זַרְעוֹ.	חֵיל פַּרְעֹה.

יָרְדוּ כְאֶבֶן מְצוּלָה:

וְגַם שָׁם לֹא שָׁקַטְתִּי.	דְּבִיר קָדְשׁוֹ הֱבִיאַנִי.
כִּי זָרִים עָבַדְתִּי.	וּבָא נוֹגֵשׂ וְהִגְלַנִי.
כִּמְעַט שֶׁעָבַרְתִּי.	וְיַיִן רַעַל מָסַכְתִּי.
זְרֻבָּבֶל.	קֵץ בָּבֶל.

לְקֵץ שִׁבְעִים נוֹשָׁעְתִּי:

For the generally ragged, and at times cryptic, style of this song, and for the somewhat seriocomic tone of certain stanzas, the author, not the translator, is primarily responsible. These defects, however, have been to a certain extent exaggerated in the English version, both by the exigencies of the rhyme-scheme and by its nature. In Hebrew the "doublet" is a facile rhyme, and lends itself as readily to elevated as to commonplace style, to the development of serious and fanciful themes as to humorous handling. In English it is comparatively difficult; and apart from the work (continued on p. 344)

ROCK OF MY SALVATION[1]
(*Ma'oz Zur Yeshu'ati*)

SOLOMON SOLIS-COHEN

Mighty, praised beyond compare,
 Rock of my salvation,
Build again my house of prayer,
 For Thy habitation!
Offering and libation, shall a ransomed nation
 Joyful bring
 There, and sing
Psalms of Dedication!

Woe was mine in Egypt-land,
 (Tyrant kings enslaved me);
Till Thy mighty, out-stretched Hand
 From oppression saved me.
Pharaoh, rash pursuing, vowed my swift undoing—
 Soon, his host
 That proud boast
'Neath the waves was rueing!

To Thy Holy Hill, the way
 Madest Thou clear before me;
With false gods I went astray—
 Foes to exile bore me.
Torn from all I cherished, almost had I perished—
 Babylon fell,
 Ze-ru-ba-bel
Badest Thou to restore me!

[1] *When Love Passed By and Other Verses*, Solomon Solis-Cohen. The Rosenbach Co., 1929, pp. 94–95.

כָּרֹת קוֹמַת בְּרוֹשׁ בִּקֵּשׁ. אֲגָגִי בֶּן־הַמְּדָתָא.

וְנִהְיָתָה לוֹ לְמוֹקֵשׁ. וְנַאֲוָתוֹ נִשְׁבָּתָה.

רֹאשׁ יְמִינִי נִשֵּׂאתָ. וְאוֹיֵב שְׁמוֹ מָחִיתָ.

רוֹב בָּנָיו. וְקִנְיָנָיו.

עַל הָעֵץ תָּלִיתָ:

יְוָנִים נִקְבְּצוּ עָלַי. אֲזַי בִּימֵי חַשְׁמַנִּים.

וּפָרְצוּ חוֹמוֹת מִגְדָּלַי. וְטִמְּאוּ כָּל הַשְּׁמָנִים.

וּמִנּוֹתַר קַנְקַנִּים. נַעֲשָׂה נֵס לְשׁוֹשַׁנִּים.

בְּנֵי בִינָה. יְמֵי שְׁמֹנָה.

קָבְעוּ שִׁיר וּרְנָנִים:

חֲשׂוֹף זְרוֹעַ קָדְשֶׁךָ וְקָרֵב קֵץ הַיְשׁוּעָה

נְקוֹם נִקְמַת עֲבָדֶיךָ מֵעוֹשֵׂי הָרְשָׁעָה,

כִּי אָרְכָה לָנוּ הַיְשׁוּעָה, וְאֵין קֵץ לִימֵי הָרָעָה.

דְּחֵה אַדְמוֹן בְּצֵל צַלְמוֹן,

וְהָקֵם לָנוּ רוֹעֶה שִׁבְעָה.

of such masters of rhapsody as Poe and Swinburne, has been best employed in burlesques (e. g. the Ingoldsby Legends) and in sentimental ditties (e. g. those of Tom Moore).

Nevertheless the translator believes that a better representation of the spirit of the *Ma'oz Zur* has been attained by giving its essential ideas as faithfully as possible in the meter of the original, than could have resulted from a literal rendering or from even a successful attempt to impart to the English verses a dignity and polish absent from the Hebrew. The familiar melody and the deep feeling of national continuity and of faith in the continuance of divine protection that underlies the uncouth phrasing, have maintained a strong hold upon Catholic Israel. These characteristics it has been the effort to preserve.

Then the vengeful Haman wrought
    Subtly, to betray me;
In his snare himself he caught—
    He that plann'd to slay me.
(Haled from Esther's palace; hanged on his own gallows!)
    Seal and ring
    Persia's king
Gave Thy servant zealous.

When the brave Asmonéans broke
    Javan's chain in sunder,
Through the holy oil, Thy folk
    Didst Thou show a wonder—
Ever full remainèd the vessel unprofanèd;
    These eight days,
    Lights and praise,
Therefore were ordainèd.

Lord, Thy Holy Arm make bare,
    Speed my restoration;
Be my martyr's blood Thy care—
    Judge each guilty nation.
Long is my probation; sore my tribulation—
    Bid, from Heaven,
    Thy shepherds seven
Haste to my salvation![1]

---

[1] This Hanukkah song is from the Ashkenazic Liturgy.

מִזְמוֹר שִׁיר חֲנֻכַּת הַבַּיִת לְדָוִד:

אֲרוֹמִמְךָ יְהֹוָה כִּי דִלִּיתָנִי   וְלֹא־שִׂמַּחְתָּ אֹיְבַי לִי:

יְהֹוָה אֱלֹהָי   שִׁוַּעְתִּי אֵלֶיךָ וַתִּרְפָּאֵנִי:

יְהֹוָה הֶעֱלִיתָ מִן־שְׁאוֹל נַפְשִׁי   חִיִּיתַנִי מִיָּרְדִי־בוֹר

זַמְּרוּ לַיהֹוָה חֲסִידָיו   וְהוֹדוּ לְזֵכֶר קָדְשׁוֹ:

כִּי רֶגַע בְּאַפּוֹ   חַיִּים בִּרְצוֹנוֹ

בָּעֶרֶב יָלִין בֶּכִי   וְלַבֹּקֶר רִנָּה:

וַאֲנִי אָמַרְתִּי בְשַׁלְוִי   בַּל־אֶמּוֹט לְעוֹלָם:

יְהֹוָה בִּרְצוֹנְךָ הֶעֱמַדְתָּ לְהַרְרִי עֹז   הִסְתַּרְתָּ פָנֶיךָ הָיִיתִי נִבְהָל:

THIRTIETH PSALM

[Chanted in the Synagogue]

A Psalm; a Song at the Dedication of the House; of **David.**

I will extol Thee, O Lord, for Thou
    hast raised me up,
And has not suffered mine enemies
    to rejoice over me.

O Lord my God,
I cried unto Thee, and Thou didst
    heal me;
O Lord, Thou broughtest up my
    soul from the nether-world;
Thou didst keep me alive, that I
    should not go down to the pit.
Sing praise unto the Lord, O ye
    His godly ones,
And give thanks to His holy name.
For His anger is but for a moment,
His favour is for a life-time;
Weeping may tarry for the night,
But joy cometh in the morning.

Now I had said in my security:
'I shall never be moved.'
Thou hadst established, O Lord, in
    Thy favour, my mountain as a
    stronghold—
Thou didst hide Thy face; I was
    affrighted.

אֵלֶיךָ יְהֹוָה אֶקְרָא   וְאֶל־אֲדֹנָי אֶתְחַנָּן:

מַה־בֶּצַע בְּדָמִי   בְּרִדְתִּי אֶל שָׁחַת

הֲיוֹדְךָ עָפָר   הֲיַגִּיד אֲמִתֶּךָ:

שְׁמַע־יְהֹוָה וְחָנֵּנִי   יְהֹוָה הֱיֵה עוֹזֵר לִי:

הָפַכְתָּ מִסְפְּדִי לְמָחוֹל לִי   פִּתַּחְתָּ שַׂקִּי וַתְּאַזְּרֵנִי שִׂמְחָה:

לְמַעַן יְזַמֶּרְךָ כָבוֹד וְלֹא יִדֹּם   יְהֹוָה אֱלֹהַי לְעוֹלָם אוֹדֶךָּ:

Unto Thee, O Lord, did I call,
And unto the Lord I made
    supplication:
'What profit is there in my blood,
    when I go down to the pit?
Shall the dust praise Thee? shall it
    declare Thy truth?
Hear, O Lord, and be gracious
    unto me;
Lord, be Thou my helper.'

Thou didst turn for me my mourn-
    ing into dancing;
Thou didst loose my sackcloth, and
    gird me with gladness;
So that my glory may sing praise
    to Thee, and not be silent;
O Lord my God, I will give thanks
    unto Thee for ever.

עַל הַנִּסִּים, וְעַל הַפֻּרְקָן, וְעַל הַגְּבוּרוֹת, וְעַל הַתְּשׁוּעוֹת, [וְעַל
הַנִּפְלָאוֹת, וְעַל הַנֶּחָמוֹת] [וְעַל הַמִּלְחָמוֹת] שֶׁעָשִׂיתָ לַאֲבוֹתֵינוּ, בַּיָּמִים
הָהֵם [וּ]בַּזְּמַן הַזֶּה:

בִּימֵי מַתִּתְיָהוּ, בֶּן־יוֹחָנָן כֹּהֵן גָּדוֹל חַשְׁמוֹנַא[א]י וּבָנָיו, כְּשֶׁעָמְדָה
מַלְכוּת יָוָן הָרְשָׁעָה עַל־עַמְּךָ יִשְׂרָאֵל, לְהַשְׁכִּיחָם [וּלְשַׁכְּחָם] תּוֹרָתֶךָ,
וּלְהַעֲבִירָם מֵחֻקֵּי רְצוֹנֶךָ. וְאַתָּה, בְּרַחֲמֶיךָ הָרַבִּים עָמַדְתָּ לָהֶם בְּעֵת
צָרָתָם. רַבְתָּ אֶת־רִיבָם, דַּנְתָּ אֶת־דִּינָם, נָקַמְתָּ אֶת־נִקְמָתָם. מָסַרְתָּ
גִבּוֹרִים בְּיַד חַלָּשִׁים, וְרַבִּים בְּיַד מְעַטִּים, [וּטְמֵאִים בְּיַד טְהוֹרִים]
וּרְשָׁעִים בְּיַד צַדִּיקִים, [וּטְמֵאִים בְּיַד טְהוֹרִים] וְזֵדִים בְּיַד עוֹסְקֵי
תוֹרָתֶךָ. וּלְךָ עָשִׂיתָ שֵׁם גָּדוֹל וְקָדוֹשׁ בְּעוֹלָמֶךָ, וּלְעַמְּךָ יִשְׂרָאֵל עָשִׂיתָ,
תְּשׁוּעָה גְדוֹלָה וּפֻרְקָן [וּפֻרְקָן] כְּהַיּוֹם הַזֶּה. וְאַחַר כֵּן [וְכַּךְ] בָּאוּ בָנֶיךָ
לִדְבִיר בֵּיתֶךָ, וּפִנּוּ אֶת־הֵיכָלֶךָ, וְטִהֲרוּ אֶת־מִקְדָּשֶׁךָ, וְהִדְלִיקוּ נֵרוֹת
בְּחַצְרוֹת קָדְשֶׁךָ. וְקָבְעוּ שְׁמוֹנַת יְמֵי [וּשְׁמוֹנָה יָמִים] (חֲנֻכָּה) אֵלּוּ, לְהוֹדוֹת
וּלְהַלֵּל [וּבְהַלֵּל וּבְהוֹדָאָה], וְעָשִׂיתָ עִמָּהֶם נִסִּים וְנִפְלָאוֹת וְנוֹדָה] לְשִׁמְךָ
הַגָּדוֹל [וְסֶלָה]:

The following is added to the 'Amidah and
to the Grace after meals

We thank Thee also for the miracles, for the redemption, for
the mighty deeds and saving acts [wonders and consolations],
wrought by Thee, (as well as for the wars) which Thou didst
[perform] (wage) for our fathers in days of old, at this season.

In the days of the Hasmonean, Mattathias son of Johanan,
the High Priest, and his sons, when the iniquitous power of
Greece rose up against Thy people of Israel to make them forget-
ful of Thy Law, and to force them to transgress the statutes of
Thy will, then didst Thou in Thine abundant mercy rise up for
them in the time of their trouble; Thou didst plead their cause,
Thou didst judge their suit, Thou didst avenge their wrong;
Thou deliveredst the strong into the hands of the weak, the
many into the hands of the few, the impure into the hands of
the pure, the wicked into the hands of the righteous and the
arrogant into the hands of them that occupied themselves with
Thy Law; for Thyself Thou didst make a great and holy name
in Thy world, and for Thy people Israel Thou didst work a
great deliverance and redemption as at this day. And thereupon
Thy children came into the [sanctuary] (oracle) of Thy house,
cleansed Thy temple, purified Thy sanctuary, kindled lights in
Thy holy courts, and appointed these eight days of Hanukkah
to give thanks and praises [for the wonders and miracles Thou
didst perform for them and for which we must gratefully thank]
(unto) Thy great name.

During the daily morning service, the complete
Hallel (Psalms 113-118) is chanted

*The Service of the Central Conference of American Rabbis
is as follows:*[1]

Friday Evening Service, pp. 47–51.
    Added to the regular service.
        Psalm 30.
        Responsive Reading.
        An excerpt from I Maccabees.

Saturday Morning Service, pp. 103–106.
    Added to the regular service.
        Responsive Reading.
        A prayer of thanksgiving read by the minister.

Private Devotion for Hanukkah in the home, as follows:

Before the kindling of the lights, the following is said:

Praised be Thou, O Lord our God, Ruler of the world, who hast sanctified us by Thy commandments and bidden us kindle the Hanukkah lights.

Praised be Thou, O Lord our God, Ruler of the world, who didst wondrous things for our fathers at this season in those days.

Praised be Thou, O Lord our God, Ruler of the world, who hast granted us life, sustained us and permitted us to celebrate this joyous festival.

(Then the blessings in Hebrew)

---

[1] See *Union Prayer Book*, revised edition, Central Conference of American Rabbis, Cincinnati, 1934.

After kindling the lights, say the following:

Praised be Thou, O Lord our God, King of the universe, for the inspiring truths of which we are reminded by these Hanukkah lights.

We kindle them to recall the great and wonderful deeds wrought through the zeal with which God filled the hearts of the heroic Maccabees. These lights remind us that we should ever look unto God, whence comes our help.

As their brightness increases from night to night, let us more fervently give praise to God for the ever-present help He has been to our fathers in the gloomy nights of trouble and oppression.

The sages and heroes of all generations made every sacrifice to keep the light of God's truth burning brightly. May we and our children be inspired by their example, so that at last Israel may be a guide to all men on the way of righteousness and peace.

Responsive Reading
(Psalm 121)

Minister

I will lift up mine eyes unto the mountains;
From whence shall my help come?

Congregation

My help cometh from the Lord,
Who made heaven and earth.
He will not suffer thy foot to be moved;
He that keepeth thee will not slumber.
Behold, He that keepeth Israel
Doth neither slumber nor sleep.

The Lord is thy keeper;
The Lord is thy shade upon thy right hand.
    The sun shall not smite thee by day,
    Nor the moon by night.
The Lord shall keep thee from all evil;
He shall keep thy soul.
    The Lord shall guard thy going out and thy coming in.
    From this time forth and for ever.

A HANUKKAH PARTY

A HANUKKAH PARTY

Jerrie Meyer

In planning a Hanukkah party in a home, it is well to have in addition to the service a short program of recitation and of dances and if possible either a dramatic candle-lighting-drill or some other dramatic presentations interesting to children. This may either precede or follow the distribution of gifts.

In planning a program for the school or for stage presentations before an adult organization, it is well to have a short service and address and a musical or dramatic program.

Therefore descriptions are here given of appropriate dances and of a dramatic candle-drill with suggestions for costume and properties.

Programs are given as models.

PROGRAM — UNITS

Units	Participants	Minutes	Pages
SONG: { Ma'oz Zur ROCK OF MY SALVATION	Solo or chorus	Two	316–319
CANDLE-DRILL	Eleven 9 male, 2 female	Ten	345
A READING	One	Five	137 or 141
A RECITATION	One or two	Five	248–76
DANCES:			
DANCE OF TOP	One male or female	One	336
DANCE OF THE PANCAKES	Four male or female	Two	337–8
DANCE OF HAPPINESS	Group male or female	Two	340
DANCE OF CANDLES	Eight 4 male, 4 female	Two	339
PANTOMIME:			
SPIRIT OF GIVING	Group and leader	Five	340
HANUKKAH RIDDLES	A questioner, male Four children 2 boys, 2 girls	Three	107 ff.
SONGS	Entire company		

SHORT PROGRAMS

1.

Recitation
Dance of Top
Play
Candle-Drill
Dance of Happiness
Spirit of Giving
Distribution of Gifts
Refreshment

2.

Hymn
Lighting of Candles
Play
Dance of Pancakes
Recitation
Address
Singing

3.

Singing
Dance of Happiness
A Story
Play
Hanukkah Riddles
Candle-Drill
Dance of Top
Distribution of Gifts

EQUIPMENT NEEDED FOR A STAGE PERFORMANCE

FOR THE CANDLE DRILL

Use 8 stools or 8 boxes arranged in steps to simulate a Menorah. A full set of lights is required:

> a. Flood (at side)—Amber on one side and
>   white on the other.
>
> b. Foot—Rose and white.
>
> c. Border (above)—Rose.
>
> d. Spot—White.

Place the White Spotlight above the Menorah. Focus it on the CANDLES to give the effect of a lamp. In a home, no lights are required.

COSTUMES

Each CANDLE should be dressed in cardboard painted white and shaped like a wax-candle, and wear a wig of yellow wool, pointed high for a wick. A better effect can be had if the wool has been dipped in melted wax and shaped. The flame may be represented by orange colored cheese-cloth collars.

Instead of cardboard it is possible to use crepe paper for the costumes; instead of wigs, hats shaped like wicks.

Dress FREEDOM in white and let her carry a cup shaped like the cup of the Hanukkah-Menorah.

Dress ISRAEL in Palestinian garb; or in white and blue.

FOR DANCES

The TOP wears a starched muslin costume, ivory in color; on each side, painted in black, one of the four Hebrew letters נ, ג, ה, ש.

The PANCAKES should wear brown paper or burlap costumes of appropriate shape, and have hands and faces powdered brown.

The SPIRIT OF GIVING wears a costume of silver tissue or of crepe paper and a crown of the same material. The GIFTS should be dressed to represent playthings, books, coins, etc. Use painted muslin or crepe paper.

FOR RIDDLES

The QUESTIONER should wear a purple domino costume, and have a white beard and wig.

The QUESTIONED are modern children, boys and girls, in everyday garb.

MUSIC

DANCES

I

Dance of Top
(Music—'*Al Ha-nissim*, p. 367)

FIRST MOVEMENT

Enter center; turning constantly to left to indicate the winding of the top.

On reaching center front stop in upright position.

This takes two measures of music.

SECOND MOVEMENT

Twirl to the right, moving right, *four counts*. Continue twirling to the rear, *four counts*. Forward, still twirling, *four counts*. Jump up and down, *four counts*.

This takes eight measures of music.

THIRD MOVEMENT

Twirl in complete circle.

This takes two measures of music.

FOURTH MOVEMENT

Fall gradually to show in turn the letters on each side. For direction use each of the four corners of room. End the dance lying on floor so that one letter is exposed to audience.

This takes the remaining four measures of music.

———

II

DANCE OF PANCAKES (p. 368)

Four PANCAKES make an entrance by running into the center of the stage. Then they take places side by side in a row facing the audience.

This takes place without music.

FIRST MOVEMENT

All four hop from right to left foot, side to side seven times; then turn and hop, landing on both feet, facing audience.

This takes four measures of music.

Repeat on next four measures of music, but end by facing partners.

All in all, eight measures of music have been used.

SECOND MOVEMENT

The outside partners run backwards using eight small steps. The inside partners run forward to meet and face the outside partners.

This takes ten measures of music.

THIRD MOVEMENT

Hop around each other, using the same step as in the first movement, and run back so that the four pancakes again face the audience in front center.

This takes twelve measures of music.

FOURTH MOVEMENT

Take four slide steps to the right. Four slide steps to the left. Each pancake makes its own circle, using four slide steps, and finishes by facing audience.

This takes eight measures of music.

FIFTH MOVEMENT

Repeat the Fourth Movement. Then run off and return with refreshments for the guests.

III

DANCE OF CANDLES (p. 369)

FIRST MOVEMENT

The CANDLES take four slide steps to the right, two steps toward ISRAEL; two steps back and turn and step to the side once.

This takes four measures of music.

SECOND MOVEMENT

The CANDLES arrange themselves as partners; facing one another, still keeping circular formation. The four outside CANDLES walk, each around his respective partner. The inside four CANDLES repeat.

This takes four measures of music.

THIRD MOVEMENT

Holding hands in the circle the CANDLES take four slide steps to the right; two slide steps toward ISRAEL, two steps back, and turn and face the stools.

This takes four measures of music.

FOURTH MOVEMENT

To the remaining measures the CANDLES walk to the stools and turn and face outward.

ISRAEL moves toward the CANDLES; as each CANDLE is lit it mounts its stool.

IV

Dance of Happiness (p. 370)
(Music—Palestinian Folk Tune)

In the center stage is a table with an unlighted Menorah.

The group forms a grand circle, dancing around the table.

The step used is one-two-three; stamp, go to the right, at the end, open the circle and kindle the candles reciting the Blessings —(See p. 340).

When this dance is the Finale of the CANDLE DRILL, the circle dances around the "human Menorah."

Instead of pronouncing the Blessings, recite: Lamps of Dedication (p. 254).

PANTOMIME

Spirit of Giving

The SPIRIT OF GIVING enters slowly. When she reaches center stage she turns and beckons, then one by one—children dressed as PLAYTHINGS, BOOKS, COINS enter, dancing in a manner appropriate to the GIFT presented; as the dance ends the GIFT stands by the SPIRIT OF GIVING to form a figure with its companions.

Then the GIFTS distribute presents, either by pantomime or actually.

HANUKKAH

(Dance of Top, one minute)

A. *1st movement.* *(2 measures.)*　*2nd movement.* *(8 measures.)*

1. Enter from center turning and 2. Twirl to Right, moving right,
[finish center.

Twirl to rear,　　Twirl forward.

3rd movement. *(2 measures.)*
𝆏 *poco rit.*

Jump up and down.　3. Twirl in complete circle

4th movements. *(4 measures.)*
𝆑 *a tempo*

fall on one side.　Second side.　4. Third side.　Fourth side.

367

DANCE OF PANCAKES

(One and one half minutes)

B. *1st movement. (4 measures.)* *(Repeat 4 more*
With spirit

1. Hop from R to L seven times turn and hop.   Repeat first

measures.)   *2nd movement. (10 measures.)*

movement but end facing partners.   2. Outside partners run back-

wards 8 steps—Inside partners run forward and face partners.

3rd movement. (12 measures.)

3. Hop around each other using first movement and then run

forward until original place is reached.

4th movement.

4. Take four slide

(8 measures.)

steps to R and four to L.   Each pancake makes its own circle using four

5th movement.
(Repeat last 8 measures.)

slide steps and finish.

Repeat last 8 measures for 5th movement which allows the children to end by
running off.

HANEROS HALOLU

(Dance of the Candles, two minutes)

C.   *1st movement.*   *(4 measures.)*   *2nd movement.*

1. Four slide steps to R two to-ward Israel, two steps   2. Four child-
   [back turn and step to side once.

(4 measures.)   *3rd movement.*   *(4 measures.)*

ren walk around their four partners.   3. Holding hands take four slide
   [Reverse this figure

4th movement.   *(19 measures.)*

steps to R, two steps to-ward Israel 4. Use remaining music to walk to places.
   [two steps back and turn.

ff rall.

PALESTINE FOLK TUNE

(Dance of Happiness, two minutes)

One-two-three stamp and continue using the same step in a large circle.

Qu - - ma e cha so - - va sov

al - - ta nu cha shu va shov

en kan rosh ve - en kan sof yad el yad

al ta a zov yom sha qa ve yom yiz rach

a nu ne fen ach el ach min hak far u

min hak rack ba cher mesh u va a' nach.

Repeat.

THE CANDLE DRILL

THE CANDLE DRILL[1]

Emily Solis-Cohen, Jr.

CHARACTERS IN THE ORDER OF THEIR APPEARANCE

(acting-time 10 minutes)

VOICE

ISRAEL

FREEDOM: THE SHAMMASH

MATTATHIAS: *First Candle*

HANNAH: *Second Candle*

ELEAZAR: *Third Candle*

JUDAH the MACCABEE: *Fourth Candle*

JOHANAN: *Fifth Candle*

SIMON: *Sixth Candle*

ELEAZAR: *Seventh Candle*

JONATHAN: *Eighth Candle*

MUSIC

MA'OZ ZUR, entrance

HA-NEROT HA-LALU, March and Drill

[1] Reprinted from the *Hanukkah Envelope*, published by Young Judea.

SCENE

*The first verse of MA'OZ ZUR is chanted from behind the
curtain which is rising slowly, revealing a row of eight vacant stools,
rear left.*

*After a moment the score (without words) of HA-NEROT HA-
LALU is heard. At the same time the eight CANDLES appear rear
center, ready for the entrance march. Slowly, in single file they enter.
As the head of the column reaches front stage ISRAEL appears, rear
center, and advances center front. The CANDLES form behind
ISRAEL. Then they dance in a circle around him. (See p. 365,
DANCE OF CANDLES).*

VOICE

Speaks from the distance

Hinneni—Behold me.

ISRAEL

*Turns and sees advancing toward him the figure of FREEDOM,
carrying a vial of oil.*

ISRAEL

Exclaims

Upon the mountain tops the joyful feet,
Of Heaven's Messenger, with tidings sweet.

FREEDOM

Advances—offering the oil to ISRAEL

With me Abram set forth to worship God;
And I with Moses o'er vast deserts trod;
I spoke with Israel in the Wilderness:—

"Proclaim My name and I thy way shall bless."
I, FREEDOM, walk on heights and plains and field
Where valiant men have formed my living shield.
From them I garnered oil of dedication,
In it, O Israel, light the world's salvation.

ISRAEL

Taking vial

Redeeming now with brawn his sacred soil,
Israel, O Freedom, takes your hallowed oil.

FREEDOM and ISRAEL

Move together slowly to the CANDLES *and recite in Hebrew the
Blessings for the lights (p. 340) and repeat in English:*

Blessed art Thou, Lord our God, Ruler of the Universe, who
hath kept us alive, and enabled us to enjoy this season, and to
recite the blessings of God's light.

Blessed art Thou, Lord our God, Ruler of the Universe, who
wrought wonderful deliverance for our forefathers, in days of
old, in this season.

Blessed art Thou, Lord our God, Ruler of the Universe. Thou
hast sanctified us with Thy Commandments and ordained that
we kindle the Lamp of Dedication.

FREEDOM

Steps aside while ISRAEL'S *gesture indicates that he is lighting
the* FIRST CANDLE.

ISRAEL

This light I light in MATTATHIAS' name.

FIRST CANDLE

This light is lit in MATTATHIAS' name—
And lo, the message flareth forth in flame,
While upward lifts the Maccabean cry:
Mi L'adonai, Mi L'adonai Elai!

FREEDOM

"Who fights with God?" he asks, and in reply

CANDLES

In unison

As one, your children, ISRAEL, answer "I."

ISRAEL

Moves to the SECOND CANDLE

This light I light for martyred HANNAH'S sake.

SECOND CANDLE

For HANNAH'S sake, O Holy Candle, burn.
In lands of hate, repeat her message stern:
"My sons whom ye oppress will heed my plea,
And die as martyrs die, and perish free."

FREEDOM

A mother bids sons die, tyrants, take care!

ISRAEL

Kindles THIRD CANDLE

Enkindled be in ELEAZAR'S name.

THIRD CANDLE

"Eat your own food," they said, "and call it
    swine."
"I would not, and I died. This light be sign—
Life is not sweet that's had by mocking lie;
For truth and one's own honor, let men die."

FREEDOM

Old men perish, and the young men see.

ISRAEL

Walks to each of the five remaining CANDLES
These tapers light for Maccabeans five.

FOURTH, FIFTH, SIXTH, SEVENTH,
EIGHTH CANDLES

Recite in unison

Within the hearts of Jews we keep alive
The memory of Asmonean brothers five:
Judah, God's Hammer, called the Maccabee—
Johanan, Simon, Eleazar,—We
With Jonathan for God strove valiantly;
New-risen foes God's shrine profane; swiftly
    they flee,
If kindled is our light eternally.

FREEDOM

Far flare the lights of Zion's dedication,
To all, O Israel, make this proclamation!

Addresses ISRAEL

"The Syrian legion lives but in a name,
Judah's legion, carrying Sinai's flame,
Armored in Law, and girt in sacred right,
Upon Mount Scopus kindled Wisdom's light.

ISRAEL

Our gates are freedom and our walls are praise,
Justice doth rule our house, and Peace our ways.

By the time the last CANDLE *has spoken and has mounted its stool, the Menorah is formed. The spotlight is focused on the* CANDLES *so that they glow*

FREEDOM and ISRAEL

In unison pointing to the first FOUR CANDLES

These lights we lit for all the mighty deeds, wonders and comforts that Thou hast performed for our forefathers in days of old at this season, by the hands of Thy holy priests.

Pointing to the last FOUR CANDLES

These lights we lit for all the deeds, wonders and consolations that Thou art performing for us, in our day and at this season by the hands of Thy valiant servants.

ENTIRE COMPANY

Shine, lamps of Dedication, shine;
Your hallowed radiance be the sign
That still there burns undimmed by years,
Not quenched, but fed by blood and tears,
In Israel's heart, clear, steadfast, bright,
The flame it caught from Sinai's height.

CANDLE DRILL FOR HANUKKAH[1]

*For nine girls, whose ages do not matter,
but whose sizes are important*

Jessie E. Sampter

All the girls are dressed alike, to represent CANDLES, *in straight plain dresses, from the throat to the feet, of deep yellow cheese cloth or crepe paper, with peaked caps of the same material. Each one carries a wand covered with the same material, and with a tassel of bright reddish orange strips of tissue paper at the end, to represent the flame. Care should be taken in choosing the two colors, in order that they may harmonize. The tallest girl represents the* SHAMMASH *and must be able to lead in the dance. The next two girls must be a little shorter and of one size; so again with the next two, and so on, so that when all the girls are arranged in "menorah" order, with the* SHAMMASH *in the center, they taper down toward each side, the two smallest being one at each end.*

The girls march in, to appropriate music, the SHAMMASH *leading, the two girls of the next size following, and so on, the two smallest girls coming last. They do a march and wand dance—or flame dance—which begins with "follow master," the* SHAMMASH *going through various motions and poses which are followed by the others. Other figures may then be done, the girls dividing into fours and the* SHAMMASH *dancing in the center. Throughout, the flame motive should be used. In the last figure, the* SHAMMASH *collects the wands from all the other girls and holds them in a bouquet. Each girl, as she relinquishes her wand, drops to the ground in a squatting position, in the "menorah" order (see above), the group leaving a space in the center where the* SHAMMASH *is afterwards*

[1] The Bloch Publishing Co., N.Y., 1932.

to stand. The CANDLES *are now ready to be lighted. The* SHAM-
MASH *now passes to the center of the group, standing there, and
while waving the bouquet of wands gently from side to side over her
head, recites the following. The music may stop or play very softly
during all the recitations.*

SHAMMASH

Candles, O candles of dedication,
Now shall you be relit!
Again to dedicate your nation
Your shining row is set;
The Temple lies in desolation,
But we are living yet,
And this is our reconsecration,
A people that can not forget.
Candles, O candles, long extinguished,
Again your light shall flame!
O people, scattered, tortured, anguished,
Your pride all turned to shame,
Is there no light? Is hope extinguished?
Arise, a miracle proclaim!
Our Land is won, our foe is vanquished!
Now bring the oil to light the flame!

The SHAMMASH *passes from her place to the left, behind the other*
CANDLES, *and stands beside and in front of the last* CANDLE.
She hands to her one of the wands, saying as she does so:

O little candle, old yet new,
What will your flaming brightness do?

The CANDLE *receives the flame, rises, gives it a high shake, and then waves it very gently while reciting:*

I am the oldest of candles
Of our people in our land:
When Abraham came from Aram
I burned at his right hand,
I am the candle of flocks and herds,
Of tending cows and sheep,
And for my people in my land
A living hope I keep.
For they must tend the ewe again,
And nurse the little lamb,
And milk the cow and churn the cream,
And tend the foal and dam.
For was not Moses chosen
To lead us to our Land
Because he nursed a little lamb
And bore it in his hand?

During the other recitations, the previously lighted CANDLES *are kept softly moving, without strain or effort. The stick may be held before the face, so that the tassel will be about parallel with the cap. The* SHAMMASH *now passes around behind the others to the smallest* CANDLE *at the other end, to soft music, and repeats action and verse as before (see above), the same being repeated in the same manner with each* CANDLE, *and the* SHAMMASH *passing from side to side, so that the two tallest candles are lighted and arise last*

SECOND CANDLE

I am the second candle
Of a people on its soil,
    For I have burned to light the way
Of the farmer at his toil.
    I am the candle of growing things,
Of plow and rake and seed,
    And by my light the husbandman
A living folk shall feed.
    By me Elisha drove his plow
And Boaz succored Ruth;
    By me our people living now
Alone can live in truth.
    By me the grape is garnered,
The fig and olive grown,
    And the bounty of an honest folk
Shall by their fruits be known.

THIRD CANDLE

I am the candle of making things
Of stone and clay and wood;
    For God, when first He made the world,
And saw that it was good,
    Made man in His own image
That man might learn to make,
    And in that great creating love
His rightful part should take.
    'Tis I whereby Bezalel
Shaped silk and linen fine,
    The candlestick, the table,
The ark and all the shrine.

And by my light my people
Shall build in gracious ways,
 And know that work in making things
Is but a form of praise.

FOURTH CANDLE

 I am the candle of learning things
Of light that fills the mind,
 Of passing on from man to child
All tasks of every kind.
 I am the candle of Torah,
Of wisdom, of the truth,
 The light that kept our people
Eternal in its youth.
 By me that speech was treasured
Whereby the prophets taught.
 So children play and sing today
In the tongue of ancient thought.
 I never was extinguished!
How brightly must I burn
 To light my people to that Land
Where it shall live and learn!

FIFTH CANDLE

 I am the candle of purity;
I made the Temple clean
 Before again its lamp could shine
Or sacrifice be seen.

I was that light of holiness
That sanctified the priest,
　　And in the new redemption
My light is not the least.

For holiness needs cleanliness,
And Zion's sons defiled,
　　With filth and fever in their midst,
Can rear no kingly child.

So we must cleanse the alley,
And bring the waters down,
　　Ere God's own house can shine again
On Zion's holy town.

SIXTH CANDLE

I am the candle of service;
Our new born nationhood
　　Again needs many hands to toil
For our ancient people's good.

I ask to light no leaders,
Nor fame nor honor mine;
　　In the service of my people
For any task I shine.

I helped to light the Levites
That joined in Temple song;
　　When honest Jews do work or trade,
They bear my light along.

I am the candle of doing well,
Of dealing straight and fair.
　　And when my people build my land,
Oh, may they find me there!

SEVENTH CANDLE

I am the candle of brotherhood
Whose brightness shines afar,
Whose light gives strangers welcome
Wherever my people are;
For I was lit in Egypt
By suffering and despair;
The need of human brotherhood
We learned in anguish there.

Esau and Edom, our brothers,
We shall not now forget!
The Arab shares our Land with us,
And we are brothers yet.

So let us live with kindness
And seek for peace always,
That God may send redemption
O soon, in our own days!

EIGHTH CANDLE

I am the candle of that faith
That kept our people whole,
The light of worship and of trust
Whose flame is Israel's soul.

Without me all were barren,
The sky would be as brass,
And every virtue soon would die,
And every effort pass.

I burned to hear the promise
Our father Abraham heard;
By me the scribes of Ezra
Renewed the holy word.

By me alone the land can live
And yet my light is dim,
But God has chosen Israel
To keep that flame for Him.
When all the other candles
Are pleasing in His sight,
I shall arise in glory
And fill the world with light.

The SHAMMASH *now dances around all the other* CANDLES *and then returns to her place in the center, and the drill ends with all singing* MA'OZ ZUR, *the while the flames wave.*

BIBLIOGRAPHY

There is an extensive literature on Hanukkah in various languages, particularly in Hebrew, French, German, and English. Except for German books on music and German anthologies similar in scope to the present volume, this bibliography lists English titles only.

This book is designed not only for reading but for use in the class-room and in the home for the preparing of exercises and entertainments to commemorate Hanukkah. For additional titles for this purpose it is recommended that the current catalogues of the Bloch Publishing Company and other Jewish Book-houses be consulted as well as those of local and national Boards of Jewish Education and Departments of Synagogue Extension.

In addition to bulletins the Jewish Welfare Board has stereopticon slides which may be rented.

A. L. O. E., Hebrew Heroes: A tale Founded on Jewish History, T. Nelson and Sons, London and New York, 1870.

ABRAHAMS, ISRAEL, Festival Studies, First Illustrated Edition, Edward Goldston, Limited, London, 1934.

ABRAHAMS, ISRAEL, Jewish Life in the Middle Ages, New edition enlarged and revised on the basis of the Author's Material, by Cecil Roth. Edward Goldston, Limited, London, 1932.

ABRAHAMS, ISRAEL, The Shulchan Aruch (in Chapters on Jewish Literature), The Jewish Publication Society of America, Philadelphia, 1899.

AGNON, S. J., and HERRMANN, H., ed., Moaus Zur, ein Channukkabuch, Jüdischer Verlag, Berlin, 1918.

AGUILAR, GRACE, The Women of Israel; or Characters and Sketches from the Holy Scriptures, and Jewish History, Illustrative of the Past History, Present Duties, and Future Destiny of the Hebrew Females, as Based on the Word of God, R. Groombridge, London, 1845.

ALTMAN, ADDIE RICHMAN, The Story of Channukah, and Judas Maccabeus (in The Jewish Child's Bible Stories), Bloch Publishing Company, New York, 1915.

APOCRYPHA, revised edition, Thomas Nelson and Sons, New York, 1894.

APOCRYPHA AND PSEUDEPIGRAPHA of the Old Testament, in English with Introductions and Critical and Explanatory Notes to the Several Books, edited in conjunction with many scholars by R. H. Charles, Oxford, at the Clarendon Press, 1913.

ART, Jewish, Hebraica, documents d'art juif: orfèvrerie, peinture: préface de Henri Guttmann, Librairie des arts décoratifs, Paris, 1930.

BARTON, GEORGE A., A History of the Hebrew People (in The Language of the Bible), The Century Company, New York, 1930.

BENJAMIN, IRMA A., Shadows of our Past; a Hanukkah entertainment; A prologue, shadowgraphs, an epilogue, Bloch Publishing Company, New York, 1924.

BENTWICH, NORMAN, Hellenism, The Jewish Publication Society of America, Philadelphia, 1920.

BENTWICH, NORMAN, Josephus, The Jewish Publication Society of America, Philadelphia, 1914.

BENTWICH, NORMAN, Philo Judaeus of Alexandria, The Jewish Publication Society of America, Philadelphia, 1910.

BERKOWITZ, HENRY, The Symbol of Lights, an allegorical presentation of the lessons of Judaism. For Sunday School use, Poems, Biblical quotations, and Sermonettes, Philadelphia, 1893.

BEVAN, A. A., Origin of the Name Maccabee (in Journal of Theological Studies, XXX [1929], pp. 191–193).

BEVAN, EDWYN R., Hellenistic Judaism (in Legacy of Israel, by Bevan and Singer, editors), Oxford University Press, 1927.

BEVAN, EDWYN R., Later Greek Religion, London, 1927.

BEVAN, EDWYN R., The House of Seleucus, Edward Arnold, London, 1902.

BIALIK, C. N., Selected Poems, tr. by Maurice Samuel, New York, 1926.

BINDER, A. W., Chanukkah Songster, contains a complete Children's Musical Service and other hymns in English and Hebrew, Bloch Publishing Company, New York, 1922.

BINDER, A. W., Jewish Year in Song, G. Schirmer, New York, 1928.

BINDER, A. W., Judas Maccabeus, an Oratorio for Children, Bloch Publishing Company, New York, 1923.

BINDER, A. W., Palestine in Song, Metro Music Co., New York, 1937.

BRAVERMAN, LIBBIE L., Program for a Hanukkah Assembly (in The Jewish Teacher, vol. II, no. 1, November, 1933).

BRUCH, MAX, Hebräische Gesänge, Breitkopf and Haertel, Leipzig, 1888.

BRUCH, MAX, Three Hebrew Melodies, Breitkopf and Haertel, Leipzig, n. d.

BURY, J. B., The Hellenistic Age, Cambridge, 1923.

CHALIF, LOUIS H., Textbook on Dancing, Nos. 1 and 2, New York, The Chalif Russian Normal School, New York, n. d.

CHOMSKY, ELSIE, A Holiday Project as a Center of Interest in the Curriculum (in Jewish Education, vol. V, no. 2, pp. 95–100, April-June, 1933).

COHEN, ISABEL E., Readings and Recitations for Jewish Homes and Schools, The Jewish Publication Society of America, Philadelphia, 1895.

COLEMAN, EDWARD D., The Bible in English Drama, an annotated list of plays including translations from other languages, New York Public Library, New York, 1931.

COLSON, F. H., and WHITAKER, H. G., Philo Judaeus, an English translation, G. P. Putnam's Sons, New York, 1929.

COMINS, H. Z., and LEAF, R., Arts-Crafts for the Jewish Club, Union of American Hebrew Congregations, Cincinnati, 1934.

CONDER, CLAUDE REIGNIER, Judas Maccabeus and The Jewish War of Independence, new edition, published for the Committee of The Palestine Exploration Fund, A. P. Watt and Son, London, 1879, 1894.

COOPERSMITH, HARRY, Chanukah, Feast of Lights (in Little Books of Jewish Songs), Board of Jewish Education, Chicago, 1928.

CUMONT, FRANZ, The Oriental Religions in Roman Paganism, Open Court Press, Chicago, 1911.

CURTISS, S. I., The Name Maccabee Historically and Philologically Examined, Leipzig, 1876.

DEMBITZ, LEWIS N., Jewish Services in Synagogue and Home, The Jewish Publication Society of America, Philadelphia, 1898.

FINKELSTEIN, LOUIS, The Pharisees, 2 vols., The Jewish Publication Society of America, Philadelphia, 1938.

FLANTER, EMIL, compiler, Im Strahlenglanze der Menorah, ein neues Channukkah-Buch, Berlin, 1920.

FRIEDLÄNDER, MICHAEL, The Jewish Religion, 3rd ed., revised and enlarged, London, 1913.

GASTER, MOSES, The Scroll of the Hasmoneans (Megillath Bene Hasmunai), International Congress of Orientalists, Transactions of Ninth Congress, 1892, vol. 2, pp. 3–32, London, 1893.

GOLDBERG, I., and BENDERLY, S., Outline of Jewish Knowledge, vol. III, Bureau of Jewish Education, New York, 1931.

GOLDFARB, I., and GOLDFARB, S. E., The Jewish Songster, Bloch Publishing Company, New York, 1918.

GOODENOUGH, ERWIN R., New Light on Hellenistic Judaism (in Journal of Bible and Religion, Jan., Feb., Mar., 1937).

GRAETZ, HEINRICH, History of the Jews, vol. I, The Jewish Publication Society of America, Philadelphia, 1891.

GREENSTONE, JULIUS H., Methods of Teaching the Jewish Religion in Junior and Senior Grades, Jewish Chautauqua Society, Philadelphia, 1915.

GREENSTONE, JULIUS H., The Religion of Israel, The Hebrew Sunday School Society, Philadelphia, 1902.

GROSSMANN, LOUIS, The Hanukkah Festival, Suggestions for a Program in Sunday Schools, Hebrew Union College, Cincinnati, 1914.

HALPER, B., Post-Biblical Hebrew Literature, an Anthology, The Jewish Publication Society of America, Philadelphia, 1921.

HANUKKAH and Purim Service, reprinted from Moses' Sabbath School Hymnal, Bloch Publishing Company, New York, 1928.

HASTINGS, JAMES, Ed., Encylopedia of Religion and Ethics, Charles Scribner's Sons, New York, 1927, vols. 5 and 10.

HEBREW SUNDAY SCHOOL SOCIETY of Philadelphia, Selected Hymns for Jewish Religious Schools (music and words), Philadelphia, 1929.

HERFORD, R. TRAVERS, Pirke Aboth, The Jewish Institute of Religion Press, New York, 1925.

HERFORD, R. TRAVERS, The Pharisees, The Macmillan Company, New York, 1924.

HILL, G. F., Catalogue of the Greek Coins of Palestine (Galilee, Samaria, and Judea), British Museum, Department of Coins and Medals, London, 1914.

HOENIG, SIDNEY B., Hanukah Anagrams (in The Orthodox Union, vol. IV, no. 3, Dec., 1936).

IDELSOHN, A. Z., Ceremonies of Judaism, National Federation of Temple Brotherhoods, 2nd enlarged edition, Cincinnati, 1930.

IDELSOHN, A. Z., Jewish Liturgy and Its Development, Henry Holt and Company, New York, 1932.

IDELSOHN, A. Z., Jewish Music In Its Historical Development, Henry Holt and Company, New York, 1929.

IDELSOHN, A. Z., Sefer Hashirim, Berlin, 1912.

ISAACS, A. S., Under the Sabbath Lamp, The Jewish Publication Society of America, Philadelphia, 1919.

JEWISH ENCYCLOPEDIA, The, New York and London, 1901–1906.

JEWISH HOME INSTITUTE BOOKLETS, Chanukah Festival Course, Bureau of Jewish Education, New York, n. d.

JEWISH NATIONAL FUND, A Hanuca Evening; program for a festival function, Keren Kayemeth (Typewritten), Jerusalem, 1932.

JEWISH NON-ROYALTY PLAYS AND PAGEANTS, National Play Bureau (Federal Theater Project, Works Progress Administration, publication, no. 8), Jan., 1937.

JEWISH WELFARE BOARD, Hanukkah Programs (mimeographed), New-York, 1934.

JOSEPH, MORRIS, Judaism as Creed and Life, The Macmillan Company, London and New York, 1910.

JOSEPHUS, FLAVIUS, Antiquities of the Jews, Bk. XII.

KAISER, REV. ALOIS, and SPARGER, REV. WM., A Collection of the Principal Melodies of the Synagogue. From the Earliest Time to the Present. With a preface by Cyrus Adler, Chicago, 1893.

KITTEL, RUDOLF, Great Men and Movements in Israel, The Macmillan Company, New York, 1929.

KOHLER, K., Chanuka and Christmas, in The Menorah, vol. 9, No. 6, The Menorah Publishing Company, New York, 1890.

LAZARUS, EMMA, Poems, Houghton, Mifflin and Company, 1899.

LAZARUS, EMMA, Songs of a Semite, The American Hebrew, New York, 1882.

LAZARUS, M., The Ethics of Judaism, The Jewish Publication Society of America, Philadelphia, 1901.

LEARSI, RUFUS, The Severed Menorah (in Kasriel the Watchman), The Jewish Publication Society of America, Philadelphia, 1925.

LEHRMAN, S. M., Hanucah (in Jewish Festivals), Shapiro, Vallentine and Company, London, 1936.

LEVINGER, ELMA EHRLICH, As The Candles Glow (in Tales Old and New), Bloch Publishing Company, New York, 1926.

LEVINGER, ELMA EHRLICH, Chanukah Entertainments, a Handbook, Department of Synagogue and School Extension, Cincinnati, 1924.

LEVINGER, ELMA EHRLICH, Chanukah—The Feast of Lights (in In Many Lands), Bloch Publishing Company, New York, 1936.

LEVINGER, ELMA EHRLICH, The Story of the Jew for Young People, Jewish Book House, New York, 1935.

LEVINGER, ELMA EHRLICH, With the Jewish Child in Home and Synagogue, Bloch Publishing Company, New York, 1930.

LOWENTHAL, MARVIN, A World Passed By, A Guide Book for Travellers, Harper and Brothers, New York and London, 1933.

LUDLOW, JAMES M., Deborah, A Tale of the Times of Judas Maccabaeus, Fleming H. Revel Company, New York, 1901.

MADDEN, FREDERIC WILLIAM, Jewish Numismatics; being a supplement to the History of Jewish Coinage and Money in the Old and New Testaments, published in 1864; London, 1874–1876.

MARGOLIS, MAX L., and MARX, ALEXANDER, A History of the Jewish People, The Jewish Publication Society of America, Philadelphia, 1927.

MELAMED, DEBORAH M., The Three Pillars, The Women's League of the United Synagogue of America, New York, 1927.

MISCH, MARION L., Selections for Homes and Schools, The Jewish Publication Society of America, Philadelphia, 1911.

MOISE, PENINA, Secular and Religious Works, with a brief sketch of her life, Council of Jewish Women, Charleston, S. C., 1911.

MOORE, GEORGE FOOTE, Judaism, 3 volumes, Harvard University Press, Cambridge, 1927–1930.

MURRAY, GILBERT, Five Stages of Greek Religion, Oxford, 1925.

OESTERLEY, W. O. E., and ROBINSON, T. H., A History of Israel, vol. II, Oxford, 1932.

OESTERLEY, W. O. E. and BOX, G. H., The Religion and Worship of the Synagogue from the New Testament Period, New York, Charles Scribner's Sons, 1907. London, 1911.

OPPENHEIM, MORITZ, The Jewish Year, Illustrated by Pictures of Old-Time Jewish Family Life, Customs and Observances from the Paintings by M. O., with explanatory text by Louis Edward Levy (large fol.), Philadelphia, 1895.

PERLES, F., The Name Makkabaios (in Jewish Quarterly Review, XVII, p. 404, New Series), Philadelphia, 1926–27.

PHINEAS, Hanukkah (a poem in Mitteilungen des Forschungs-institutes fuer hebraeische Dichtungen, vol. I), Berlin, 1933, pp. 163–174.

POEMS FOR YOUNG JUDEANS, An Anthology, 4th edition, Young Judea, New York, 1925.

RADIN, MAX, The Jews Among the Greeks and Romans, The Jewish Publication Society of America, Philadelphia, 1915.

RAISIN, J. S., The Haskalah Movement in Russia, The Jewish Publication Society of America, Philadelphia, 1913.

RANKIN, O. S., The Festival of Hanukkah (in The Labyrinth, edited by S. H. Hooke), The Macmillan Company, New York, 1935.

RANKIN, O. S., The Origins of the Festival of Hanukkah; The Jewish New-Age Festival, Edinburgh, 1930.

REIFENBERG, A., Rare and Unpublished Jewish Coins (in Palestine Exploration Fund Quarterly Statement, LXVII [1935], pp. 79–84).

ROSENFELD, MORRIS, Songs From The Ghetto, prose translation by Leo Wiener, Small Maynard and Co., Boston, 1900.

ROTH, CECIL, A Bird's-Eye View of Jewish History, Union of American Hebrew Congregations, Cincinnati, 1935.

SACHAR, A. L., A History of the Jews, Alfred A. Knopf, New York, 1930.

SACHS, KURT, Musik des Altertums, Ferdinand Hirt, Breslau, 1924.

SACHS, BENJAMIN, The Story of Chanuka, Pittsburgh, 1913.

SAMPTER, JESSIE E., The Last Candles, The Zionist Organization of America, New York, 1918.

SCHAUSS, HAYYIM, The Jewish Festivals, Union of American Hebrew Congregations, Cincinnati, 1937.

SCHECHTER, SOLOMON, A Glimpse of the Social Life of the Jews in the Age of Jesus, the Son of Sirach (in Studies in Judaism, 2d Series), The Jewish Publication Society of America, Philadelphia, 1908.

SCHÜRER, EMIL, A History of the Jewish People in the Time of Jesus Christ, Div. I, tr. by John MacPherson, Div. II, tr. by Sophia Taylor and Peter Christie, Edinburgh, 1895–90; 2nd edition, Charles Scribner's Sons, New York, n.d.

SOLIS-COHEN, EMILY, JR., The Magic Top (in The Breakfast of the Birds, translated from the Hebrew of Judah Steinberg), The Jewish Publication Society of America, Philadelphia, 1917.

SOLIS-COHEN, EMILY, JR., The Sacrifice at Modin (in David the Giant Killer and Other Tales of Grandma Lopez), The Jewish Publication Society of America, Philadelphia, 1908.

SOLIS-COHEN, SOLOMON, When Love Passed By and Other Verses, The Rosenbach Company, Philadelphia and New York, 1929.

SONG-FILM FOR HANUKKAH, Bureau of Jewish Education, New York, n.d.

SPIEGEL, S., Hebrew Reborn, The Macmillan Company, New York, 1930.

STANDARD BOOK OF JEWISH VERSE, THE, compiled by Joseph Friedländer, edited by George Alexander Kohut, Dodd, Mead and Company, New York, 1917.

TRAGER, HANNAH, Festival Stories of Child Life in a Jewish Colony in Palestine, Rutledge, London, 1920.

UNION HYMNAL, Songs and Prayers for Jewish Worship, Central Conference of American Rabbis, 3rd ed., Cincinnati, 1932.

UPTON, GEORGE PUTNAM, The Standard Oratorios, Judas Maccabeus, A. C. McClurg and Company, Chicago, 1909.

VERET, PAUL, Chanukah, Project for classroom use, Associated Talmud Torahs of Philadelphia, 1932.

WEILERSTEIN, SADIE ROSE, The Chanukah Lights (in What
    Danny Did), Bloch Publishing Company, New York, 1932.
WISE, ISAAC M., The First of the Maccabees, A Historical Novel,
    The Bloch Publishing and Printing Co., Cincinnati, n. d.

ZEITLIN, S., The History of the Second Jewish Commonwealth,
    prolegomena, Dropsie College, Philadelphia, 1933.
ZEITLIN, S., "Hanukkah," in Jewish Quarterly Review, XXIX
    (1938), pp. 1–36.

ACKNOWLEDGMENTS

A number of friends, authors, and publishing houses have helped in the production of this book either through personal service or by extending permission to reprint from their former publications. To all of them the editor extends her sincere thanks for their gracious assistance.

In especial, acknowledgments are due to:

Mrs. Israel Abrahams for permission to reprint the article "Hanukkah in Olden Times" from *Festival Studies* by Doctor Israel Abrahams.

Mrs. H. Berkowitz for permission to reprint the poem, "The Menorah," by Miriam Del Banco from *Song Service for Hanukkah*, arranged by Doctor Henry Berkowitz.

Bloch Publishing Co. for permission to reprint a number of their publications:

> *The Light That Never Failed*, by E. E. Levinger,
> "Hanukkah Lights," from *What Danny Did*, by S. R. Weilerstein,
> *The Candle Drill for Hanukkah*, by Jessie E. Sampter.

Justice Louis D. Brandeis for permission to use a quotation from an address delivered by him in 1912.

Dr. Solomon Solis-Cohen for permission to use a number of his poems.

Council of Jewish Women, the Charleston Section, for permission to reprint the poem, *Feast of Dedication*, by Penina Moise.

Professor Israel Davidson for calling the editor's attention to the poem for the Sabbath of Hanukkah in *Ayeleth Ha-shahar*.

Doubleday, Doran and Co. for permission to reprint the poem "Hanukkah Lights" by Morris Rosenfeld, from *Apples and Honey*.

Groombridge, R. for permission to reprint an excerpt from Grace Aguilar's *Women of Israel*.

Houghton, Mifflin and Co. for permission to reprint several poems from the poetical works of Emma Lazarus.

Jewish Exponent for permission to reprint the poem, *Hanukkah*, by Cecelia G. Gerson.

Jewish Publication Society of America for permission to reprint a number of previously published stories.

Jewish Theological Seminary of America for permission to reproduce several of the Menorahs in its Museum.

Keren Kayemeth of Jerusalem for permission to translate and publish the poem, *Lights*, by J. Fichman.

Elma Ehrlich Levinger for permission to reprint several of her poems and the story, *The Light That Never Failed*.

Menorah Journal for permission to reprint *The Menorah* by Theodor Herzl.

S. M. Salomon for permission to reproduce a number of pictures from the Salomon Collection *Hebraica*.

Philip M. Raskin for permission to reprint the poem, *My Hanukkah Candles*.

Rabbi Efraim Rosenzweig for permission to use his poems.

Doctor Jonah B. Wise for permission to reprint a chapter from the novel, *The First of the Maccabees* by Isaac M. Wise.

Sadie R. Weilerstein for permission to reprint one chapter from *What Danny Did*.

Young Judea for permission to reprint several poems by Mrs. Levinger, *The Call*, by H. Snowman, and *Hail the Maccabee*, by Israel Goldberg, as well as the *Candle Drill* by Jessie E. Sampter.